SHARING THE LIGHT OF FAITH

National Catechetical Directory for Catholics of the United States

United States Catholic Conference
Washington, D.C.

The document *Sharing the Light of Faith* was developed by the USCC Committee on Education and approved by the U.S. bishops prior to the publication of the *Catechism of the Catholic Church* and the *General Directory for Catechesis*. The content of this document remains valid; it should be read, however, in light of the *Catechism* and the *GDC*.

ISBN 1-55586-001-X

First Printing, May 1979
Eleventh Printing, February 1999

Scriptural Prayer

May the God of Our Lord Jesus Christ,
the Father of glory, grant you a spirit
of wisdom and insight to know him clearly.
May he enlighten your innermost vision
that you may know the great hope
to which he has called you, the wealth
of his glorious heritage to be distributed
among the members of the church,
and the immeasurable scope of his power
in us who believe.

Eph 1,17ff

Contents

CROSS-REFERENCES

The small numbers in the margins are cross-references to the more important passages treating the same or similar topics in other parts of the document. The numbers preceded by the letter "c." refer to chapters; those without this letter refer to article numbers.

Abbreviations

DOCUMENTS OF VATICAN II

Bishops: *Decree on the Bishops' Pastoral Office in the Church (Christus Dominus)*

Christian Education: *Declaration on Christian Education (Gravissimum Educationis)*

Church: *Dogmatic Constitution on the Church (Lumen Gentium)*

Eastern Churches: *Decree on Eastern Catholic Churches (Orientalium Ecclesiarum)*

Ecumenism: *Decree on Ecumenism (Unitatis Redintegratio)*

Laity: *Decree on the Apostolate of the Laity (Apostolicam Actuositatem)*

Missionary Activity: *Decree on the Church's Missionary Activity (Ad Gentes)*

Modern World: *Pastoral Constitution on the Church in the Modern World (Gaudium et Spes)*

Non-Christian Religions: *Declaration on the Relationship of the Church to Non-Christian Religions (Nostra Aetate)*

Priestly Formation: *Decree on Priestly Formation (Optatam Totius)*

Priests: *Decree on the Ministry and Life of Priests (Presbyterorum Ordinis)*

Religious Freedom: *Declaration on Religious Freedom (Dignitatis Humanae)*

Religious Life: *Decree on the Appropriate Renewal of the Religious Life (Perfectae Caritatis)*

Revelation: *Dogmatic Constitution on Divine Revelation (Dei Verbum)*

Sacred Liturgy: *Constitution on the Sacred Liturgy (Sacrosanctum Concilium)*

Social Communication: *Decree on the Instruments of Social Communication (Inter Mirifica)*

Quotations from the above documents are taken from *The Documents of Vatican II*, Walter M. Abbott, S.J., general editor. ©Copyright 1966 by The America Press. Used with permission. All rights reserved.

OTHER CHURCH DOCUMENTS

A Call to Action (Paul VI, 1971): *A Call to Action*, Apostolic Letter on the Occasion of the Eightieth Anniversary of the Encyclical *Rerum Novarum*, May 14, 1971.

BT: *Basic Teachings for Catholic Religious Education*, Prepared by the National Conference of Catholic Bishops in consultation with the Holy See. January 1973.

GCD: *General Catechetical Directory*, Prepared by the Sacred Congregation for the Clergy and approved by Pope Paul VI on March 18, 1971. © Copyright 1971 by the United States Catholic Conference. All rights reserved.

JW: *Justice in the World*, Prepared by the Second General Assembly of the Synod of Bishops and confirmed by Pope Paul VI on November 30, 1971.

On Evangelization (Paul VI, 1975): *On Evangelization in the Modern World (Evangelii Nuntiandi)*, an Apostolic Exhortation of Pope Paul VI, December 8, 1975.

Paths of the Church (Paul VI, 1964): *Paths of the Church (Ecclesiam Suam)*, Encyclical Letter of Pope Paul VI, August 6, 1964.

Peace on Earth (John XXIII, 1963): *Peace on Earth (Pacem in Terris)*, Encyclical Letter of Pope John XXIII, April 11, 1963.

Sexual Ethics (Doctrine of the Faith, 1975): *Declaration on Certain Questions Concerning Sexual Ethics*, Sacred Congregation for the Doctrine of the Faith, December 29, 1975.

TJD: *To Teach As Jesus Did, A Pastoral Message on Catholic Education*, National Conference of Catholic Bishops, November 1972.

TLCJ: *To Live in Christ Jesus, A Pastoral Reflection on Moral Values*, National Conference of Catholic Bishops, 1976.

OTHER SOURCES

Catholic Schools in a Declining Church (1976): Greeley, Andrew M., McCready, William C., and McCourt, Kathleen, *Catholic Schools in a Declining Church*. Sheed and Ward, Inc., Kansas City, 1976.

Religion and American Youth (1976): Potvin, Raymond H., Hoge, Dean R., Nelsen, Hart M., *Religion and American Youth with Emphasis on Catholic Adolescents and Young People*. Publications Office, United States Catholic Conference, 1976.

The Religion of Children (1976): Nelsen, Hart M., Potvin, Raymond H., Shields, Joseph, *The Religion of Children*. Publications Office, United States Catholic Conference, 1976.

Preface

I am the light of the world.
No follower of mine
shall ever walk in darkness;
no, he shall possess
the light of life.
Jn 8, 12

1. Introduction

Jesus Christ lives and, with His Father, unceasingly sends forth the Holy Spirit, who abides in believers' hearts as the source of light and love. No one walks in darkness who possesses the life-giving Spirit.

In the 1960s the Second Vatican Council gave testimony to the presence of Christ, the light of nations, within His Church. It reaffirmed the Church's mission to lead people to God, heal human anxieties, uphold human dignity, and bear witness as a community united through the bond of love. Recognizing that many people see Christ's light only in the lives of Christians, the Council called upon the members of the Church to make this light shine more brightly by their words and deeds and so lead others to Christ.

PART A: BACKGROUND INFORMATION ON THIS DIRECTORY

2. Mandate

The Council called for the renewal of catechetics.[1] To assist this renewal, it prescribed that a directory be prepared dealing with fundamental principles of catechesis, organizations, and the composition of books on the subject.[2]

The *General Catechetical Directory*, prepared by the Sacred Congregation for the Clergy, after consultation with conferences of bishops around the world, was approved by Pope Paul VI on March 18, 1971. It draws together and organizes principles and guidelines for catechesis for the universal Church. It emphasizes the Church's concern that the faith of Catholics be informed and living. It urges bishops' conferences to prepare national directories applying its principles and guidelines. *Sharing the Light of Faith, National Catechetical Directory for Catholics of the United States* (NCD) has been prepared in response.

Algimantas Kezys

8,15,73,
112,242a)

3. Collaboration of the Eastern and Western Catholic Churches

This document has been developed jointly by members of Eastern and Western Churches of the Catholic Church with jurisdictions in the United States, and has been approved by the bishops of all these Churches. Though it is written largely from the perspective of the Western Church, special effort has been made to inform and interest all Catholics concerning the rich diversity found within Catholic unity. It is hoped that, while respecting the integrity and proper traditions of the Eastern and Western Churches, it will assist all Catholics in certain aspects of catechesis.

4. Consultation process

The NCD has been prepared in dialogue with large numbers of Catholics and other interested persons in the United States. This was done in response to the bishops' desire for dialogue: within the Catholic community; between the Catholic Church and the other Christian churches, as well as with representatives of other religions; and between the Church and the human family.[3]

The process of dialogue included three extensive consultations with the Church at large and with scholars, involving hundreds of thousands of people and resulting in tens of thousands of recommendations. The NCD was the subject of regional meetings of the bishops in the spring of 1975, during which laity, religious, and clergy joined with them in discussing catechetical needs. The NCD also reflects the deliberations and conclusions of the Fourth General Assembly of the Synod of Bishops convened at the Vatican in 1977 to discuss "Catechesis in Our Time, With Special Reference to the Catechesis of Children and Young People."

5. Sources

It is appropriate at the outset to say something about the term "catechetical" in this document's title. It comes from the ancient word "catechesis,"

32-33

which appears often in the documents of the Church. Catechesis refers to efforts which help individuals and communities acquire and deepen Christian faith and identity through initiation rites, instruction, and formation of conscience. It includes both the message presented and the way in which it is presented. The NCD therefore draws upon the Church's biblical, patristic, historical, liturgical, theological, missiological, and catechetical heritages. It also makes use of sound contemporary developments in the sacred and human sciences, as well as the "signs of the times" — the contemporary cultural situation. Another source is the wisdom of God's people, united with their bishops under the guidance of the Holy Spirit.

6. Audience

This NCD has been prepared particularly for those responsible for catechesis in the United States. Among those who will benefit, directly or indirectly, are parents and guardians exercising their responsibilities as the primary educators of children; professional and paraprofessional catechists at all levels; men and women religious; deacons and priests involved in this ministry; and members of diocesan and parish council education committees or boards with catechetical duties. The NCD is also of basic importance to writers and publishers of catechetical texts and other materials for catechesis.

7. Authority

This NCD is an official statement of the National Conference of Catholic Bishops of the United States and has been reviewed and approved by the Sacred Congregation for the Clergy according to established norms.[4]

Not all parts of this document are of equal importance. The teaching of the Church in regard to revelation and the Christian message is to be held by all; the norms or criteria identified in article 47 pertaining to all catechesis must be observed.[5] The other portions of the NCD are also important, but the treatment of such matters as stages of human development, methodology, catechetical roles and training, organization and structures, resources, etc. is subject to change in light of new knowledge or different circumstances.

c.III, c.V, c.VI

Because the methods and cultural context of catechesis are very likely to change and new Church documents on the subject will be published, this document will be reviewed periodically for updating and improvement. Approximately five years after its approval by the Holy See, it will be submitted to an extensive evaluation, in a manner to be determined by the National Conference of Catholic Bishops.

PART B: OVERVIEW OF CATECHESIS

8. A brief background to contemporary catechesis

The Church continues the mission of Jesus, whose teaching has come down to us through the apostles. The ministry of catechesis serves the Church in that mission. Great importance has always been attached to catechesis, but its methods and emphases have varied in different times and places, from apostolic times to the present, according to changing circumstances and needs. Such differences appear in the catechetical traditions and histories of the Eastern and Western Churches or, as they are also called, the Oriental and Occidental Churches.

Historical records indicate that catechesis was introduced into what is now the United States during the late 16th and early 17th centuries by Spanish and French missionaries in their ministry to the American Indians. Archbishop John Carroll of Baltimore, the first Catholic bishop in the United States (1789-1815), had a strong interest in religious instruction. Later generations of Catholics have consistently manifested the same concern.

John Willig

Michal Heron

3

215,232-
233

In the United States during the 19th century many catechisms and other instructional materials for catechizing were published in English as well as virtually all the other languages spoken by the Catholic immigrants. The *Baltimore Catechism* (published 1885; revised 1941) became the dominant text in Catholic religious education in the United States until shortly before the Second Vatican Council (1962-1965). Also of critical importance was the decision of the Third Plenary Council of Baltimore that parish schools be built near all churches and that, except in unusual circumstances, parents be required to send their children to these schools. This policy gave great impetus to the growth of the parochial schools, in which millions of Catholic children and youth have received, and continue to receive, extensive religious education.

The 20th century has been especially eventful for catechesis in the United States. Some developments are mentioned in the next article. Many others are cited throughout this NCD as accepted elements of contemporary catechesis.

The Confraternity of Christian Doctrine (CCD) has played a major role in the development of catechetics in the United States during this century. First established here in 1902, the CCD developed especially under the leadership of Bishop Edwin V. O'Hara. In 1934 the bishops set up a national office of the confraternity, with Bishop O'Hara as first chairman. Within a few years the CCD spread into virtually every part of the country.

15,73,112,
242a)

Extensive immigration of Eastern Rite Catholics occurred mainly from the end of the 19th century to the early 1920s. Most came from the Middle East or from Central and Eastern Europe. There are now more than one million in this country. During the 1940s and 1950s, many members of these Churches began to rediscover their religious and cultural traditions; they have developed instructional texts and materials to meet their unique needs.

9. Hopeful signs in catechetics in the United States

While catechetical ministry in the United States faces many problems, there are also many hopeful signs and trends. These will be discussed before some of the contemporary problems.

10,c.I,
197-202

Increasingly, catechetics is taking into account significant contemporary developments in the sacred and human sciences. For some time it has also given particular attention to social justice, prompted by scripture and the papal social encyclicals, especially since Leo XIII.

Catechesis is recognizing the contemporary concern for education in morality and values, encouraging this within the framework of the teaching of Jesus and His Church, the influence of God's Spirit, and parental guidance.

In many places, lay people are assuming increasing responsibility and leadership in catechetical work. Women, especially women religious, have for a long time made impressive contributions to catechetics. Now the role of the laity, both men and women, is expanding further, as they assume new responsibilities involving greater leadership in the Church.

USCC Creative Services

221-222

Lay involvement is receiving a significant impetus from representative and advisory bodies developed since the Second Vatican Council. Among the promising new instruments of shared responsibility are pastoral councils, boards of education committees responsible for comprehensive catechetical programs, councils of the laity, and boards of education at the diocesan, interparochial, and parochial levels. Such new structures have led to a marked increase in comprehensive catechetical planning and the skills related to it. Planning has fostered prudent use of time, resources, and personnel. It has also contributed to the understanding and observance of the principles of subsidiarity and accountability.

Adult catechesis, including parent and family education and allied programs for the enrichment of married life, has become more prominent. The rite of the Christian initiation of adults is being introduced for both the catechumenate and adult catechesis. Of particular interest are small Christian communities which provide an atmosphere for more effective catechesis, including the *comunidad de base* found especially in the Hispanic community.[6]

Among other positive developments are the growing tendency in youth ministry to include catechesis within a total ministry to this age group; greater commitment to serving the needs of the mentally, emotionally, and physically handicapped; heightened awareness of the needs of racial, ethnic, and cultural groups, as well as their special contributions to the Church; and the expansion of programs for the continuing education of the clergy.

It is also widely recognized that Catholic schools are to be communities of faith in which the Christian message, the experience of community, worship, and social concern are integrated in the total experience of students, their parents, and members of the faculty.

NC Photo by Tom Lorsung

Aided by the spread of graduate schools and programs of religious education, as well as summer schools, seminars, institutes, and a wide assortment of professional publications and texts, Catholic catechists and catechetical administrators now enjoy greater opportunities for professional growth than in the past. At the same time, attention is also given to the centrality for their ministry of their personal faith commitment in and to Christ.

c.XI

Modern technology — records, audio cassettes, filmstrips, films, video cassettes, video discs, instructional, cable, public and commercial television, with satellite transmission — contributes much to catechetical efforts. It is important for communicating Christ's message to people for whom media other than the printed word are an increasingly significant part of learning and growth.

The most heartening development has been the renewed interest of many Catholics in the Bible, liturgy, and prayer. A new spiritual maturity exists in many sectors of the Catholic community in the United States today.

10. Contemporary problems in catechetics in the United States

c.I,197-202

Because catechesis is concerned with applying the certain, timeless teachings of faith to the uncertain, changing conditions of each generation, some errors of judgment, misplaced emphasis, and ill-timed innovations are likely. Recent difficulties and disagreements revolve largely around the orthodoxy and adequacy of doctrinal content in contemporary catechetical methodology. This NCD gives serious attention to these questions. No small part of the difficulty arises from the fact that today most children are catechized in a way which bears little resemblance to the ways in which their parents received religious instruction.

Contemporary catechesis also confronts a variety of problems arising from social conditions. Some of these are described in Chapter I and elsewhere in this document.

11. Conclusion

This NCD seeks to help the entire Catholic community grow in unity, love, and peace. Its purpose is correspondingly evangelical and missionary, looking toward an increase in the vitality and holiness of Christ's body which is the Church.

Though "the Church is more than ever alive," yet "it seems good to consider that everything still remains to be done; the work begins today and never comes to an end."[7] This document is presented to the Catholic community in the confidence that, as in the past, the Holy Spirit will guide the Church in our land in its catechetical ministry both now and in the future.

NC Photo

Chapter I

Some Cultural and Religious Characteristics Affecting Catechesis in the United States

Your light must shine before men,
so that they may see goodness
in your acts and give praise
to your heavenly Father.
Mt 5, 16

12. *Applying general principles*

It is a complex task to apply the principles and guidelines of the *General Catechetical Directory* to Catholic catechesis in the United States, a nation of well over 200 million people of many different racial, ethnic, and cultural backgrounds. The difficulty is increased by differences related to region, age, style of life, temperament, and other factors. While the NCD seeks to be responsive to all conditions and catechetical needs in this country, only some major aspects of contemporary culture, with special relevance to catechesis, will be noted here.

These phenomena are grouped under four headings: diversity, the influence of science and technology, a brief profile of United States Catholics, and the importance of family and home.

PART A: DIVERSITY

16,39,47,
51,72c),
137,139,
193-194,
236,242a)

13. *Race, ethnicity, and culture*

Nearly every race and ethnic group on earth is represented in the population of the United States. Relatively recent immigrations have greatly increased the Catholic population.[1] Here the oppressed and needy from many nations have sought a haven and a land of opportunity. The Church from the beginning sheltered and fostered these cultural, racial, and ethnic groups as they strove to find their way in a strange new country. Yet local churches did at times fail to appreciate, refuse to try to understand, and neglect to welcome the newcomers. Some, in fact, have left the Church and either joined other existing denominations, established their own, or joined the ranks of the unchurched.

NC Photo by Tom Lorsung

Today, however, the United States appears to be growing in appreciation of cultural diversity, recognizing the splendid beauty of all races, cultures, and ethnic groups. At the same time, peoples throughout the world look to this country for support in their struggle for human rights.

75-80

14. *The many religions*

The United States has from the beginning been a refuge for those fleeing religious persecution. Many new religions have also been founded here. Yet at present nearly 40 percent of the people are not formally affiliated with any religion. The unchurched in the United States now are estimated to number 81 million.[2]

The great religious diversity of the United States and the very large number of unchurched persons, including lapsed Catholics, together point to the need both for ecumenical activities and for continuing efforts directed to the evangelization of all.

The number and percentage of Catholics in a given area also have an obvious practical bearing on catechesis. The figures vary greatly: for example, from a high of nearly two-thirds in Rhode Island to below 2 percent in North and South Carolina. In the nation as a whole, roughly one person in every four has been baptized as a Catholic.

8,73,112,
242a)

15. *Church and Churches*

The Catholic Church in the United States is quite diverse. It includes the Catholic Church of the West and the Catholic Churches of the East. The former is sometimes called the Latin Church. The latter have their origins in the Apostolic Churches of the East — Constantinople, Alexandria, Antioch,

8

and Jerusalem — and are usually organized according to the major traditions: Byzantine, Antiochene, Chaldean, Armenian, and Alexandrian. Those with established hierarchies in the United States are the Ukrainians, Ruthenians, and Melkites, all of the Byzantine tradition, and the Maronites of the Antiochene tradition. Those without their own hierarchies here include the Romanians, Russians, Byelorussians, Italo-Albanians, and Italo-Greeks of the Byzantine tradition, and the Armenians, Syrians, Chaldeans, and Malankarese.

Over the centuries the Eastern and Western Churches have developed diverse traditions, theologies, liturgies, and forms of spirituality, all faithful expressions of the teaching of Christ. Representing cultures and world views with which most Catholics in this country are not familiar, the Eastern Churches provide significant alternative resources for catechesis. The insights of all the traditions are needed to deal with the varieties of pluralism in the United States.

16. Unity of the faith and theological pluralism[3]   37,73

Pluralism in theological expression of faith, common today, is not new in the history of the Church. Found in the New Testament and present in the early centuries in the great theological currents of the West and the East, pluralism in the course of time grew and manifested itself in a variety of theological schools.

Theological reflection is integral to the Church's life and thought. In the past, the Church not only tolerated but encouraged a pluralism of theological tendencies, reflecting attempts to provide better explanations of themes and problems addressed under different aspects. Today the Church continues to encourage pluralism for pastoral and evangelical reasons, provided always that

Rick Smolan

Nelson Brooks

the pluralism in question contributes to a genuine enrichment of the doctrine of the faith and is in constant fidelity to it. Theological expression also takes into account different cultural, social, and even racial and ethnic contexts, while at the same time remaining faithful to the content of the Catholic faith as received and handed on by the magisterium of the Church.[4]

Catechists must be sensitive to the distinction between faith and theology. There is one faith, but there can be many theologies. Yet in regard even to matters which admit of a legitimate variety of theological opinions, the common doctrine of the Church is to be taught and the belief of the faithful respected. The unequal value of various theological systems should also be recognized. Which particular theological opinions should be raised in catechesis, and when they should be raised, are to be determined by the readiness of the learners and the preparation of the teacher. When catechists are engaged in the teaching dimension of their ministry, they teach not in their own names but in the name of the Church: from it they receive a commission, and under the direction of its hierarchy they are to carry out their ministry.

60c),190, 206,212

PART B: SCIENCE AND TECHNOLOGY

17. Science and technology

The rapid progress of science and technology in the United States has put into human hands unprecedented power to reap great benefit for the human race or sow disaster upon the earth. Men and women have new capacities to attempt to solve some of the persistent problems confronting the people of the entire world; but, they also have new power to deny human dignity and even survival to much of humanity.

Science and technology hold out the promise of improving the world food supply, curing diseases and plagues, and distributing the world's goods more equitably. They can also be used to violate human freedom, curtail human rights, and kill vast numbers of people.

NC Photo

NC Photo by Chris Sheridan

18. The arms race

The greatest threat to human survival lies in the awesome power of modern weaponry. Warfare and the arms race menace civilization: atomic devices including hydrogen and neutron bombs; biological weapons capable of spreading disease and plagues to human and animal life; and chemical projectiles, with deadly gases and liquids. Furthermore, the arms race is a colossal waste of God-given resources.

Disarmament is a critical and fundamental issue. The Second Vatican Council placed the problem in perspective when it declared that people, especially leaders and rulers, must "make a true beginning of disarmament, not indeed a unilateral disarmament, but one proceeding at an equal pace according to agreement, and backed up by authentic and workable safeguards."[5]

19. Life sciences

Similarly, the unprecedented progress in life sciences, especially in the field of biology and allied disciplines, has generated new moral problems while calling into being a new specialty called bioethics, which deals with human life in all its stages.

Awareness of the intrinsic value of life and respect for human dignity are fundamental to any consideration of the problems of abortion, infanticide, the care of those who are severely handicapped, infirm, or aged, the definition of death and euthanasia, behavior control through surgery and drug therapy, genetic engineering, and population control.

105b),131, 156,167

20. Technology

Technological progress has had contradictory effects on life in this country. In becoming highly mobile and migratory, people, especially families, have been drawn further apart; yet, in another sense, the almost universal coverage of modern communications media has brought people into increasingly constant and immediate contact.

21. Mobility

Mobility is a characteristic of life in the United States. Almost one person out of five changes residence annually (though most moves are for short distances, and two people out of three live in the state in which they were born). Movers tend to be younger, better educated, and male. The majority of people, including Catholics (about three out of four), live in metropolitan areas.[6]

USDA Photo

The breakdown of family ties and community identity along with intensified loneliness are among the negative results of this mobility. Except perhaps in rural areas and surviving ethnic neighborhoods, Church leaders can no longer take for granted a sense of community; often they must instead work to develop and sustain it.

22. Communications

The impact of the communications revolution, especially television, is very powerful in the United States. The influx of information is overwhelming. A person living in the United States today is said to be exposed to more information in a week than his or her counterpart of two centuries ago was in a year.

170,15), 178,253-258,262

Many find that they are given more information than they can assimilate or evaluate. People need to acquire "literacy" in relation to the new media — that is, they need to grow in their ability to evaluate television and other contemporary media by critical standards which include gospel values.

Yet another threat to human dignity and privacy is posed by the enormous capacity of computers and data banks to store billions of data indefinitely and retrieve them readily. All manner of records, medical, personal, educational, financial, have now become available to government and even private agencies. Such records can be helpful in many ways and can work to the advantage of many people; yet at the same time the invasion of personal, corporate, and institutional privacy can pose a very real threat to human rights. Solutions lie not only in the physical protection of data banks and in legal sanctions, but also in the moral order of justice.

PART C: PROFILE OF UNITED STATES CATHOLICS

23. Positive elements

While no brief description can adequately portray Catholicism in this country, it is possible to sketch some elements of the total picture.

Most Catholics approve the changes initiated by the Second Vatican Council, despite differences concerning the implementation of its documents. There has been an increase in the weekly reception of Holy Communion. New religious forms have emerged, such as the Cursillo, charismatic renewal, prayer groups, Marriage Encounter, youth retreats, home liturgies, and parish renewal programs. Among members of the Eastern Catholic Churches there is a resurgence of interest in their Eastern traditions. Various aspects and programs of catechesis have flourished. There is continued generosity in giving time and money to worthy causes at home and abroad. Numerous examples of Christian witness exist.

24. Problems

There are also serious problems. Many Catholics express little or no confidence in organized religion, say their religious beliefs are of limited or no importance to them, and are registered in no parish.[7] Surveys indicate that, with respect to doctrine, many Catholics are poorly informed about their faith or have deliberately rejected parts of it. For example, many express doubt that the pope is infallible when he teaches solemnly in matters of faith and morals; that there can be such a thing as eternal punishment for evil; that the devil exists; that the Church has a right to teach on racial integration. There is

NC/KNA Photo

Lou Niznik

Paul S. Conklin

widespread acceptance of remarriage after divorce; of sexual relations between engaged persons; of artificial birth control; of legal abortion in certain cases.[8] Even many church-affiliated people, Catholics and others, make no conscious connection between their religious beliefs and their moral choices.

Although new forms of devotion have emerged and grown in popularity, traditional religious practice — notably including Sunday Mass attendance — has declined since the early 1960s.[9] Uncertainty, confusion, and apathy are widespread. Large numbers are Christian in name only: they have never really responded with a mature faith to the Lord and His Church. Long-term trends are not clear, but recent developments are a cause of concern even while they contain elements of hope.

While most Catholics have not seriously thought of leaving the Church,[10] a growing number have abandoned active membership. This phenomenon varies considerably with age and education, generally decreasing with age and increasing with the level of education. People under 30 who have attended college have been most affected.[11]

182, 201b)

Atheism, however, does not appear to be a major problem. Very few (3 percent) of the people of the United States deny that there is a personal God or a higher power of some kind.[12]

Clearly, evangelization and catechesis are needed to solve some of these problems. The sophistication, self-awareness, and maturity with which different people approach doctrinal and moral issues vary greatly, for a variety of reasons. It is necessary to present and give witness to the Church's authentic teaching in a way which respects the sincerity of those who are seeking to know what is true and do what is right.[13] Many persons need a gradual integration into the community of believers. Assistance in this regard is offered in the pertinent sections of this NCD.

190

PART D: FAMILY AND HOME IN THE UNITED STATES

25. Importance of the home and community in catechesis

177-178, 201a)

Education, broadly defined, includes the entire process by which culture is transmitted from one generation to the next. Educational research supports the view that the home is the critical educational institution. Study after study identifies home and family as vital forces strongly affecting school achievement. Throughout the world the home is the crucial factor in determining children's overall performance. Behavioral disorders and social pathology in children and youth frequently begin in family disorganization: arising not only from within the family itself, but from the circumstances in which the family finds itself and from the way of life which results.

Family and community are also extremely important in the catechetical process. While other factors are involved (e.g., age, sex, size of community, present study of religion, parental approval of the friends of their children, etc.), the impact of parents is primary among the human factors which influence this process. This is the principal reason for the current emphasis on preparation for parenthood and parent education, as well as a subsidiary motive for adult education.[14]

Michal Heron

The vital influence of parents on the social and religious development of their children must be more widely recognized. Family life needs to be strengthened so that children and youth will derive their values from the home, rather than from potentially undesirable sources outside the home. The Church, especially through the parish, should provide an intensified support system for family life.

26. Changes in families

In the past quarter-century in the United States the family has experienced progressive fragmentation and isolation, along with changes in its structure and child-bearing role. Catholic families have been affected together with the rest. Changes are more rapid among younger families with young children, increase with economic deprivation and industrialization, and reach a peak among low-income families living in the central core of larger cities.

27. Illustrations of change in families

a) Divorce

There are now over one million divorces a year in the United States. Millions of children and young people under 18 have experienced family breakup on account of divorce. Nearly one-third of all school-age children are not living with both natural parents.

b) One-parent families

The number of one-parent families has risen with the increased rate of divorce, desertion, and births outside of marriage. Currently about one family in every five with school-age children is headed by one parent.

NC Photo by Chris Sheridan

One-parent households are much more common in large cities and among younger families. They occur least often in rural and suburban areas. However, patterns of fragmentation found a few years ago only in major metropolitan centers are now also present in smaller urban areas. Families in similar circumstances (as to age, region, education, income, etc.) now tend to be affected in much the same way.

c) Unwed mothers

After families divided by divorce, the most rapidly growing category of one-parent families is that of families headed by unwed mothers.

The number of live births out of wedlock tripled between 1960 and the mid-1970s. A preponderant number of women who become pregnant out of wedlock and give birth to their children do not place them for adoption. The overwhelming proportion of out-of-wedlock births occur to women under 25.

d) Families where both parents work

In more than half of the families with school-age children both parents work outside the home or are seeking such work. Most have full-time jobs. In about one-third of the families with preschool children, both parents work. Needless to say, extensive parental absence from the home is more likely in one-parent families.

"Catholic Northwest Progress" Photo

The great increase in the number of working mothers has been a major factor in the expansion of nursery schools, day care centers of all kinds, and ordinary babysitting. Millions of school-age youngsters ("latchkey children") return from school to empty homes. They contribute, at a rate far out of proportion to their numbers, to the ranks of those with academic difficulties or behavioral problems.

e) Family size

The average size of households in the United States has dropped significantly in recent years. A dramatic decline in childbearing has been a major factor.

f) Delay of marriage

People are marrying later now than in the past; and more and more persons of both sexes choose to remain single. Many postpone or refrain from marriage for career or vocational reasons. At the same time, a substantial number of men and women are living together without marriage and, generally, without having children.

28. *Effects of change on families*

These trends appear to be nationwide and are having profound effects on society and religion. They underline the fact that the members of many families need extensive support if they are to grow in faith and live according to the example of Christ and the teaching of His Church.

29. *Conclusion*

This overview has presented some contemporary cultural and religious factors confronting catechesis in the United States. Many more could be mentioned (e.g., the special characteristics of children and youth, young adults, and the elderly; the special obstacles to catechesis presented by illiteracy, extreme poverty, drug abuse, alcoholism, etc.).

c.VIII
c.VII

Continuing research is needed so that those engaged in catechesis will understand contemporary social phenomena and be better equipped to bring people to Christian maturity by means which take these phenomena into realistic account. There is a particularly urgent need for analysis of the current status of the family, the roles of men and women within the family and society generally, and the alterations brought about by social and economic changes.

The picture presented here and elsewhere in this NCD is a sober one. Two points need to be borne in mind: first, because catechesis occurs in a cultural and social context, the catechist must take the negative as well as the positive aspects of the situation into account; second, God's kingdom has already been established, and Christ's followers are called to manifest and work for the ever fuller realization of that kingdom in all areas of life.

Michal Heron

Paul S. Conklin

15

Chapter II

The Catechetical Ministry of the Church

O Lord,
let the light of your countenance
shine upon us!
Ps 4,7

30. *Mission of the Church*

The Church continues the mission of Jesus, prophet, priest, and servant king. Its mission, like His, is essentially one — to bring about God's kingdom — but this one mission has three aspects: proclaiming and teaching God's word, celebrating the sacred mysteries, and serving the people of the world. Corresponding to the three aspects of the Church's mission and existing to serve it are three ministries: the ministry of the word, the ministry of worship, and the ministry of service. In saying this, however, it is important to bear in mind that the several elements of the Church's mission are inseparably linked in reality (each includes and implies the others), even though it is possible to study and discuss them separately.

PART A: CATECHESIS — A FORM OF MINISTRY OF THE WORD

31. *Forms of ministry of the word*

The ministry of the word takes different forms, depending on circumstances and on the particular ends in view.[1] Proclamation and teaching of God's word are present in evangelization, catechesis, liturgy, and theology, in a manner appropriate to each.

32. *Catechetical ministry*

c.VI
c.VII

Like other pastoral activities, catechetical ministry must be understood in relation to Jesus' threefold mission. It is a form of the ministry of the word, which proclaims and teaches.[2] It leads to and flows from the ministry of worship, which sanctifies through prayer and sacrament.[3] It supports the ministry of service, which is linked to efforts to achieve social justice and has traditionally been expressed in spiritual and corporal works of mercy.[4]

40,115,117,
170,13),
182-189,
192-196,
201-202,
225-227

Catechesis is an esteemed term in Christian tradition. Its purpose is to make a person's "faith become living, conscious, and active, through the light of instruction."[5] While aiming to enrich the faith life of individuals at their particular stages of development, every form of catechesis is oriented in some way to the catechesis of adults, who are capable of a full response to God's word.[6] Catechesis is a lifelong process for the individual and a constant and concerted pastoral activity of the Christian community.

33. *Task of catechesis: to foster mature faith*

174

Faith grows and matures. People of mature faith recognize the real and lasting value of human activity in this world, while also directing their "thoughts and desires to the full consummation of the kingdom in eternal life."[7] They "constantly [strive] for conversion and renewal, and [give] diligent ear to what the Spirit says to the Church."[8] They live in communion with God and other people, willingly accepting the responsibilities which arise from these relationships.[9] Maturity of faith implies that one "knows the mystery of salvation revealed in Christ, and the divine signs and works which are witnesses to the fact that this mystery is being carried out in human history."[10] A mature Christian has an active sacramental and prayer life.[11] Such a person tests and interprets human events, "especially the signs of the times," in a wholly Christian spirit,[12] and is zealous to spread the gospel in order to make the Church known as the sign and instrument of the salvation and unity of the human race.[13]

Such faith is a grace, a gift of God. Growth in faith is intimately related to one's response to this gift. (Cf. Col 2,6f) So "the life of faith admits of various degrees," both in acceptance of God's word and in the ability to explain and apply it.[14] (The act of faith is considered at greater length in Chapter III, while the stages on the way to mature faith are examined in Chapter VIII.)

54,57-58,84, 98,175,188, 213

34. Catechesis and pre-evangelization

Catechesis presupposes prior pre-evangelization and evangelization. These are likely to be most successful when they build on basic human needs — for security, affection, acceptance, growth, and intellectual development — showing how these include a need, a hunger, for God and His word.

Often, however, catechesis is directed to individuals and communities who, in fact, have not experienced pre-evangelization and evangelization, and have not made acts of faith corresponding to those stages. Taking people as they are, catechesis attempts to dispose them to respond to the message of revelation in an authentic, personal way.

There is a great need in the United States today to prepare the ground for the gospel message. Many people have no religious affiliation. Many others have not committed their lives to Christ and His Church, even though they are church members. Radical questioning of values, rapid social change, pluralism, cultural influences, and population mobility — these and other factors underline the need for pre-evangelization.

14
24

35. Catechesis and evangelization

Although evangelization and catechesis are distinct forms of the ministry of the word, they are closely linked in practice. Evangelization "has as its purpose the arousing of the beginnings of faith."[15] It seeks to bring the good news "into all the strata of humanity," in this way "transforming humanity from within and making it new."[16] It aims at interior change, conversion of "the personal and collective conscience of people, the activities in which they engage, and the lives and concrete milieux which are theirs."[17]

Such change and renewal are also goals of catechesis, which disposes people "to receive the action of the Holy Spirit and to deepen conversion," and does so "through the word, to which are joined the witness of life and prayer."[18]

To consider evangelization only as a verbal proclamation of the gospel robs it of much of its richness; just as it does not do justice to catechesis to think of it as instruction alone. Like evangelization, catechesis is incomplete if it does not take into account the constant interplay between gospel teaching and human experience — individual and social, personal and institutional, sacred and secular.

Michal Heron

36. Catechesis and liturgy

44,97,c.VI

From its earliest days the Church has recognized that liturgy and catechesis support each other. Prayer and the sacraments call for informed participants; fruitful participation in catechesis calls for the spiritual enrichment that comes from liturgical participation.

While every liturgical celebration has educative and formative value, liturgy should not be treated as subservient to catechesis. On the contrary, catechesis should "promote an active, conscious, genuine participation in the liturgy of the Church, not merely by explaining the meaning of the ceremonies, but also by forming the minds of the faithful for prayer, for thanksgiving, for repentance, for praying with confidence, for a community spirit, and for understanding correctly the meaning of the creeds."[19]

Sacramental catechesis has traditionally been of two kinds: preparation for

19

the initial celebration of the sacraments and continued enrichment following their first reception. The first is elementary or general in nature; it aims to introduce catechumens to the teaching of scripture and the creed. The second reflects on the meaning of the Christian mysteries and explores their consequences for Christian witness. Preparatory sacramental catechesis can be for a specified period of time — some weeks or months; the catechesis which follows is a lifelong matter. In the early Church sacramental catechesis focused on the Sacraments of Initiation: Baptism, Confirmation, and Eucharist. Over the course of time similar catecheses have been developed for the other sacraments: Reconciliation, Matrimony, Holy Orders, and the Anointing of the Sick.

16,73

37. Catechesis and theology

Catechesis draws on theology, and theology draws in turn on the richness of the Church's catechetical experience. Both must be at the service of the Church. Though intimately related, they are distinguishable in practice by their goals, methods, and criteria.

Theology seeks fuller understanding of the gospel message through reflection on the life of Christians and the formal teachings of the Church. It employs systematic and critical methods. It uses philosophy, history, linguistics, and other disciplines in attempting to understand and express Christian truth more clearly.

Catechesis also makes use of the sacred and human sciences. It does this not as theology does — for systematic study and analyses of the faith — but in order to better proclaim the faith and, in cooperation with the Holy Spirit, lead individual Christians and the community to maturity of faith, a richer living of the fullness of the gospel message.

NC Photo by Tom Lorsung

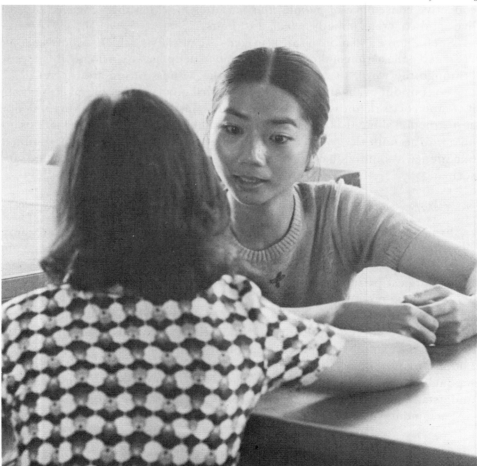

NC Photo

102-105,
159,190

Catechesis in morality is an essential element of catechetical ministry.

The Gospels contain Jesus' moral teaching as transmitted by the apostolic Church. The epistles, especially those of St. Paul, denounce conduct unbecoming to Christians and specify the behavior expected of those who have been baptized into Christ. (Cf., e.g., Eph 4,17-32; Col 3,5-11)

Through the ages moral teaching has been an integral part of the Catholic message, and an upright life has been a hallmark of a mature Christian. Catechisms have traditionally emphasized a code of Christian conduct, sometimes summarized under three headings: a sense of personal integrity; social justice and love of neighbor; and accountability to God as a loving Father who is also Lord of all.

Catechesis therefore includes the Church's moral teaching, showing clearly its relevance to both individual ethics and current public issues. It takes into account the stages through which individuals and communities pass as they grow in ability to make moral judgments and to act in a responsible, Christian manner. Catechesis expresses the Church's moral teaching clearly and emphasizes the faithful acceptance of this teaching — an acceptance which carries a twofold responsibility on the part of individuals and the community: to strive for perfection and give witness to Christian beliefs and values and to seek to correct conditions in society and the Church which hinder authentic human development and the flourishing of Christian values.

PART B: FORMS OF CATECHESIS

39. *General diversity of catechetical activity*

Conducted in a variety of circumstances and directed to widely diverse audiences, catechetical activity takes many forms. There is catechesis for different age levels — children, pre-adolescents and adolescents, young adults and adults — and for different groups (e.g., the non-English speaking, members of particular cultural, racial, and ethnic groups, the handicapped, etc.) within each age category. It will also vary in form according to the language, vocation, abilities, and geographical location of those catechized. Its components include sharing faith life, experiencing liturgical worship, taking part in Christian service, and participating in religious instruction. Programs should be designed to take into account participants' experiences and circumstances. As far as possible, catechesis should be adapted to the needs of each individual.

Michal Heron

Furthermore, although the initiation, education, and formation of individuals and the faith community pertain especially to catechesis,[20] every pastoral activity has a catechetical dimension.

For the past century Catholic catechetical effort in the United States has focused primarily upon children and adolescents. Much of this effort has been carried on in Catholic schools. Other major catechetical programs for children and adolescents who do not attend Catholic schools have been and are being developed under the auspices of national and diocesan offices and in parishes.

40. *Adult catechesis*

32,115,117,
170,13),
182-189,
196,201-
202,225,
227

Without neglecting its commitment to children, catechesis needs to give more attention to adults than it has been accustomed to do. It should not be thought that adult catechesis is important only by reason of its relationship to the catechesis of children (i.e., adults must be catechized so that they can catechize the young) or that parent and teacher education are the whole of adult catechesis — though they are certainly forms of it. Rather, the primary reason for adult catechesis — its first and essential objective — is to help adults themselves grow to maturity of faith as members of the Church and society. The *General Catechetical Directory* views adult catechesis as the summit of the entire catechetical enterprise[21] (cf. Col 1,28); while, from another perspective, it stands at the center of the Church's educational mission.[22]

It is adult Christians who are capable of mature faith, and whose lives exemplify gospel values to the young members of the Christian community and the rest of society. They strongly influence the way in which children and catechumens perceive faith. It is essential that they express gospel values by living with the hope and joy that come with faith. The Church, for its part, must encourage its adult members to grow in faith and give them opportunities to do so.

Rick Smolan

Linda Bartlett

PART C: SOURCE AND SIGNS OF CATECHESIS

41. *Source of catechesis*

The source of catechesis, which is also its content, is one: God's word, fully revealed in Jesus Christ and at work in the lives of people exercising their faith under the guidance of the magisterium, which alone teaches authentically.[23] God's word deposited in scripture and tradition is manifested and celebrated in many ways: in the liturgy and "in the life of the Church, especially in the just and in the saints"; moreover, "in some way it is known too from those genuine moral values which, by divine providence, are found in human society."[24] Indeed, potentially at least, every instance of God's presence in the world is a source of catechesis.

42. *Signs: manifestations of the source*

c.III

The various manifestations of the source of catechesis are called signs because they point to a deeper reality: God's self-communication in the world. Drawing upon the words and deeds of revelation to express a vision of God's love and saving power, catechesis recalls the revelation brought to perfection in Christ and "interprets human life in our age, the signs of the times, and the things of this world."[25] The signs of God's saving activity have come to be classified under four general headings: biblical signs, liturgical signs, ecclesial signs, and natural signs. Though closely related, signs of each kind have special characteristics.

*52-53,59,
60a)i,143,
179,185,
190,207,
223*

43. *Biblical signs*

Catechesis studies scripture as a source inseparable from the Christian message. It seeks ways to make the biblical signs better understood, so that people may more fully live the message of the Bible. (Cf. 2 Tm 3,14-17)

Catechesis encourages people to use the Bible as a source and inspiration for prayer. It fosters informed participation in the liturgy by helping people recognize biblical themes and language which are part of the readings and sacramental rites. It reflects constantly on the biblical signs in order to penetrate their meaning more deeply.

The term "biblical signs" refers to the varied and wonderful ways, recorded in scripture, by which God reveals Himself. Among the chief signs, to be emphasized in all catechesis, are: the creation account, which culminates in the establishment of God's kingdom; the covenant made by God with Abraham and his descendants and God's new covenant in Jesus Christ which is extended to all people; the exodus from bondage to freedom and the parallel, but far more profound, passage from death to life accomplished by Christ's paschal mystery. Underlying all as an authentic biblical sign is the community of believers — the People of Israel, the Church — from among whom, under the inspiration of the Holy Spirit, certain individuals composed and assembled these holy writings and transmitted them to future generations as testimony to their beliefs and their experience of grace.

44. Liturgical signs

As explained above, catechesis has the task of preparing individuals and communities for knowing, active, and fruitful liturgical and sacramental celebration and for profound reflection upon it. How this is done is discussed in Chapter VI. Here we wish only to note that the celebration of the liturgy, the sacramental rites, and the Church Year are important sources for catechesis.

36,97

The liturgy and sacraments are the supreme celebration of the paschal mystery. They express the sanctification of human life. As efficacious signs which mediate God's saving, loving power, they accomplish the saving acts which they symbolize. In and through the sacramental rites above all, Christ communicates the Holy Spirit to the Church. "In the earthly liturgy, by way of foretaste, we share in that heavenly liturgy which is celebrated in the holy city of Jerusalem toward which we journey as pilgrims."[26]

45. Ecclesial signs

Other aspects of the Church's life besides liturgy are important for catechesis. In general, these ecclesial signs are grouped under two headings: doctrine or creedal formulations and the witness of Christian living.

Creeds and formulas which state the Church's belief are expressions of the living tradition which, from the time of the apostles, has developed "in the Church with the help of the Holy Spirit."[27] They are formulated to meet particular liturgical needs (e.g., the Apostles' Creed), to counteract specific errors (e.g., the Nicene Creed), or simply to express the common beliefs of the Church (e.g., the Credo of the People of God). "The integral, vital substance handed down through the creed provides the fundamental nucleus of the mystery of the One and Triune God as it was revealed to us through the mystery of God's Son, the Incarnate Savior living always in his Church."[28]

59,60c)

Michael Serino

Michal Heron

52,66,96,
165c)

23

Human language is limited, however, especially when it comes to expressing transcendent mysteries. Therefore it is valid to distinguish between the truth itself and the language or words in which it is expressed. One and the same truth may be expressed in a variety of ways. Catechesis must nevertheless recognize creedal statements and doctrinal formulas as indispensable instruments for handing on the faith.

The Church also gives witness to its faith through its way of life, its manner of worship, and the service it renders. The lives of heroic Christians, the saints of past and present, show how people are transformed when they come to know Jesus Christ in the Spirit. The forgiveness and reconciliation experienced by repentant sinners are signs of the Church as a healing community. Concern for and ministry to the poor, disadvantaged, helpless, and hopeless are signs that the Church is a servant. Uniting in love and mutual respect people from every corner of the earth, every racial and ethnic background, all socioeconomic strata, the Church is a sign of our union with God and one another effected in Jesus Christ. Every Christian community, characterized by its stewardship, is meant to be a sign of that assembly of believers which will reach fulfillment in the heavenly kingdom. Such a community catechizes its members by its very life and work, giving witness in a multitude of ways to God's love as revealed and communicated to us in Christ.

46. Natural signs

Its prophetic mission requires that the Church, in communion with all people of good will, examine the signs of the times and interpret them in light of the gospel.[29] Catechesis seeks to teach the faithful to test and interpret all things, including natural signs, in a wholly Christian spirit.[30]

Central human values are expressed in the arts, science, and technology; in family, culture, economic, and social life; in politics and international relations. Catechesis for adults should therefore teach them to evaluate correctly, in light of faith, contemporary cultural and sociological developments, new questions of a religious and moral nature, and the interplay between temporal responsibilities and the Church's mission to the world. It must give an intellectually satisfying demonstration of the gospel's relevance to life.[31] In short, it has the task of examining at the most profound level the meaning and value of everything created, including the products of human effort, in order to show how all creation sheds light on the mystery of God's saving power and is in turn illuminated by it.

PART D: CATECHETICAL CRITERIA

47. Norms of catechesis[32]

While it is neither possible nor desirable to establish a rigid order to dictate a uniform method for the exposition of content, certain norms or criteria guide all sound catechesis. These are developed further throughout this NCD.

First and foremost, catechesis is trinitarian and christocentric in scope and spirit, consciously emphasizing the mystery of God and the plan of salvation, which leads to the Father, through the Son, in the Holy Spirit. (Cf. Eph 1,3-14) Catechesis is centered in the mystery of Christ. The center of the message should be Christ, true God and true man, His saving work carried out in His incarnation, life, death, and resurrection.[33]

Since catechesis seeks to foster mature faith in individuals and communities, it is careful to present the Christian message in its entirety. It does so in such a way that the interrelationship of the elements of this message is

NC Photo

83-92

73,176a),
181,12),
229

apparent, together with the fact that they form a kind of organic whole. Thus their significance in relation to God's mystery and saving works is best communicated.

In practice, this means recognizing a certain hierarchy of truths. "These truths may be grouped under four basic heads: the mystery of God the Father, the Son, and the Holy Spirit, Creator of all things; the mystery of Christ the incarnate Word, who was born of the Virgin Mary, and who suffered, died, and rose for our salvation; the mystery of the Holy Spirit, who is present in the Church, sanctifying it and guiding it until the glorious coming of Christ, our Savior and Judge; and the mystery of the Church, which is Christ's Mystical Body, in which the Virgin Mary holds the pre-eminent place."[34] This hierarchy of truths does not mean that some truths pertain less to faith itself than others do, but rather that some truths of faith enjoy a higher priority inasmuch as other truths are based on and illumined by them. In presenting the truths of faith, catechesis must foster close contact with the various forms of life in the ecclesial community.[35] Sound catechesis also recognizes the circumstances — cultural, linguistic, etc. — of those being catechized. Finally, while interpreting the present life in the light of revelation, catechesis seeks to dispose people "to hope in the future life that is the consummation of the whole history of salvation."[36] (Cf. Col 1,23)

"This task of catechesis, not an easy one, must be carried out under the guidance of the magisterium of the Church, whose duty it is to safeguard the truth of the divine message, and to watch that the ministry of the word uses appropriate forms of speaking, and prudently considers the help which theological research and human sciences can give."[37] Thus, the bishop holds the primary position of authority over programs of catechesis. Under him the pastor holds the office of direct responsibility in the local Church. The teaching of what is opposed to the faith of the Catholic Church, its doctrinal and moral positions, its laws, discipline, and practice should in no way be allowed or countenanced in catechetical programs on any level.

Catechesis strives to express and foster a profound dialogue, which arises from God's loving self-communication and the trusting response of human beings in faith, under the guidance of the Spirit. The next chapter considers in greater detail this dialogue.

16,41,59, 60c),69, 74f),93, 104,181,12), 190,208, 264

13,16,39, 137,139, 193-194, 236,242a)

c.VIII 218a),217

Rick Levine

Linda Bartlett

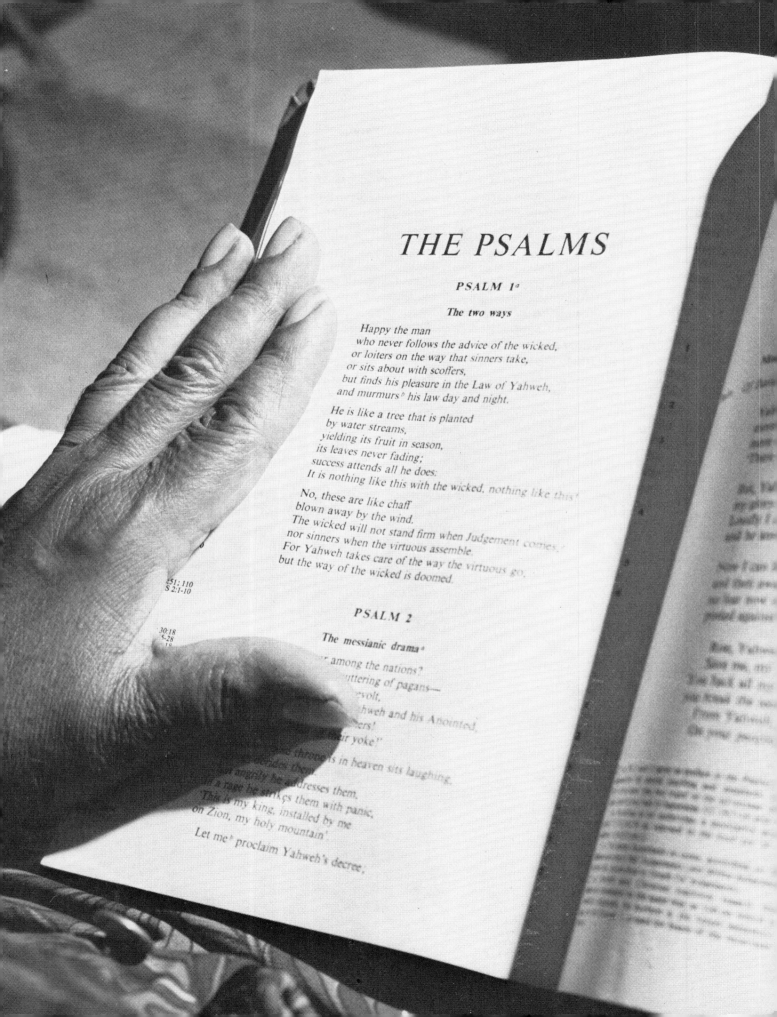

THE PSALMS

PSALM 1ᵃ

The two ways

Happy the man
    who never follows the advice of the wicked,
    or loiters on the way that sinners take,
    or sits about with scoffers,
but finds his pleasure in the Law of Yahweh,
and murmursᵇ his law day and night.

He is like a tree that is planted
    by water streams,
    yielding its fruit in season,
    its leaves never fading;
    success attends all he does:
It is nothing like this with the wicked, nothing like this!

No, these are like chaff
    blown away by the wind.
The wicked will not stand firm when Judgement comes,
nor sinners when the virtuous assemble.
For Yahweh takes care of the way the virtuous go,
but the way of the wicked is doomed.

PSALM 2

The messianic dramaᵃ

r among the nations?
uttering of pagans—
evolt,
hweh and his Anointed,
ers!
ir yoke!"

throne is in heaven sits laughing,
ondes them.
angrily he addresses them,
a rage he strikes them with panic;
"This is my king, installed by me
on Zion, my holy mountain"

Let meᵇ proclaim Yahweh's decree;

Chapter III

Revelation, Faith and Catechesis

A lamp to my feet is your word,
a light to my path.
Ps 119,105

48. Introduction

Christ gave the Church the mission of proclaiming the message of salvation and unfolding its mystery among all peoples. (Cf. Mt 28,19f) In doing this the Church is guided by God's own way of revealing Himself. From the beginning He has gradually made known the inexhaustible mystery of His love in words and deeds and, in so doing, summoned a response in faith from His people. The loving self-revelation of God and the response of humankind together constitute a profound dialogue.

PART A: GOD'S SELF-REVELATION

49. The act of revelation, a mystery of love

55

God's inner life is a deep mystery, for He is "great beyond our knowledge." (Job 36,26) The Word, however, fully comprehends the Father, and God reveals Himself through His Word. "The Word became flesh and made his dwelling among us, and we have seen his glory: The glory of an only Son coming from the Father, filled with an enduring love." (Jn 1,14)

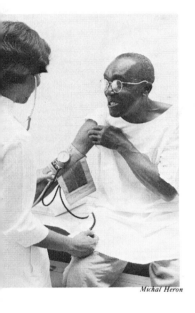

Michal Heron

The term "revelation" has both a general and a strict sense. It has been applied to the constant evidence which God provides of Himself "in created realities."[1] This manifestation of God is available to all human beings, even in the present condition of the human race.[2] Strictly speaking, however, revelation designates that communication of God which is in no way deserved by us, for it has as its aim our participation in the life of the Trinity, a share in divine life itself. This revelation is a gift of God upon which no one has a claim. Because it goes beyond anything which we can dare imagine, the proper response to this revelation is that self-surrender known as the obedience of faith. (Cf. Rom 16,26)

50. Use of the word "revelation" in this document

The word "revelation" is used in this document to refer to that divine public revelation which closed at the end of the Apostolic Age. The terms "manifestation" and "communication" are used for the other modes by which God continues to make Himself known and share Himself with human beings through His presence in the Church and the world.

51. God's self-manifestation through creation

85

God manifests Himself through creation. "Since the creation of the world, invisible realities, God's external power and divinity, have become visible, recognized through the things he has made." (Rom 1,20)

The first chapter of Genesis tells us that God spoke and created all things. Because it is "spoken" by God, creation is a great symbol of Him.[3]

Because human beings are created in God's image and likeness (cf. Gn 1,27), they are most capable of making God manifest in their lives. The more fully people live in fidelity to the image of God in them, the more clearly perceptible is the divine in human life.

Human cultures also mirror divine attributes in various ways. The religions of humanity, especially, give a certain perception "of that hidden power which hovers over the course of things and over the events of human life, at times, indeed, recognition can be found of a Supreme Divinity and of a Supreme Father too. Such a perception and such a recognition instill the lives of these peoples with a profound religious sense."[4] These are concrete examples and expressions of what can be termed God's natural revelation.[5]

52. God's revelation through Israel

Sin and its effects have been part of the human condition ever since our first parents sinned. (Cf. Rom 5,12) But God, intending our redemption, called Abraham to be the father of a people (cf. Gn 12,1ff) — a people with whom God entered into a loving relationship through the Sinai covenant: "I will dwell in the midst of the Israelites and will be their God." (Ex 29,45)

43,60a)i, 77

God spoke to His people through judges and kings, priests and prophets, sages and biblical writers. He fed His people, protected them, liberated them, loved them, corrected, punished, and forgave them. He taught them that He alone is God, compassionate and true to His promises. He invited their free response.

God inspired men and women like Moses, Miriam, Joshua, Deborah, and David to act on His behalf and interpret to others the meaning of His deeds. He inspired authors to record the words and deeds of revelation for the benefit of future generations, and to bring forth from the community the Old Testament accounts which best express His love.

53. God's revelation through His Son, Jesus Christ

87-91

Thus the stage was set for a broader and deeper covenant, God's fullest self-revelation in Jesus Christ. "God so loved the world that he gave his only Son, that whoever believes in him may not die but may have eternal life." (Jn 3,16)

St. Ephrem, in the Eastern tradition, said God imprinted upon nature and in sacred scripture symbols and figures which would manifest Him, as a preparation for revealing Himself in the humanity of Jesus. The purpose of the created universe was to manifest the Son of God and prepare humanity for His coming.[6]

God's revelation reached its supreme expression in the incarnation, life, death, burial, and resurrection of Jesus Christ, by the power of the Spirit. Jesus inaugurated God's kingdom among human beings. He confronted the sinful, dehumanizing forces which alienate people from God, from other human beings, and, indeed, from basic elements of their own personhood. Coming among us as a servant, Jesus expressed His love for the Father and for us by obediently accepting suffering and death, and so reconciling us with God. (Cf. Phil 2,6ff)

45,66,96, 165c)

The apostles were privileged eyewitnesses of God's self-revelation in Christ both before and after His resurrection. (Cf. Jn 21,24) Jesus promised to send them the Holy Spirit, who would enable them to bear witness to Him. (Cf. Jn 14,26) This apostolic witness is normative for the faith of the Church. The Church is thus convinced that "the Christian dispensation . . . as the new and definitive convenant, will never pass away, and we now await no further new public revelation before the glorious manifestation of our Lord Jesus Christ."[7] (Cf. 1 Tm 6,14; Tit 2,13)

NC Photo by Tom Lorsung

God's revelation in and through Jesus Christ, proclaimed by the apostles, is thus unique, irrevocable, and definitive. Still, the Church does not simply possess the memory of something that happened long ago. Rather "God, who spoke of old, uninterruptedly converses with the Bride of His beloved Son; and the Holy Spirit, through whom the living voice of the gospel resounds in the Church, and through her, in the world, leads unto all truth those who believe and makes the word of Christ dwell abundantly in them."[8] (Cf. Col 3,16)

"The Roman Pontiff and the bishops, in view of their office and of the importance of the matter, strive painstakingly and by appropriate means to inquire properly into that revelation and to give apt expression to its contents.

Rick Smolan

But they do not allow that there could be any new public revelation pertaining to the divine deposit of faith."[9] Pope Paul VI reiterates this teaching: "Revelation is inserted in time, in history, at a precise date, on the occasion of a specific event, and it must be regarded as concluded and complete for us with the death of the Apostles."[10]

54. God's manifestation through the Holy Spirit

God continues to manifest Himself through the Holy Spirit at work in the world and, especially, in the Church. Christ, risen and living, is present to believers through the power of the Spirit, who has united Christians since Pentecost, awakening in them the memory of the Lord's life, death, and resurrection, and making these acts present, especially through scripture and the sacraments. The Spirit's action also makes believers sensitive to God's promptings in their hearts, moving them to respond and bear witness to Him so that others, too, may come to know the Lord. (Cf. 1 Cor 2,12f)

Finally, the Spirit helps believers perceive the divine presence in history and interpret human experiences in the light of faith. As the word of the Lord helped the prophets see the divine plan in the signs of their times, so today the Spirit helps the people of the Church interpret the signs of these times and carry out their prophetic tasks.

55. God's manifestation through the daily lives of believers

51

49

Because Christ's revelation is inexhaustible, we can always know more about it and understand it better. (Cf. Eph 3,18f) We grow in such knowledge and understanding when we respond to God manifesting Himself through creation, the events of daily life, the triumphs and tragedies of history. God speaks to us in a special manner in His word — sacred scripture — and through prayer, communicating His love and beauty to us through the Holy Spirit. Above all, He communicates Himself through the sacraments, through the witness of the faithful, and through the full life and teaching of the Church.[11]

But even as He manifests Himself, God remains a mystery. "How deep are the riches and the wisdom and the knowledge of God! How inscrutable his judgments, how unsearchable his ways! For 'who has known the mind of the Lord? Or who has been his counselor?' " (Rom 11,33f) Beyond a certain point we must rely on love, expressed in contemplative prayer and lives of charity, for further growth in knowledge and experience of God.

PART B: REVELATION CALLS FOR RESPONSE IN FAITH

56. Revelation calls for response

Rick Smolan

Though the response to God's revelation and love will vary according to one's background and circumstances, the act of faith involves "total adherence . . . under the influence of grace to God revealing himself."[12] This is the faith *by which* one believes. Total adherence includes not only the mind but also the will and emotions; it is the response of the whole person, including belief in the "content of revelation and of the Christian message."[13] This latter is the faith *which* one believes. Thus faith involves both a relationship and its expression.

57. Faith and grace

The interior help of the Holy Spirit must "precede and assist" faith, "moving the heart and turning it to God, opening the eyes of the mind and giving 'joy and ease to everyone in assenting to the truth and believing it.' "[14] (Cf. Rom 1,16f) Thus one believes in response to grace.

Faith calls for responses of assent, trust, surrender, and obedience to God. Thus faith means commitment, and in this sense it is a deep personal relationship with the Lord. Moments of doubt and anxiety, arising from our weakness, can be expected in the life of faith. Nevertheless, God is faithful. The Lord Jesus reminds us: "Have faith in God and faith in me. . . . I am the way, the truth and the life." (Jn 14,1.6)

58. *Faith as a free response*

Faith is a free response to God revealing. This is "one of the major tenets of Catholic doctrine. . . . Man, redeemed by Christ the Savior and through Christ Jesus called to be God's adopted son, cannot give his adherence to God revealing Himself unless the Father draw him to offer to God the reasonable and free submission of faith."[15] At the same time, faith is also obligatory, in the sense that one who violates conscience by refusing to believe "will be condemned." (Mk 16,16)

59. *Faith expressed in words and deeds*

Faith is expressed in words and deeds.

What we are to believe is found in tradition and scripture, which together "form one sacred deposit of the word of God which is committed to the Church."[16] "Scripture is the word of God inasmuch as it is consigned to writing under the inspiration of the divine Spirit. To the successors of the apostles, sacred tradition hands on in its full purity God's word. . . . Thus, led by the light of the Spirit of truth, these successors can in their preaching preserve this word of God faithfully, explain it, and make it more widely known."[17]

The tradition which comes from the apostles is unfolded in and by the Church with the help of the Holy Spirit. (Cf. 1 Cor 12,2f) Believers grow in insight through study and contemplation. Such growth comes about "through the intimate understanding of spiritual things they experience, and through the preaching of those who have received through episcopal succession the sure gift of truth."[18]

As the community of believers grows in understanding, its faith is expressed in creeds, dogmas, and moral principles and teachings. The meaning of dogmatic formulas "remains ever true and constant in the Church, even when it is expressed with greater clarity or more developed."[19] Because they are expressed in the language of a particular time and place, however, these formulations sometimes give way to new ones, proposed and approved by the magisterium of the Church, which express the same meaning more clearly or completely.[20]

What we believe is also expressed in the deeds of the Church community. The "deeds" in question are worship — especially the celebration of the Eucharist, in which the risen Christ speaks to His Church and continues His saving work — and acts performed to build up Christ's body through service to the community of faith or voluntary service in the universal mission of the Church. (Cf. Eph 4,11f) While it is true that our actions establish the sincerity of our words, it is equally true that our words must be able to explain our actions. In catechesis Catholics are taught a facility in talking about their faith, lest they be silent when it comes to explaining what they are doing and why.

Belief can also be expressed in the visual arts, in poetry and literature, in music and architecture, in philosophy, and scientific or technological achievements. These, too, can be signs of God's presence, continuations of His creative activity, instruments by which believers glorify Him and give witness to the world concerning the faith that is in them.

33,54,84, 98,175, 188,213

AP Photo

45,60c)

Linda Bartlett

PART C: A CATECHETICAL APPROACH TO REVELATION AND FAITH

60. Catechetical guidelines concerning revelation and faith

These general guidelines for catechesis arise from what has been said.

a) Catechists should draw upon all the sources: biblical, liturgical, ecclesial, and natural.

i) Biblical, liturgical, and ecclesial sources

Catechists have vast resources available to them in the Church. These include the Bible, liturgical rites, the Church Year, dogma, doctrines, moral principles and laws, Church history, and theological insights, both ancient and modern. (For liturgical and ecclesial sources, cf. articles 44 and 45.)

*43,52-53,59,
143,179,185,
190,207,223*

The Bible has an essential and indispensable role to play in Christian catechesis. "Ignorance of the scriptures is ignorance of Christ."[21] Catechesis keeps ever in mind the vision of the Second Vatican Council: every Catholic reading, knowing, understanding, and loving the sacred scriptures. The Bible is not just a book to be read and studied. It contains God's word, which should be the object of our prayerful meditation. As a source of inspiration and spiritual nourishment, the Bible ought to be a constant companion.

Michal Heron

Catechists will be thoroughly familiar with both the New and Old Testaments. Hearing scripture read in the liturgy and reading it privately deepen their understanding of the Christian message. Courses in scripture are imperative in preparing catechists to make better use of God's word as a major catechetical source.

Homes, classrooms, and other places of catechesis should have an approved[22] edition of the Bible. In time, students should have and use their own copies of the scriptures.

Paul S. Conklin

52,77

Catechesis explains the number and structure of the books of the Old and New Testaments, speaks of them as God's inspired word, and treats their major themes, such as creation, salvation, and final fulfillment. The Bible is presented as a collection of divinely inspired books, each with its human author or authors, history of composition, and literary form or forms. Such information helps one understand "what meaning the sacred writers really intended, and what God wanted to manifest by means of their words."[23]

The books of the New Testament, especially the Gospels, enjoy preeminence as principal witness of the life and teachings of Jesus, the Incarnate Word. Everyone, according to ability, should become acquainted with the infancy narratives, the miracles and parables of Jesus' public life, and the accounts of His passion, death, and resurrection. Catechesis also develops the principal themes found in the epistles, and gives some attention to the literary characteristics of all the New Testament books, besides providing an introduction to critical exegesis. Major themes of the Old Testament are also to be known as preparing for Christ: creation and redemption, sin and grace, the covenant with Abraham and the chosen people, the exodus from Egypt and the Sinai covenant, the Babylonian captivity and the return, the Emmanuel and suffering servant passages in Isaiah, etc. Individuals are encouraged to meditate on the meaning of the scriptures for their lives. There is value in committing particular passages to memory.

In adult catechesis the work of biblical scholars is studied as a means to achieving "deeper insight into the sense intended by God speaking through the sacred writer."[24] However, critical scholarship of itself is not the ultimate source of the full interpretation of the sacred texts. This interpretation is the gift of the Holy Spirit given to the Church and guarded by the magisterium.

ii) Natural sources

As Jesus often used the experiences of His listeners as the starting point of

His parables, catechists should use examples from daily life, the arts, and the sciences to draw out the meaning of God's revelation and show its relevance for contemporary life.

b) Catechists note the historical character of revelation and faith.

God's revelation occurred through a process of unfolding. "In times past, God spoke in fragmentary and varied ways to our fathers through the prophets; in this, the final age, he has spoken to us through his Son." (Heb 1,1) The Fathers of the Church, especially in their baptismal catechesis, took note of the historical dimension of the drama of salvation. So, in catechesis, "memory of the past, awareness of the present, and hope of the future ought to be evident."[25]

c) Catechists need to understand the development of doctrine.

45,59

Catechists need to have a clear understanding of what is meant by the development of doctrine, namely: (1) that new and deeper insights into the meanings and applications of doctrines can occur;[26] (2) that new terminology can emerge for the expression of doctrine; and (3) that, through its magisterium, the Church can define doctrines whose status as part of divine revelation and the Church's tradition is, in the absence of such definition, not explicitly evident.

Catechists teach as authentic doctrines only those truths which the magisterium teaches. When referring to speculative matters, they identify them as such.

16,190,206, 212

d) Catechists situate catechesis within the community of believers.

The Church, the Body of Christ, is always the context for catechesis. The meaning and vitality of catechesis grow especially in the parish — the praying, believing, and serving community of faith. The parish gives spiritual, moral, and material support to regular, continuing catechesis.

224

e) Catechists pray for discernment of the Spirit.

In those with whom they come in contact catechists will encounter a variety of gifts suited to the service of the Church and the world. The First Epistle to the Corinthians (chapters 12-14) offers classic guidance for perceiving and evaluating the Spirit's gifts. Catechists pray for discernment, which will enable them to be open to the authentic call of the Spirit and to help others be open.[27]

f) Catechists emphasize God's living presence.

In order to speak convincingly of revelation and faith one must be alert to God's living presence. Christ is uniquely present in the Eucharist. He is also present in the other sacraments and in prayer, as well as in other people, in daily life, the signs of the times, and occasions of service: "I assure you, as often as you did it for one of my least brothers, you did it for me." (Mt 25,40)

g) Catechists give guidance on private revelation.

Divine public revelation is the basis of Catholic faith. While some private manifestations (also called private revelations) can occur, claims of these are to be approached with caution. Catechesis stresses that alleged heavenly messages or miraculous events must be investigated and approved by the local bishop before being given any credence.

Paul S. Conklin

61. Conclusion

In speaking of God's self-revelation and of our grace-inspired response of faith, our consequent belief in the truth of what God has revealed, our assent to this truth and trusting surrender, this chapter has referred to the profound dialogue between God and humankind. Catechesis draws attention to this dialogue and seeks to shed light upon it. The next chapter considers the Church: the assembly of believers who respond to God's self-giving by forming and sustaining a community of faith, hope, and love.

Chapter IV

The Church
and Catechesis

Your light has come,
the glory of the Lord
shines upon you.
Nations shall walk by your light.
The Lord shall be your light
forever. . . .
Is 60,1.3.19

62. Introduction

This chapter discusses the meaning of church. It provides catechetical principles and guidance concerning the Catholic Church's mission and concerning its relationship to other Christian churches and communities, the Jewish people, other major religions, and those who profess no religion.

PART A: MEANING OF CHURCH

63. Mystery of divine love

"The Church is a mystery. It is a reality imbued with the hidden presence of God."[1] Born of the Father's love, Christ's redeeming act, and the outpouring of the Holy Spirit, it reflects the very mystery of God.

97

As a divine reality inserted into human history, the Church is a kind of sacrament. Its unique relationship with Christ makes it both sign and instrument of God's unfathomable union with humanity and of the unity of human beings among themselves. Part of the Church's mission is to lead people to a deeper understanding of human nature and destiny and to provide them with more profound experiences of God's presence in human affairs.

As a mystery, the Church cannot be totally understood or fully defined. Its nature and mission are best captured in scriptural parables and images, taken from ordinary life, which not only express truth about its nature but challenge the Church: for example, to become more a People of God, a better servant, more faithful and holy, more united around the teaching authority of the hierarchy.

93

64. People of God

The Church is also a human reality, a community of believers, the People of God. Jesus called men and women to become free from the slavery of sin, to pass through the saving waters of Baptism, to believe, worship, and witness to all He said and did. The first letter of Peter calls this new people "a chosen race, a royal priesthood, a holy nation, a people he claims for his own to proclaim the glorious works of the One who called you from darkness into his marvelous light." (1 Pt 2,9)

93

65. One Body in Christ

This new People of God is "one Body in Christ." (Rom 12,5) Through His death and resurrection the Son redeemed humankind, overcoming sin and division. (Cf. 2 Cor 5,15) Although glorified now at the right hand of the Father, the Lord Jesus remains incarnate in the world through the Church, His body. Through the Spirit we are vivified and made one in Christ, the head of this body of which we are members.

The Church expresses and celebrates its identity above all in the Eucharist. St. Paul, who often[2] refers to the Church as the Body of Christ, brings together the meaning of the Eucharist and the Church in his first letter to the Corinthians: "Is not the cup of blessing we bless a sharing in the blood of Christ? And is not the bread we break a sharing in the body of Christ? Because the loaf of bread is one, we, many though we are, are one body, for we all partake of one loaf." (I Cor 10,16f)

Christ unceasingly bestows the Spirit on the members of the Church, thus joining them with Himself in His continuing mission in and to the world. St. Paul pleads with the members of Christ's body to live in a manner worthy of

Robert Hollis

their calling. (Cf. Eph 4,1) They are to grow to "form that perfect man who is Christ come to full stature." (Eph 4,13) They are to build the body which is the Church in love and unity. (Cf. Eph 4,16)

66. The Church as servant

45,53,96, 165c)

Like Christ, who came into the world "not to be served by others but to serve" (Mt 20,28), the Church seeks to minister to all peoples. It has a mission to heal and reconcile as its founder did. (Cf. 2 Cor 5,18f) It must perform the corporal and spiritual works of mercy, assisting the needy, whatever their condition. (Cf. Mt 25,35-40) The good and faithful servant acts out of concern and love, not for personal gain or glory. (Cf. Lk 22,27) One way in which the Church fulfills its role as servant is its teaching ministry: in today's world one of its chief forms of service is its witness to a transcendent God, to unchanging truths, and to the gospel message.

67. The Church as sign of the kingdom

29-30,43, 53,68-69

The Church — that community of loving believers in the risen Lord — is called to be a sign of God's kingdom already in our midst. It is called to serve the kingdom and to advance it among all peoples of the world. In seeing the Church, people should have at least a glimpse of the kingdom, a glimpse of what it will be like to be united in love and glory with one another in Christ the Lord, king of heaven and earth.

To be a sign of the kingdom already here, the Church on every level — most immediately on the parish level — must be committed to justice, love, and peace, to grace and holiness, truth and life, for these are the hallmarks of the kingdom of God. (Cf. Roman Missal, Preface for the Feast of Christ the King)

NC Photo by Tom Lorsung

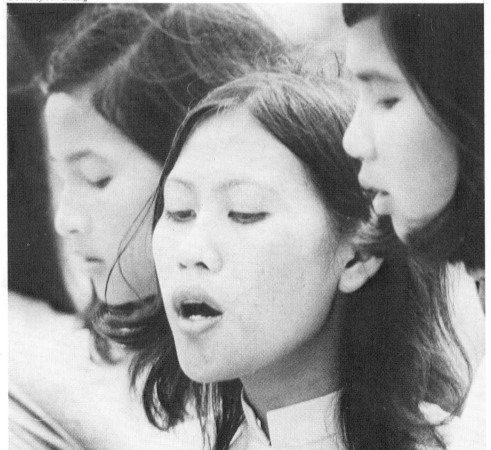

NC/KNA Photo

72b)

93

68. The pilgrim Church

The Church on earth represents the initial manifestation of the kingdom of God. Like pilgrims on a long, hard journey to a holy place, the Church's members have to bear the burden of their own sins, weakness, and frailty on the way to God's eternal city. Along the way they amend their sinful habits and resume their quest for union with God. The power of the risen Lord gives this pilgrim Church "strength to overcome patiently and lovingly the afflictions and hardships which assail her from within and without, and to show forth in the world the mystery of the Lord in a faithful though shadowed way, until at last it will be revealed in total splendor."[3]

As mystery, people, one body in Christ, servant, sign of the kingdom, and pilgrim, the Church is conceived as God's family, whose members are united to Christ and led by the Spirit in their journey to the Father. The Church merits our prayerful reflection and wholehearted response.

72d),93

69. The Church as a hierarchical society

At the same time, as the Second Vatican Council teaches, the Church is also a visible society established by Christ with ordained ministers to serve its members.

132-133,
218a)

The pope, Christ's vicar on earth, is the chief shepherd and supreme authority. Patriarchs[4] and other bishops join with the pope in service to the whole membership of the Church through the faithful performance of their Christ-given roles as teachers, sanctifiers, and rulers. The body of bishops united with the Roman pontiff, and never apart from him, has supreme and full authority over the universal Church.[5] Priests and deacons collaborate intimately with their bishops in the service of God's people.

Michal Heron

Paul S. Conklin

The clergy serve the Church through authentic Christian teaching, sacramental ministry, and direction in various organizations and activities for God's kingdom. Of special importance for unity of faith are the Church's official teachings on matters of faith and morals authoritatively promulgated by the pope and bishops. These teachings give the faithful assurance of truth in their profession of faith and their adherence to moral standards and ideals.

132-133, 217

70. The call of Christians to community

94

Under the impulse of the Spirit, the Church from its very beginning has been a community of believers. "Those who believed shared all things in common." (Acts 2,44)

"Community" involves a sharing of beliefs, experiences, ideals, and values. Christian community leads one to put aside selfish goals and private interest for the sake of a common good. It is based on the willingness of all community members, as good stewards, to accept responsibility, individually and corporately, for the way each lives, uses his or her time, talent, and treasure, and responds to the needs and rights of others. (Cf. Gal 6,2)

Michal Heron

The early Christians celebrated their identity as a worshiping community in word and sacrament. "They devoted themselves to the apostles' instruction and communal life, to the breaking of the bread and prayers." (Acts 2,42)

Now, as then, the Church is called to hear and proclaim Jesus' saving gospel. At worship the community again hears in faith Christ's living message and is reminded of how to live in obedience to His law of love. In the breaking of the bread, God's people experience the risen Christ: their hope of salvation is reaffirmed. With the great "Amen" of faith after the eucharistic prayer, the Church acknowledges Christ as the source of its communal identity and pledges to live out that grace by visible witness.

71. Missionary nature of the Church

11,67,72c), 74d)e),93, 185,210, 224,228b), 229,232

Because the Church is "missionary by her very nature,"[6] all Christians, in obedience to the mandate of the Church's founder, are called to proclaim the gospel "to the whole of creation." (Mt 16,15) They do this in various ways. Some — ordained ministers, professed religious, and lay persons — serve in foreign countries, among other cultures, or among the unchurched or non-practicing in the United States — wherever there are people to be evangelized. Others do so by their generosity and support of home and foreign missionary societies. All have an obligation to promote the growth of the kingdom by constant prayer and personal sacrifice.

72. Marks of the Church

Certain signs or marks identify this community of faith. In the Creed Christians confess their belief in the one, holy, catholic, and apostolic Church. These four marks simultaneously describe the Church and identify its mission. They are gifts bestowed upon the Church by the Lord — but gifts which the Church must also strive to realize ever more fully in its life.

a) One

At the Last Supper Jesus prayed for the Church's unity, "That all may be one, as you, Father are in me, and I in you." (Jn 17,21) How is this unity to be perceived?

First, in the celebration of the Eucharist, which is both a sign and a cause of unity. Second, in the affirmation by the Church's members that there is but "one Lord, one faith, one baptism, one God and Father of all" (Eph 4,5), which reminds us of the unity yet to be achieved among Christians and among

75-76,95

all people. (Cf. Eph 4,13) Third, in explicit efforts by the members of the Church to become a community of deeper faith, hope, and love, where Christ's peace reigns. (Cf. Col 3,15) Finally, in the fact that, while the Holy Spirit is the Church's principle of unity, the pope, patriarchs, and bishops embody that principle in a special way. "The Roman Pontiff, as the successor of Peter, is the perpetual and visible source and foundation of the unity of the bishops and of the multitude of the faithful. The individual bishop . . . is the visible principle and foundation of unity in his particular church."[7]

b) Holy

68,93

Its union with Christ gives the Church a holiness which can never fail and empowers it to foster holiness in its members. This holiness, engendered by the Spirit, is expressed in the lives of Christians who strive to grow in charity and to help others do the same. (1 Cor 3,16f) The lives of saintly men and women, and the rich tradition of prayer and mysticism, remind us that holiness resides in the following of Christ. Pilgrim and sinful people that they are, the members of the Church nevertheless give visible evidence of God's holiness through acts of repentance and conversion, and through striving daily for holiness.

c) Catholic

Jesus commissioned the Church to carry the gospel to all nations. The catholicity or universality of the Church rests on the fact that the gospel message is capable of being integrated with all cultures. It corresponds to all that is authentically human. Potentially, therefore, according to the mind of its

Rick Smolan

NC/KNA Photo

founder, the community of believers embraces an exceptionally broad range of authentic religious expressions and a membership as diverse as the human race.

But catholicity resides also in the fraternal diversity of the Churches within the Catholic communion — in the variety of rites and the multiplicity of local dioceses. Moreover it is manifested by the presence of this one, same society throughout the world.

d) Apostolic

This sign has both a historical and dynamic significance.

Historically, it means that the Church traces itself back to Christ and the apostles. "You form a building which rises on the foundation of the apostles and prophets, with Christ Jesus himself as the capstone." (Eph 2,20) As successors of the apostles, bishops "receive from Him the mission to teach all nations and to preach the gospel to every creature."[8]

Dynamically, the apostolic sign refers to continuing fidelity to Christ's loving and saving work and message, to ministry and service inspired by the evangelical vision and teaching of the original apostles.

Rick Smolan

73. *The Church and the Churches*

God's Church is a community of baptized persons of all nations and cultures and also a communion of local Churches. St. Paul addressed and sent greetings to "the Church of God which is in Corinth" (1 Cor 1,2), "to the churches in Galatia" (Gal 1,2), and to "the Church of the Thessalonians" (2 Thes 1,1). These local Churches later became dioceses, as we understand that term today, each expressing the totality of the Catholic Church. In Europe these local Churches — dioceses — were organized under the bishop of Rome, the patriarch of the West, and followed in their liturgical practices what came to be known as the Latin Rite. In the East several patriarchates came into being, each with its distinct institutions, liturgical rites, and Christian way of life. Their presence in the United States is described in article 15.

8,15,112, 242a)

The Second Vatican Council recognized this diversity as a positive reality. "That Church, Holy and Catholic, which is the Mystical Body of Christ, is made up of the faithful who are organically united in the Holy Spirit through the same faith, the same sacraments, and the same government and who, combining into various groups held together by a hierarchy, form separate Churches or rites. Between these, there flourishes such an admirable brotherhood that this variety within the Church in no way harms her unity, but rather manifests it. For it is the mind of the Catholic Church that each individual Church or rite retain its traditions whole and entire, while adjusting its way of life to the various needs of time and place."[9]

The Eastern and Western Churches in communion with the bishop of Rome as supreme head of the universal Church (cf. Mt 16,17ff) perform a special ministry in making their unity visible in the world. At the same time, each particular Church has its own identity and traditions, which are to be respected. Each should govern itself according to its own proper procedures.[10]

The universal Church needs the witness which the particular Churches can give one another; for no one theology or liturgical tradition can exhaust the richness of Christ's message and His love. To carry out its mission to preach the gospel to all peoples, the Church must always strive more fully to understand and practice catholicity, that wholeness of the gospel message which characterizes the Church in its fullness. In fostering the expression of all the traditions which comprise the universal Church, it will be clear that the Church's unity is not based on a particular language, rite, spiritual tradition, or theological school, but upon the one cornerstone, Jesus Christ. (Cf. 1 Pt 2,4-8)

16,37

74. Catechetical guidelines

One of the principal tasks of catechesis is to witness to the Church as a sign and instrument of intimate union with God and the unity of humankind. The following guidelines, in addition to those suggested by the text, are relevant.

a) The Church's inner reality as mystery and its outward reality as a human community should both be emphasized.

b) Biblical images are selected which shed light on the Church's nature and mission.

c) Emphasis should be given to those common beliefs and experiences, especially the Eucharist, those ideals and values which are the basis of shared life and unity in the Catholic community.

d) People should be encouraged to reflect the marks of the Church in their lives by working for unity, striving to grow in holiness, participating in the missionary efforts of the Church, and increasing their understanding of and loyalty to the Church's apostolic nature.

129

e) Catechists, including clergy, religious, and especially parents, should encourage young men and women to consider missionary careers at home and abroad.

f) Emphasis should be placed on the need for fidelity to Christ's preaching and mission. (Cf. Mk 16,15f) The special role of the magisterium in guaranteeing the authentic teaching of the gospel should be explained. (Cf. Eph 2,20)

g) Catechists should foster understanding and unity among Catholics by accurately presenting the history and practices of each Church tradition in the context of the universal Church. The following principles are pertinent in this regard.

i) The Catholic Church is manifest and recognizable in the local Churches which express and celebrate the authentic faith.

ii) The communion of local Churches witnesses to the catholicity of the Church and to legitimate diversity in the profession of the one faith in Jesus Christ as Lord.

PART B: THE CHURCH IN DIALOGUE

72a),76,
95

75. Other Christian churches

The Catholic Church perceives itself to have a special relationship with those Eastern Churches which are not in full communion within it. This relationship arises from the fact that these Eastern Churches possess "true sacraments, above all — by apostolic succession — the priesthood, and the Eucharist."[11] The "entire heritage of spirituality and liturgy, of discipline and theology, in their various traditions, belongs to the full Catholic and apostolic character of the Church."[12]

In a very positive way the Catholic Church also recognizes the separate churches and ecclesial communities in the West with which it has a special affinity and close relationship arising from the long span of earlier centuries when Christians lived in ecclesiastical communion.[13] Several among these have maintained Catholic traditions and institutions, and are in closer relationship to the Catholic Church.

In our times Christians have become more eager for the restoration of unity, in response to Jesus' prayer that His followers might be one. (Cf. Jn 17,20f) Many are striving to discern and obey God's will in this matter. The quest for unity has led the Catholic Church to engage in ecumenical dialogue with other Christian churches and has made it more aware of the common witness to the Lord already given to the world by Christians. The religious pluralism of the

NC Photo by Chris Sheridan

United States offers an important opportunity to advance ecumenism.

Catholics pray that Christ's Spirit will draw us to unity, so that all may worship Father, Son, and Holy Spirit with one voice and one heart. Urged by the divine call, catechesis has an important role in creating an environment for the growth of Christian unity.

76. *Catechetical guidelines for ecumenism*

While Christians are called to support and encourage ecumenism, catechesis should point out that human efforts alone cannot restore Christian unity. Catechesis can, however, foster ecumenism in a variety of ways: by clearly explaining Catholic doctrine in its entirety and working for the renewal of the Church and its members; by presenting information about other Christians honestly and accurately, avoiding words, judgments, and actions which misrepresent their beliefs and practices; by communicating the divine truths and values Catholics share with other Christians and promoting cooperation in projects for the common good. Ecumenical dialogue and common prayer, especially public and private petitions for unity, are to be encouraged. Catechetical textbooks should conform to the guidelines found here and in the *Directory for Ecumenism* according to the age and readiness of learners.[14] When circumstances seem to call for teaching religion to children and youth in an ecumenical setting, this should be done only with the knowledge and guidance of the local ordinary.

NC Photo by Chris Sheridan

Catechesis should be especially sensitive in dealing with the Orthodox Churches which have so much in common with the Catholic tradition. Dialogue and collaboration should be as extensive and cordial as possible.[15] Members of the Eastern Churches in communion with Rome make a unique contribution to the ecumenical movement by remaining faithful to their Eastern heritage.

Catechesis should also be sensitive in dealing with the separated churches and ecclesial communities of the West, many of which share much in common with Catholic tradition. The numerous bilateral studies and proposed agreements should be suitably presented.

Paul S. Conklin

77. *The Jewish people*

43,52,
60a)i

There are several reasons why Catholics in the United States should be especially sensitive to relationships with the Jewish people. First, Catholics and Jews share a common heritage — a heritage not only of biblical revelation rooted in faith in the one true God and the liberation of the exodus event, but also in the family origins of Jesus, Mary, and the apostles. Second, the members of the largest Jewish population in the world are our fellow citizens. Finally, the tragic, scandalous, centuries-long persecution of the Jewish people, including the terrible holocaust in Central Europe and active persecution up to this day, calls for the specific and direct repudiation of anti-Semitism in any form and for determination to resist anti-Semitism and its causes.

Christ's passion and death "cannot be blamed on all the Jews then living, without distinction, nor upon the Jews of today." The Church "deplores the hatred, persecutions, and displays of anti-Semitism directed against the Jews at any time and from any source."[16]

In seeking together to grow in appreciation of one another's heritages, Catholics and Jews should cooperate in scholarship, particularly in reference to sacred scripture, and in social action programs, and should promote a mutual understanding of the Christian and Jewish traditions as they address political, moral, and religious problems in the United States.[17]

78. The Moslem people

The Catholic Church esteems the people of Islam. Catholics share with Moslems certain beliefs; in God as creator of the human race and all-powerful maker of heaven and earth; in Abraham as a pre-eminent patriarch in the history of salvation; in Jesus Christ as God's prophet; in Mary as the virgin mother. Catholics and Moslems also share a deep reverence for the worship of God through prayer, fasting, and almsgiving.

Familiarity with the history of Islam, especially the centuries-old quarrels and hostilities between Christians and Moslems, is basic to mutual understanding. Collaboration in promoting spiritual and moral values in society, common to both Catholic and Moslem traditions, is an obligation for Catholics. The safeguarding and fostering of social justice, moral values, freedom, and world peace based on belief in God challenges both Catholics and Moslems.[18]

14

79. Other religions

God's Word "gives light to every man." (Jn 1,9) Almost all religions strive to answer the restless searchings of the human heart through teachings, rules of life, and sacred ceremonies.[19]

Millions of people around the globe follow traditional religions, handed down from time immemorial, whose rites and mores generate among them a sense of solidarity. Students and teachers should learn about these religions in order to aid the Church's missionary endeavor, which seeks to reach these people and incorporate them into its worship, belief, and life for the sake of Christ Jesus while redeeming those elements of their religious and cultural traditions which can become part of ecclesial life.

The Catholic Church regards the positive and enriching aspects of these religions with honor and reverence. In particular it searches for common bonds with religions such as Hinduism and Buddhism.

This interest should spur catechists to:

1) Present an accurate account of the essential elements of traditional non-Christian religious beliefs, as perceived by their adherents in the light of their own religious experience.

2) Develop an appreciation of their insights and contributions to humanity.

3) Promote joint projects in the cause of justice and peace.

NC Photo by Tom Lorsung

14

80. Relationship to those who profess no religion

There are many varieties and degrees of religious skepticism and disbelief. Some who profess no formal religion nevertheless believe in God and base their lives on this belief. Others, doubting God's existence, do not regard the question of whether He does or does not exist as important or relevant in their lives. Still others profess not to believe in God at all.

Whether they are believers or non-believers, however, all people are created in God's image and likeness and are, therefore, worthy of respect and esteem. The Catholic Church champions the dignity of the human vocation — a calling to union with God — and holds out lasting hope to those who do not expect to enjoy any destiny higher than earthly existence.

In supporting and working for human rights and freedom, the Church is confident that its message is in harmony with the most authentic and profound desires of the human heart. Further, it is the mission of the Church to evangelize so that all people may see Christ as both the perfect human being and "the image of the invisible God." (Col 1,15)

Catholics must strive to understand those who profess no faith and to collaborate with all persons of good will in promoting the human values common to all.[20]

Ecumenical activity with other Christians and with non-Christians aims at growth in mutual understanding. Catechesis must, however, present ecumenism in such a way as to guard against the danger of religious indifferentism. Indifferentism would be expressed, for instance, in the idea that it makes no difference whether one believes in Christ or not as long as one follows one's conscience and is sincere.

81. Conclusion

Arising from an outpouring of the Spirit, the Church is a divine mystery; but as People of God and pilgrim, it is also a human reality. These themes come together in the image of the Body of Christ, especially when the Church celebrates its identity in word and sacrament. The Church's communal beauty is seen in the visible signs of unity, holiness, catholicity, and apostolicity. Committed to service and to dialogue with all people of good will, the Church seeks to extend the fruits of Christ's saving death and joyful resurrection to each individual and all peoples.

This chapter has referred to the teaching authority of the hierarchy as an instrument of service for the preservation of the unity of Catholic belief. Next we turn to the more outstanding elements of this Catholic belief.

Linda Bartlett

AP Photo

45

Chapter V

Principal Elements
of the
Christian Message
for Catechesis

---

*I have come to the world
as its light,
to keep anyone who believes in me
from remaining in the dark.*
Jn 12, 46

82. Introduction

Having spoken of the Church, we now consider the more outstanding elements of the message of salvation, which Christ commissioned the Catholic Church to proclaim and teach to all nations and peoples.[1]

Certain duplications with other sections of the NCD are necessary here in order to present in sequence the elements of the Christian message which catechesis highlights in relation to the one God; creation; Jesus Christ; the Holy Spirit; the Church; the sacraments; the life of grace; the moral life; Mary and the saints; and death, judgment, and eternity.

PART A: THE MYSTERY OF THE ONE GOD

83. The mystery of the Trinity

The history of salvation is the story of God's entry into human affairs to save human beings from sin and bring them to Himself.

In the Old Testament God revealed Himself as the one, true, personal God, creator of heaven and earth (cf. Is 42,5), who transcends this world. By words and actions God prepared for the ultimate disclosure of Himself as a Trinity: Father, Son, and Holy Spirit. (Cf. Mt 3,16; 28,19; Jn 14,23.26)

The mystery of the Holy Trinity was revealed in the person, words, and works of Jesus Christ. He revealed His Father as "our" Father and Himself as God's eternal and divine Son. He also made known a third divine person, the Holy Spirit, the lord and giver of life, whom the Father and He, as risen Lord, send to His Church. He calls His disciples to become God's children through the gift of the Spirit which He bestows on them. (Cf. Jn 1,12; Rom 8,15)

84. True worship of God in the modern world

God is all-good, holy, just and merciful, infinitely wise and perfect. He has made firm commitments to human beings and bound them to Himself by solemn covenants. He has each individual always in view. He frees, saves, and loves His people with the love of a father and spouse. His goodness is the source of our eternal hope (cf. 1 Pt 1,3f) and should prompt us to worship Him.

God is worshiped in the sacred liturgy, in which people offer themselves to Him through Christ in and by the power of the Holy Spirit. People also worship God in individual and community prayer. Those who wish to love and obey God seek to carry out His will in their every activity and to use rightly and increase the talents He has given them. (Cf. Mt 25,14ff) From His goodness He bestows on people the grace which they need to "profess the truth in love" (Eph 4,15) and to bring forth the fruits of love, justice, and peace, all to His glory.

Many people today pay little or no attention to God. Others are persuaded that God is distant, indifferent, or altogether absent. Because modern life tends to focus on the tangible rather than on the transcendent, it cannot be said to offer a climate favorable to faith. Yet desire for God, no matter how hidden and unconscious, is present in every human being.

PART B: CREATION

85. The beginning of the history of salvation

The entire universe was created out of nothing. The Old Testament treats God's creative action as a sign of His power and love, proving that He is always

Paul S. Conklin

NC Photo by Sigmund J. Mikolajczyk

33,57-58, 98,175, 188,213

14,24,199- 201

51

with His people. (Cf. Is 40,27f; 51,9-16) The creation of visible and invisible things, of the world and of angels, is the beginning of the mystery of salvation.[2] Our creation by God[3] is His first gift and call to us — a gift and call meant ultimately to lead to our final glorification in Christ. In Christ's resurrection from the dead, God's same all-powerful action stands out splendidly. (Cf. Eph 1,19f) The unity of soul and body which constitutes the human person is disrupted by death but will be restored to us by God in our resurrection.

The creation of the human person is the climax of God's creative activity in this world. Made in God's likeness, each person possesses a capacity for knowledge that is transcendent, love that is unselfish, and freedom for self-direction. Inherent in each unique human person called into existence by God, these qualities reflect the essential immortality of the human spirit.

Creation should be presented as directly related to the salvation accomplished by Jesus Christ. In reflecting on the doctrine of creation, one should be mindful not only of God's first action creating the heavens and the earth, but of His continuing activity in sustaining creation and working out human salvation.

Actively and lovingly present on behalf of human beings, throughout human history, God is present among us today and will remain present for all generations. Only at the end of the world, when there will be "new heavens and a new earth" (2 Pt 3,13), will His saving work come to final completion.

86. Knowledge of God and the witness of Christian love 51,55

As scripture testifies, we can come to know God through the things He has made.[4] Reason, reflecting on created things, can come to a knowledge of God as the beginning and end of all that is.[5]

Yet unbelievers commonly need the help of other people to find God. To their plea — "Show us a sign" — Christ's followers today can respond as did the first generation Christians (cf. Acts 2,42-47): by the compelling witness of lives which manifest steadfast and mature faith in God, express personal love of Christ, and include works of justice and charity.[6]

Though our final goal is in eternity, faith in God and union with Christ entail an obligation to seek solutions for human problems here and now.

Linda Bartlett

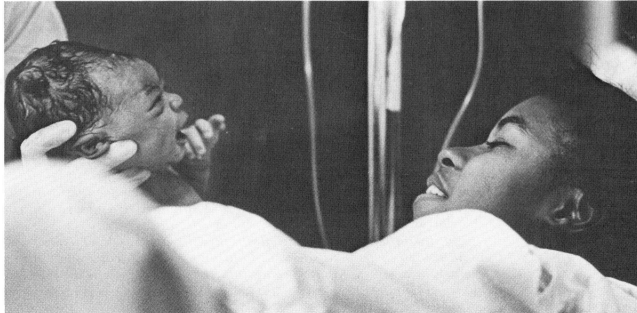

87. *Son of God, the firstborn of all creation, and savior*

In taking on human flesh through the ever-virgin Mary and entering human history, God's Son, Jesus Christ, renewed the world from within and became for it an abiding source of supernatural life and salvation from sin.

He is the firstborn of all creation. He is before all. All things hold together in Him; all have been created in Him, through Him, and for Him. (Cf. Col 1,15f)

Obedient unto death, even to death on a cross, He was exalted as Lord of all, and through His resurrection (cf. Phil 2,5-11) was made known to us as God's Son in power. (Cf. Rom 1,4) He is the "firstborn of the dead" (Col 1,18); He gives eternal life to all. (Cf. 1 Cor 15,22) In Him we are created new. (Cf. 2 Cor 5,17) Through Him all creatures are saved from the slavery of corruption. (Cf. Rom 8,20f) "There is no salvation in anyone else" (Acts 4,12) nor has there ever been.

88. *Jesus, center of all God's saving works*

In Jesus Christ the Christian is joined to all history and all human beings. The story of salvation, set in the midst of human history, is no less than the working out of God's plan for humankind: to form His people into the whole Christ, "that perfect man who is Christ come to full stature." (Eph 4,13)

Realizing this, Christians address themselves to their fundamental task: to the full extent of their abilities and opportunities, through the power of Jesus the savior (cf. 1 Cor 15,28), to bring creation to give the greatest possible glory to God.

Michal Heron

89. *True God and true man in the unity of the Divine Person*

Jesus Christ is truly divine, God's only-begotten Son (cf. Jn 1,18): "God from God, light from light, true God begotten not made, of one substance with the Father." (Nicene Creed)

Jesus is also truly human. As such, He thinks with a human mind, acts with a human will, loves with a human heart. He was made truly one of us, like us in all things except sin.[7] He accorded unparalleled respect and concern to the human person, reaching out to all — virtuous and sinners, poor and the rich, fellow-citizens and foreigners — and showing special solicitude for the suffering and rejected.

NC Photo by Phillip A. Stack

90. *Christ, savior and redeemer of the world*

God so loved sinners that He gave His Son to reconcile the world to Himself. (Cf. Jn 3,16f; 2 Cor 5,19) All people have been saved by the Son's obedience to His Father's will. (Cf. Rom 5,19)

In carrying out His earthly mission as the Messiah, Jesus fulfilled Old Testament prophecy and history. He preached the gospel of the kingdom of God and summoned people to interior conversion and faith. (Cf. Mk 1,15) He persisted in His ministry despite resistance, threats, and apparent failure.

Out of filial love for His Father (cf. Jn 14,31) and redemptive love for us, He gave Himself up to death (cf. Gal 2,20; 1 Jn 3,16) and passed through death to the glory of the Father. (Cf. Phil 2,9ff; Eph 1,20)

By His life, death, and resurrection He redeemed humankind from slavery to sin and the devil. Truly risen, the Lord is the unfailing source of life and of the outpouring of the Holy Spirit upon the human race.[8] He is the firstborn among many brothers and sisters (cf. Rom 8,29), and creates in Himself a new humanity.

91. *Christ, our life*

Thus the meaning and destiny of human life are most fully revealed in Jesus Christ. He tells us that God, whom we are to love and serve above all else (cf. Dt 6,5; Mt 22,37), loves us more than we can hope to understand, and offers us His love irrevocably. "Neither death nor life, neither angels nor principalities, neither the present nor the future, nor powers, neither height nor depth nor any other creature, will be able to separate us from the love of God that comes to us in Christ Jesus, our Lord." (Rom 8,38f) Jesus is the new covenant, the sacred and enduring bond, between God and humankind.[9]

"Whatever came to be in him, found life . . . any who did accept him he empowered to become children of God." (Jn 1,4.12) Christ, in whom the divine and the human are most perfectly one, manifests in the world God's hidden plan to share His life with us, to pour out His own Spirit upon all flesh (cf. Acts 2,17), so that we who were formed in His image should be called, and be, His children (cf. 1 Jn 3,1; Gal 4,5ff), addressing Him in truth as "our Father."

Christ also reveals the response we are to make to our calling and gives us the power to make it. This is the power of God's own Spirit. "All who are led by the Spirit of God are sons of God." (Rom 8,14) The indwelling Holy Spirit gives hope and courage, heals weakness of soul, and enables one to master passion and selfishness. The Spirit prompts people to seek what is good and helps them to advance in such virtues as charity, joy, peace, patience, kindness, forbearance, humility, fidelity, modesty, continence, and chastity. (Cf. Gal 5,22f)

Christ teaches that love of God and love of neighbor spring from the same Spirit and are inseparable. (Cf. 1 Jn 4,12f.20f) We are to love all human beings, even enemies, as we love ourselves;[10] even more, we are to obey Christ's new command to love all others as He has loved us. (Cf. Jn 13,34; 15,12f)

By this command Christ tells us something new — about God, about love, and about ourselves. His commandment to love is "new" not simply because of the scope and unselfishness of the love involved, but because it summons human beings to love with a divine love called charity, as the Father, Son, and Spirit do. This call carries with it the inner gift of their life and the power of their love, for Christ does not command what is impossible.

Christ's life is one of total obedience to the Father in the Spirit. His obedience entailed hunger and thirst and weariness, obscurity and rejection, suffering and death. By accepting the suffering which came to Him as He walked the way of loving obedience, Jesus did not deny His humanity but realized it perfectly. In giving His Son the glorious victory over death, the Father showed His pleasure with the Son's loving obedience. (Cf. Phil 2,8-11)

St. Paul tells us to "put on the Lord Jesus Christ." (Rom 13,14) This means imitating Christ in our daily lives — loving, forgiving, healing, reconciling — living as He lived.

Paul S. Conklin

53

PART D: THE HOLY SPIRIT

92. *The Holy Spirit in the Church and in the life of the Christian*

The Holy Spirit continues Christ's work in the world. Christ promised the coming of the consoling Paraclete. (Cf. Jn 14,16; 15,26) He pledged that the Spirit of truth would be within us and remain with His Church. (Cf. Jn 14,17) And the Holy Spirit came at Pentecost (cf. Acts 2,1-4), never to depart. As Christ is present where a human being is in need (cf. Mt 25,31-40), so the Spirit is at work where people answer God's invitation to believe in Him and to love

Him and one another. While the Spirit animates the whole of creation and permeates the lives of human beings, He is present in a special way in the Church, the community of those who acknowledge Christ as Lord. Our lives are to be guided by the same Holy Spirit, the third person of the Trinity.

"The Lord Jesus so arranged the ministry of the apostles and so promised to send the Holy Spirit, that both they and the Spirit were to be associated in effecting the work of salvation always and everywhere. . . . He vivifies ecclesiastical institutions as a kind of soul and instills into the hearts of the faithful the same mission spirit which motivated Christ Himself."[11]

62-74

PART E: THE CHURCH

63

93. People of God

The Church, founded by Christ, had its origin in His death and resurrection. It is the new People of God, prepared for in the Old Testament and given life, growth, and direction by Christ in the Holy Spirit. It is the work of God's saving love in Christ.

66,70,
94,96

In the Catholic Church are found the deposit of faith, the sacraments, and the ministries inherited from the apostles. Through these gifts of God, the Church is able to act and grow as a community in Christ, serving human beings and mediating to them His saving word and activity.

The Church shares in Christ's prophetic office.[12] Assembled by God's word, it accepts that word and witnesses to it in every quarter of the globe. So the Church is missionary by its very nature, and all its members share responsibility for responding to Christ's command to carry the good news to all humanity.[13]

The Church is also a priestly people.[14] (Cf. Rv 1,6) All of its members share in Christ's priestly ministry. By regeneration and the anointing of the Holy Spirit, the baptized are consecrated as a priestly people. Though the ministerial or hierarchical priesthood differs, not only in degree, but in essence from the priesthood of the faithful, nevertheless, they are interrelated.[15] "At a lower level of the hierarchy are deacons, upon whom hands are imposed 'not unto the priesthood, but unto a ministry of service.' "[16]

Lou Niznik

By God's design the Church is a society with leaders — i.e., with a hierarchy. As such, it is a people guided by its bishops, who are in union with the pope, the bishop of Rome, the vicar of Christ. The pope has succeeded to the office of Peter, with its responsibility for care and guidance of the whole flock of Christ (cf. Jn 21,15ff), and is the head of the college of bishops. The community of faith owes respect and obedience to its bishops; while "exercising his office of father and pastor, a bishop should stand as one who serves."[17]

47,70, 72d)

The pope and the bishops have the office of teaching, sanctifying, and governing the Church, and enjoy the gift of infallibility in guiding the Church when they exercise supreme teaching authority.[18]

The pope, in virtue of his office, enjoys infallibility when, as the supreme shepherd and teacher of all the faithful, he defines a doctrine of faith or morals. Therefore his definitions of themselves, and not from the consent of the Church, are correctly called irreformable. Even when he is not speaking *ex cathedra* his teachings in matters of faith and morals demand religious submission of will and of mind.[19]

"Bishops, teaching in communion with the Roman pontiff, are to be respected by all as witnesses to divine and Catholic truth. In matters of faith and morals, the bishops speak in the name of Christ and the faithful are to accept their teaching and adhere to it with a religious assent of soul."[20]

Priests and deacons share in a special way in the teaching role of their bishops. Within the local community they are called to be special signs of unity with the bishop and with the whole Church.

Rick Smolan

At the same time, "the body of the faithful as a whole, anointed as they are by the Holy One (cf. Jn 2,20.27), cannot err in matters of belief. Thanks to a supernatural sense of the faith which characterizes the people as a whole, it manifests this unerring quality when, from the bishops to the entire laity, it shows universal agreement in matters of faith and morals."[21]

The Holy Spirit preserves the Church as Christ's body and bride, so that, despite the sinfulness of its members, it will never fail in faithfulness to Him and will meet Him in holiness at the end of the world. The Spirit also helps the Church constantly to purify and renew itself and its members, for whose sake the Church, guided by the Spirit, can update itself in those areas where change is permitted.

65,68, 72b)

94. The Church as community

70

The Church is a community of people assembled by God, whose members share the life of Christ. Within this assembly all enjoy a basic equality. All are called to holiness. All are united by close spiritual bonds. All share "one Lord, one faith, one baptism." (Eph 4,5)

95,156-157,191

In the Church every vocation is worthy of honor. Every gift is given for the good of all. All are called to build up the Body of Christ.[22] All share in the dignity of being Christian.

74e),116, 129-133, 170,14, 180b),182

Throughout the history of the Church some of its members have devoted themselves to the service of God and the Christian community through commitment to an evangelical form of life based on vows of chastity, poverty, and obedience. Today such men and women serve the Church in a wide variety of ministries.

All members of the Church should seek to foster vocations to the religious life and secular institutes. The rich vision of Christian life lived out in chastity, poverty, and obedience is of benefit to all the faithful, who should offer prayers and encouragement for the growth of religious communities and secular institutes.

95. *The quest for unity*

Christ willed the unity of all who believe in Him; thus the world would know that He was sent by the Father. (Cf. Jn 17,20f) Catholics should be deeply, personally concerned about the present sad divisions which separate Christians. It is essential that they pray and work for Christian unity, with full communion and organic unity as the goal. Catholics should take the first steps in ecumenical dialogue, while working also to make the Church more faithful to Christ and its apostolic heritage.[23]

Catholics are aware of the uniqueness of the Catholic Church which possesses the fullness of the ordinary means of salvation — a fullness in which they desire all people to share. At the same time, they also recognize that they can be enriched by the authentic insights of other religious traditions.[24]

Catholic life and education must also be concerned with a still wider unity: the unity of all persons under God. The Church rejects as un-Christian any discrimination because of race, national or ethnic origin, color, sex, class, or religion. God has given every human being intrinsic dignity, freedom, and eternal importance. "If anyone says, 'My love is fixed on God,' yet hates his brother, he is a liar. One who has no love for the brother he has seen cannot love the God he has not seen." (1 Jn 4,20)

96. *The Church as institution for salvation*

The Church is a structured institution whose Christ-given mission is to bring the message of salvation to all people.[25] (Cf. Mt 28,16-20) Though it is not of the world and can never conform itself to the world, the Church does engage in dialogue with the world and strives to be seen by it as faithful to the gospel. Christians should therefore seek "to serve the men and women of the modern world ever more generously," aware that in committing themselves to the pursuit of justice they "have shouldered a gigantic task demanding fulfillment in this world," but one concerning which they "must give a reckoning to Him who will judge every man on the last day."[26]

Yet the Church is "inspired by no earthly ambition."[27] It will be perfect only in heaven, and it is heaven, toward which God's people are journeying, that the Church has always in view.

PART F: THE SACRAMENTS

97. *Actions of Christ in the Church (the universal sacrament)*

Christ's saving work is continued in the Church through the power of the Holy Spirit.

The Church has been entrusted with special means for this purpose: the sacraments which Christ instituted. They are outward signs of God's grace and humankind's faith. They effectively show God's intention to sanctify us and our willingness to grow in sanctity. In this way they bring us God's grace.[28]

The Church itself is in Christ like a sacrament, or sign and instrument of intimate union with God, and of the unity of the whole human race.[29]

It is principally through these actions — His actions — called sacraments that Christ becomes present to His people, conferring His Spirit on them and making them holy by drawing them into union with Himself. Though entrusted to the Church, the sacraments are always to be thought of as actions of Christ, from whom they receive their power. It is Christ who baptizes, Christ who offers Himself in the sacrifice of the Mass, Christ who forgives sins in the Sacrament of Reconciliation.

The purpose of the sacraments is to sanctify humankind, build up the Body of Christ, and give worship to God. As signs, they also instruct: the very act of celebrating them disposes people more effectively to receive and grow in the life of grace, to worship God, and to practice charity. It is therefore of capital importance that people be thoroughly familiar with the sacramental signs and turn often to them for nourishment in the Christian life.[30] The sacraments are treated in detail in Chapter VI, Parts A and B.

PART G: THE LIFE OF GRACE

98. Sin and grace

Sin is the greatest obstacle human beings face in their efforts to love God and their brothers and sisters and work out their salvation.

Original sin is the first obstacle. Made by God in the state of holiness, human beings from the dawn of history abused their liberty at the devil's urging. They set themselves against God and sought fulfillment apart from Him.[31] "Through one man sin entered the world and with sin death, death thus coming to all men inasmuch as all sinned." (Rom 5,12) Every human being is "born in sin" in the sense that "it is human nature . . . fallen, stripped of the grace that clothed it, injured in its own natural powers and subjected to the dominion of death, that is transmitted to all."[32]

116

In addition to the effects of original sin, there is personal sin, committed by the individual. Such sin is different from unavoidable failure or limitation. It is willful rejection, either partial or total, of one's role as a child of God and a member of His people. By it sinners knowingly and deliberately disobey God's command to love Him, other people, and themselves in a morally right way. They turn aside or even away from their lifetime goal of doing God's will. This they do either by sins of commission or sins of omission — i.e., not doing what one is morally obliged to do in a particular circumstance. (Classic illustrations are found in the story of the good Samaritan: cf. Lk 10,25-37 and Mt 25,41-46.)

165b)

Personal sin resides essentially in interior rejection of God's commands of love, but this rejection is commonly expressed in exterior acts contrary to God's law. A grave offense (mortal sin) radically disrupts the sinner's relationship with the Father and places him or her in danger of everlasting loss.[33] Even lesser offenses (venial sins) impair this relationship and can pave the way for the commission of grave sins.

USCC Creative Services

Sin and its effects are visible everywhere: in exploitative relationships, loveless families, unjust social structures and policies, crimes by and against individuals and against creation, the oppression of the weak and the manipulation of the vulnerable, explosive tensions among nations and among ideological, racial and religious groups, and social classes, the scandalous gulf between those who waste goods and resources, and those who live and die amid deprivation and underdevelopment, wars and preparations for war. Sin is a reality in the world.

Rick Smolan

"But despite the increase of sin, grace has far surpassed it." (Rom 5,20) Grace is God's generous and free gift to His people. It is union with God, a sharing in His life, the state of having been forgiven one's sins, of being adopted as God's own child and sustained by God's unfailing love. Grace is possible for us because of Christ's redemptive sacrifice.

33,54, 57-58, 84,175, 188,213

God remained faithful to His love for us, sending His own Son "in the likeness of sinful flesh" (Rom 8,3) into the midst of this sinful world. Because of sin human beings are helpless if left to themselves, unable even to do the good they know and truly wish to do. (Cf. Rom 7,14f) But God has saved us from sin through Jesus. So that by His obedience many might be made righteous (cf. Rom 5,19), He was faithful unto death. This was His final, irrevocable act of absolute self-giving in love to God and to human beings.

Christ's offer of grace, love, and life is valid forever. Transcending space and time, He is present to all and offers to each person the life that is His. Christ ardently desires that all receive His gift and share His life. It is freely offered, there for the taking, unless in their freedom people reject His call and choose not to be united with Him.

The sacraments are important means for bringing about the Christian's union with God in grace. They are sources of grace for individuals and communities, as well as remedies for sin and its effects.

We who have been baptized in Christ are to consider ourselves "dead to sin but alive for God in Christ Jesus." (Rom 6,11) "Since we live by the Spirit, let us follow the Spirit's lead." (Gal 5,25)

99. Call to conversion

Even so, achieving the final triumph over sin is a lifelong task. Christ's call to conversion is ever timely, for sin remains in the world and its power is strong in human beings. "My inner self agrees with the law of God, but I see in my body's members another law at war with the law of my mind; this makes me the prisoner of the law of sin in my members." (Rom 7,22f)

Disciples of Jesus who accept Him as their way and desire to love God and one another as they have been loved must acknowledge their sinfulness and undergo conversion: "a profound change of the whole person by which one begins to consider, judge, and arrange his life according to the holiness and love of God."[34] In a special way Christians engage in a continuing process of conversion through the Sacrament of Penance, in which sins are forgiven and we are reconciled with God and with the community of faith. Christ's followers are to live the paschal mystery proclaimed at Mass: "Dying, you destroyed our death, rising you restored our life."[35] Central to Christ's life and mission, this paschal mystery must have an equally central place in the life and mission of one who aspires to be Christ's disciple.

Living in His spirit, therefore, Christians are to deny themselves, take up the cross each day, and follow in His steps. (Cf. Lk 9,23f) Christ's atoning sacrifice is "the vital principle in which the Christian lives, and without which Christianity is not."[36] As brothers and sisters of Jesus who are also His followers and members of His body, Christians must accept suffering and death as He did, and in so accepting them share His life. "If we have been united with Him through likeness to His death," so also "through a like resurrection" we shall be raised from the dead by the glory of the Father. (Rom 6,4f) By union with Christ one has already begun to share the risen life here on earth. (Cf. 2 Pt 1,4)

100. Fulfillment in and through Christ

All people seek happiness: life, peace, joy, wholeness and wholesomeness of being. The happiness human beings seek and for which they are fashioned is given in Jesus, God's supreme gift of love. He comes in the Father's name to bring the fulfillment promised to the Hebrew people and, through them, to all people everywhere. He is Himself our happiness and peace, our joy and beatitude.

Of old the divine pattern for human existence was set forth in the decalogue. In the new covenant Jesus said: "He who obeys the commandments he has from me is the man who loves me; and he who loves me will be loved by my Father." (Jn 14,21; cf. 15,14) In the beatitudes (Mt 5,3-12; Lk 6,20-23)

124-125

Rick Smolan

105,154

105

Jesus, our brother, promises us the dignity of life as God's sons and daughters, the eternal enjoyment of a destiny which, now glimpsed imperfectly, has yet to appear in its glorious fullness. Through these beatitudes Jesus also teaches values to be cherished and qualities to be cultivated by those who wish to follow Him.

Living according to these values by the grace of Christ, one even now possesses the promised fulfillment in some measure. As God's reign takes root within us we become "gentle and humble of heart" like Jesus (Mt 11,29) through deeds done in holiness, and thus "a kingdom of justice, love, and peace"[37] is furthered in this world.

PART H: THE MORAL LIFE

101. Human and Christian freedom   190

God reveals to us in Jesus who we are and how we are to live. It is His plan that we freely respond, making concrete in the particular circumstances of our lives what the call to holiness and the commandment of love require of us. This is not easy. Nor may our decisions be arbitrary, for "good" and "bad," "right" and "wrong" are not simply whatever we choose to make them. On the contrary, there are moral values and norms which are absolute and never to be disregarded or violated by anyone in any situation. Fidelity to moral values and norms of this kind can require the heroism seen in the lives of the saints and the deaths of martyrs. This heroism is the result of Christ's redemptive love, accepted and shared.

Psychological difficulties or external conditions can diminish the exercise of freedom slightly, considerably, or almost to the vanishing point. Therefore

NC Photo by Steve Anderson

conditions favorable to the exercise of genuine human freedom must be promoted, not only for the sake of our temporal welfare but also for the sake of considerations bearing upon grace and eternal salvation.

38,105,
159

102. Guidance of the natural moral law

God's guidance for the making of moral decisions is given us in manifold forms. The human heart is alive with desire for created goods, and behind this desire is longing for God. "Athirst is my soul for God, the living God." (Ps 42,3) Desire for created goods and longing for the uncreated good are not in contradiction, since Christ came to perfect human nature, not to destroy it. He is the goal to whom all creatures tend, for whom all creatures long, in whom all hold together. (Cf. Col 1,15-20) Everything good and worthwhile in the adventure of a human life is such because it shows forth in some way the glory of God and points back to Him. Though all other goods draw people in part to their perfection as individuals, members of human communities, and stewards of the world, union with God is the supreme and only perfect fulfillment. Created goods and loves are His gifts, and they tell us of their giver and His will for humanity. Those who follow Christ will value all that is truly human and be reminded by it of His call.

NC Photo

Human beings rejoice in friends, in being alive, in being treated as persons rather than things, in knowing the truth. In doing so they are rejoicing in being themselves — images of God called to be His children. Truth and life, love and peace, justice and friendship go into what it means to be human. True morality, then, is not something imposed from without; rather it is the way people accept their humanity as restored to them in Christ.

In giving these material and spiritual goods and the desire for them, God wills that human beings be open to them and eager to foster them in themselves and others. All these goods form a starting point for reflecting upon the meaning and purpose of life. In the life of every person are reflected many elements of the "divine law — eternal, objective and universal — whereby God orders, directs, and governs the entire universe and all the ways of the human community."[38] All these goods together bear witness to the existence of what is often called the natural moral law. No disciple of Christ will neglect these goods. One is not possessed of His Spirit if one tosses them aside with contempt, spurning the loving gifts of the Father, grasps at them selfishly and denies them to others, or acts as if they, not their giver, were the ultimate end and meaning of life.[39]

190

103. Conscience and personal responsibility

Even when people have become conscious of these fundamental goods and have cultivated an attitude of cherishing them in themselves and others, more remains to be done. It is still necessary to decide how to realize and affirm them in concrete circumstances. Such decisions are called judgments of conscience. In the final analysis, they take place in the "most secret core and sanctuary" of the person, where one "is alone with God."[40]

We live in good faith if we act in accord with conscience. Nevertheless moral decisions still require much effort. Decisions of conscience must be based upon prayer, study, consultation, and an understanding of the teachings of the Church. One must have a rightly formed conscience and follow it. But one's judgments are human and can be mistaken; one may be blinded by the power of sin or misled by the strength of desire. "Beloved, do not trust every spirit, but put the spirits to a test to see if they belong to God." (1 Jn 4,1; cf. 1 Cor 12,10)

Clearly, then, it is necessary to do everything possible to see to it that judgments of conscience are informed and in accord with the moral order of which God is creator. Common sense requires that conscientious people be open and humble, ready to learn from the experience and insight of others, willing to acknowledge prejudices and even change their judgments in light of better instruction. Above and beyond this, followers of Jesus will have a realistic approach to conscience which leads them to accept what He taught and judge things as He judges them.

104. Guidance of the Church

Where are we to look for the teachings of Jesus, hear His voice, and discern His will?

In scripture, whose books were written under the inspiration of the Holy Spirit. In prayer, where people grow in knowledge and love of Christ and in commitment to His service. In the events of human life and history, where Christ and His Spirit are at work. In the Church, where all these things converge. This is why the Second Vatican Council said: "In the formation of their consciences, the Christian faithful ought carefully to attend to the sacred and certain doctrine of the Church."[41]

There are many instruments and agents of teaching in the Church. All have roles in drawing out the richness of Christ's message and proclaiming it, each according to his or her gift.

The pope and the bishops in communion with him have been anointed by the Holy Spirit to be the official and authentic teachers of Christian life. For Jesus "established His holy Church by sending forth the apostles as He Himself had been sent by the Father. (Cf. Jn 20,21) He willed that their successors, namely the bishops, should be shepherds in His Church even to the consummation of the world."[42] It is their office and duty to express Christ's teaching on moral questions and matters of belief. This special teaching office within the Catholic Church is a gift of the Lord Jesus for the benefit of all His followers in their efforts to know what He teaches, value as He values, and live as free, responsible, loving, and holy persons. (Cf. Lk 10,16) The authoritative moral teachings of the Church enlighten personal conscience and are to be regarded as certain and binding norms of morality.

Michal Heron

Following Christ's teaching and example in the family of the Church, people become more like Him and more perfect as the Father's children. Christ brings the life of the Father and fills His followers' lives with His Spirit. In face of the challenges encountered in living the Christian life the best answer is this: "In him who is the source of my strength, I have strength for everything." (Phil 4,13)

Rick Smolan

100,154

105. Specifics in the teaching of morality

The obligations which flow from love of God and human beings should be taught in a specific, practical way. The Church has a duty to apply moral principles to current problems, personal and social. Catechesis should therefore include the Christian response not only to perennial challenges and temptations but to those which are typically contemporary.

The specifics of morality should be taught in light of the Ten Commandments (cf. Appendix A), the Sermon on the Mount, especially the beatitudes, and Christ's discourse at the Last Supper. Whatever approach is used, students should know the decalogue as part of their religious heritage. Among the matters to be treated are the spiritual and corporal works of mercy, the theological and moral virtues, the seven capital sins, and traditional formulations concerning the Christian moral life which express the wisdom, drawn from experience and reflection, of those who have gone before us in the faith. Catechesis in Christian living should also include instruction in the laws of the Church, among which should be included what are called the "Precepts of the Church." (Cf. Appendix B) The Bible and the lives of the saints provide concrete examples of moral living.

What follows is by no means intended to cover all areas and issues of morality. The purpose is simply to indicate the practical approach which catechesis should take.

a) Duties toward God

Toward God, a Christian has a lifelong obligation of love and service. Christ is the model, and His life was, above all, a life of total obedience to the Father. For us, too, God's will must be first in our scale of personal values.

One's attitude toward God should be that of a son or daughter toward an all-good, all-loving Father — never judging and acting as if one were independent of Him, gladly making Him the object of worship and prayer, both liturgical and private.

NC Photo by Robert H. Davis

For the follower of Christ the first day of every week, commemorating the resurrection, is a special day, the Lord's day. Catechesis on the resurrection calls attention to the special significance of Sunday. Each Sunday should be kept as a day for special personal renewal, free from work and everyday business. It is both a privilege and a serious duty of the individual Catholic, as well as the Catholic faith community, to assemble on Sunday in order to recall the Lord Jesus and His acts, hear the word of God, and offer the sacrifice of His body and blood in the eucharistic celebration. This is, in fact, a precept of the Church following the commandment of God.

No one and nothing should occupy God's place in one's life. Otherwise one's attitude and behavior are idolatrous. (Superstition, witchcraft, and occultism are specific examples of idolatry, while such things as excessive love of money and material possessions, pride, and arrogance can be called "idolatrous" in the sense that they, too, reflect the attitude of one who gives to something else the place in his or her life which should be reserved for God.) People who seek to honor God will not blaspheme or commit perjury. They will show respect for persons, places, and things related to God. Clearly, obligations to God rule out atheism, heresy, and schism.

b) Duties toward other people

Toward other people, the Christian has specific obligations in justice and in charity. Every human being is of priceless value: made in God's image, redeemed by Christ, and called to an eternal destiny. That is why we are to recognize all human beings as our neighbors and love them with the love of Christ. We must be concerned both for the spiritual condition of others and for their temporal condition. Our concern will therefore extend to their authentic freedom, their spiritual and moral well-being, their intellectual and cultural welfare, their material and physical needs (e.g., housing, food, health, employment, etc.). Such concern will be expressed in action, including efforts to build a cultural, social, and political order based on peace and justice — locally, nationally, and internationally.

Paul S. Conklin

c.VII

A Christian's manner of judging and speaking about others should reflect the justice and charity due persons whom God has created and made His adopted children. He or she will respect and obey all lawfully exercised authority in the home, in civil society, and in the Church. A Christian will practice good manners and courtesy which, though not necessarily signs of moral goodness, are appropriate expressions of respect for others and tend to create an environment in which it is easier to be morally good.

There are many ways of sinning against one's neighbors. One can do so by being selfishly apathetic toward their real needs or by actively violating their rights: for example, by stealing, deliberately damaging their good names or property, cheating, not paying debts.

Respect for life, and for what is associated with life's transmission and preservation, enjoys a special priority in the Christian scale of moral values. Clearly Christians cannot be anti-life, cannot commit or condone the sins of murder, abortion, euthanasia, genocide, and indiscriminate acts of war. They also have a duty to work to bring about conditions in which such anti-life acts are less likely, as, for example, by supporting the responsible efforts to achieve arms control and disarmament. In view of the present tragic reality of legalized abortion practiced on a massive scale in our country, followers of Christ are obliged not only to be personally opposed to abortion, but to seek to remove circumstances which influence some to turn to abortion as a solution to their problems, and also to work for the restoration of a climate of opinion and a legal order which respect the value of unborn human life. The Church proclaims the value of the life-giving meaning of marital intercourse. It rejects the ideology of artificial contraception. The Church forbids methods of family limitation directed against the life-giving meaning of sexual intercourse. It condemns the view that sterilization and artificial contraception are morally legitimate means of family limitation.[43]

19,131, 156,167

One who seeks to follow Christ does not adopt the values and practices of a sexually permissive society. The Christian tradition holds the sexual union between husband and wife in high honor, regarding it as a special expression of their convenanted love which mirrors God's love for His people and Christ's love for the Church. But like many things human, the use of sex can be either creative or destructive. Sexual intercourse is a moral and human good only within marriage; outside marriage it is wrong. For a Christian, therefore, premarital sex, extramarital sex, adultery, homosexual behavior, or other acts of impurity or scandal to others are forbidden. A Christian practices the virtue of chastity by cultivating modesty in behavior, dress, and speech, resisting lustful desires and temptations, rejecting masturbation, avoiding pornography and indecent entertainment of every kind, and encouraging responsible social and legal policies which accord respect to human sexuality.[44]

Obligations toward neighbor also embrace many contemporary issues in the field of social justice.

c.VII

c) Duties toward self

Toward self, too, the follower of Christ has moral duties. He or she must be another Christ in the world, a living example of Christian goodness. Among the characteristics of such a person are humility and patience in the face of one's own imperfections, as well as those of others; Christ-like simplicity with respect to material things and the affluence typical of our society; and purity of word and action even in the midst of corruption.

It is critically important to guard against the capital sin of pride, which manifests itself in many ways. The same is true of sloth — spiritual, intellectual, and physical. Christians may not envy others their success, their innate or acquired qualities, their wealth or material possessions. Nor may they violate the requirements of self-control and abuse bodily health by intemperate use of drugs, alcohol, tobacco, or food.

Catechesis seeks to help people form right consciences, choose what is morally right, avoid sin and its occasions, and live in this world according to the Spirit of Christ, in love of God and neighbor. To do this requires self-discipline and self-sacrifice. It is not easy, but, in the strength which comes from the gifts of Christ and His Spirit, it is possible for sincere followers of Christ.

103,190

PART I: MARY AND THE SAINTS

106. Mary, mother of God, mother and model of the Church

The Gospel of Luke gives us Mary's words: "My spirit finds joy in God my savior, for he has looked upon his servant in her lowliness; all ages to come shall call me blessed." (Lk 1,47f) The "ever-virgin mother of Jesus Christ our Lord and God"[45] occupies a place in the Church second only to that of Christ. Mary is close to us as our spiritual mother.

Singularly blessed, Mary speaks significantly to our lives and needs in the sinlessness of her total love. Following venerable Christian tradition continued in the Second Vatican Council, the Church recognizes her as loving mother,[46] its "model and excellent exemplar in faith and charity."[47]

The special gifts bestowed on her by God include her vocation as mother of God, her immaculate conception (her preservation from original sin), and her entry into Christ's resurrection in being assumed body and soul to heaven. The special love and veneration due her as mother of Christ, mother of the Church, and our spiritual mother should be taught by word and example.[48]

107. Other saints

The Church also honors the other saints who are already with the Lord in heaven. We who come after them draw inspiration from their heroic example, look for fellowship in their communion, and in prayer seek their intercession with God on our behalf.[49] Associated with the Communion of Saints, the traditional value of indulgences may be explained.

PART J: DEATH, JUDGMENT, ETERNITY

108. Death

Michal Heron

Christians have a duty to pray for deceased relatives, friends, and all the faithful departed. They also reverence the bodies of those who have preceded them in death. The renewed funeral liturgy sets the tone for catechesis concerning death: we live, die and shall live again in the risen Christ; we look forward to a homecoming with God our loving Father. (Cf. Lk 15)

109. Judgment

Rick Smolan

Each individual has an awesome responsibility for his or her eternal destiny. The importance of the individual judgment after death, of the refining and purifying passage through purgatory, of the dreadful possibility of the eternal death which is hell, of the last judgment — all should be understood in light of Christian hope.

At the last judgment all people will fully reach their eternal destiny. The lives of all are to be revealed before the tribunal of Christ so that "each one may receive his recompense, good or bad, according to his life in the body." (2 Cor 5,10) Then "the evildoers shall rise to be damned," and "those who have done right shall rise to live" (Jn 5,29): a life eternally with God beyond what the human heart can imagine, a life of eternal enjoyment of the good things God has prepared for those who love Him.[50]

110. Final union with God

During their earthly lives Christians look forward to final union with God in heaven. They long for Christ's coming. "He will give a new form to this lowly body of ours and remake it according to the pattern of his glorified body.'' (Phil 3,21; cf. also 1 Cor 15)

The final realities will come about only when Christ returns with power to bring history to its appointed end. Then, as judge of the living and the dead, He will hand over His people to the Father. Only then will the Church reach perfection. Until that comes to pass, "some of His disciples are exiles on earth. Some have finished with this life and are being purified. Others are in glory, beholding clearly God Himself triune and one, as He is."[51]

Consoling hope, as well as salutary fear, should color one's attitude toward death, judgment, and eternity. (Cf. 1 Thes 4,13f) The Lord's resurrection signals the conquest of death, thus we have reason to live and face death with courage and joy.

111. Conclusion

This chapter has set forth the more outstanding elements of belief which the Church has received, serves, and teaches. Next we shall consider the liturgical expression of this same faith.

NC Photo

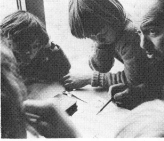

Rick Smolan

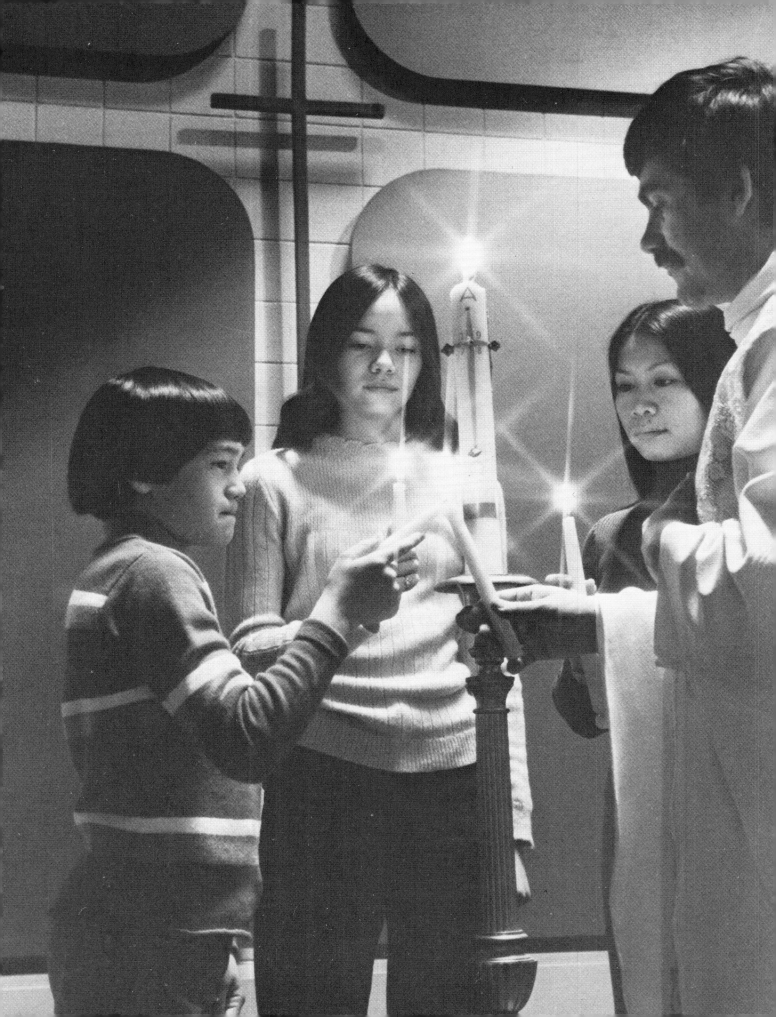

Chapter VI

Catechesis for a Worshiping Community

Send forth your light
and your fidelity;
they shall lead me on . . . .
Then will I go
in to the altar of God,
the God of my gladness and joy.
Ps 43,3f

PART A: LITURGY AND CATECHESIS

112. Introduction

The Church is a worshiping community. In worship it praises God for His goodness and glory. It also acknowledges its total dependence on God, the Father, and accepts the gift of divine life which He wishes to share with us in the Son, through the outpouring of the Spirit. Worship creates, expresses, and fulfills the Church. It is the action in and by which men and women are drawn into the mystery of the glorified Christ.

Faith and worship are intimately related. Faith brings the community together to worship; and in worship faith is renewed. The Church celebrates Christ's life, death, resurrection in its liturgy; it proclaims its faith in His presence in the Church, in His word, in the sacramental celebrations; it gives praise and thanks, asks for the things it needs, and strengthens itself to carry out its commission to give witness and service.

Different ecclesial and liturgical traditions within the Catholic Church have different ways of celebrating faith in worship. While this chapter is concerned mainly with the liturgy of the Western Church, an attempt has also been made to introduce certain perspectives of the Eastern Churches.

113. The relationship of liturgy and catechesis

There is a close relationship between catechesis and liturgy. Both are rooted in the Church's faith, and both strengthen faith and summon Christians to conversion, although they do so in different ways. In the liturgy the Church is at prayer, offering adoration, praise, and thanksgiving to God, and seeking and celebrating reconciliation: here one finds both an expression of faith and a means for deepening it. As for catechesis, it prepares people for full and active participation in liturgy (by helping them understand its nature, rituals, and symbols) and at the same time flows from liturgy, inasmuch as, reflecting upon the community's experiences of worship, it seeks to relate them to daily life and to growth in faith.

PART B: SACRAMENTS/MYSTERIES

Paul S. Conklin

114. The sacraments/mysteries as symbol

"The mystery of Christ is continued in the Church . . . in a specific way through the signs that Christ instituted, which signify the gift of grace and produce it, and are properly called sacraments."[1]

The Word of God is the full manifestation of the Father; thus He may be called a symbol, an icon, an image of the Father. Created through the Word, the world is in its very reality a symbol of its creator.

Because they have been created by His Word and in His image, human beings have the greatest capacity for symbolizing God. Jesus Christ, the Word incarnate, was the perfect symbol or sacrament of God on earth. The community of faith, which strives to follow Christ's example and live by His teachings, is the symbol or sacrament of His continued presence among us.

The sacraments, symbolic actions which effect what they symbolize, celebrate the coming of the Spirit at special moments in the life of the community of faith and its members, and express the Church's faith and interaction with Christ. The Church celebrates the mysteries of God's presence through word, bread, wine, water, oil, and the actions of the ordained ministers and the people.

The Eastern Churches call the sacraments "mysteries." The mysteries of Baptism, Chrismation (which the Western Church calls Confirmation), the Eucharist, and the other sacraments are understood as bringing the recipients into an experience of the holy. The Eastern Fathers draw an analogy between the presence of the Father in creation, the Son in the word (that is, revelation), and the Spirit in the waters of Baptism, the oil of chrism, and the Eucharist, as well as in the recipients of these mysteries. Creation viewed as a symbol, the humanity of Christ, and the tangible mysteries or sacraments — all reveal the reality of God.

Christians attribute all God's divinizing action to the Holy Spirit, God's power dwelling in creation. For example, the gesture of imposing hands in Holy Orders and the Rite of Reconciliation is meant to express the invoking of the Spirit. For this reason, too, the Eastern Churches especially highlight the calling down of the Holy Spirit (Epiklesis) in the celebration of the eucharistic liturgy.

Section 1: Sacraments — Mysteries of Initiation

115. Introduction

Christian initiation is celebrated in Baptism, Confirmation or Chrismation, and Eucharist. Through these visible actions a person is incorporated into the Church and shares its mission in the world. Baptism and Confirmation (Chrismation) enable recipients, through sharing in Christ's priestly office, to be intimately associated in the offering of the sacrifice of the Eucharist.

Full initiation into the Church occurs by stages. The *Rite of Christian Initiation of Adults* (Roman) provides a norm for catechetical as well as liturgical practice in this regard. The intimate relationship of the sacraments of Baptism, Confirmation, and Eucharist should be emphasized in the catechesis of both adults and children. Such catechesis will involve many members of the parish community who support and pray with the catechized, besides instructing them so that they may grow in understanding of the Christian message.

Paul S. Conklin

116. Baptism

Baptism cleanses people from original sin and from all personal sins, gives them rebirth as children of God, incorporates them into the Church, sanctifies them with the gifts of the Holy Spirit, and, impressing on their souls an indelible character, initiates them in Christ's priestly, prophetic, and kingly roles.[2] Furthermore, the Church has always taught that Baptism is necessary for salvation.[3]

By accepting Baptism into Christ's death and resurrection, people affirm their faith and are initiated and welcomed into the community of faith. Dedicated to and enlightened by the Spirit, made sons and daughters of God with a permanent relationship in Christ, and cleansed from sin through water and the Holy Spirit, they become a new creation.

In response to their call to share in Christ's priesthood, the baptized are to minister both to the community of faith and to the whole world. Single life, married life, the life of the evangelical counsels, and the ordained ministry are all suitable contexts for such service.

98

74e),129-133,170,14),180b),182

117. Catechesis for Baptism

Catechesis for Baptism is directed primarily to adults — adult candidates for Baptism and the parents and godparents of infants who are to be baptized. According to the *Rite of Christian Initiation of Adults*, catechumens proceed through the stages of evangelization, catechumenate, purification and enlightenment, and post-baptismal catechesis.[4] This process also provides helpful guidelines for the catechesis of parents and godparents. Authentic understanding of the significance of Baptism naturally leads to continuing catechesis.

Baptismal catechesis involves the community of the faithful, who share their faith with those being catechized. Adult catechumens and the parents of children to be baptized alike need the community's prayers, witness, and support. Pre- and post-baptismal catechesis may take many forms, such as prayer, fasting, service, and instruction.

NC Photo by Chris Sheridan

Baptismal catechesis centers on the Father's love; the life, death, and resurrection of Jesus the Son; the cleansing of original and personal sin; and the gift of the Spirit to the Church. It includes proclaiming God's word, so that those called may respond in faith.

Immediate preparation includes catechesis concerning the baptismal ritual and symbols: i.e., water as life-giving and cleansing, oil as strengthening and healing, light as driving out darkness, the community as the setting in which Christ is present.

Preparation for the Baptism of infants[5] is a "teachable" moment, when the parish community can encourage parents to reexamine the meaning which faith has in their lives. In offering catechesis to parents and sponsors, the Church shows its love for and eagerness to support them as well as their children.

Children should not be deprived of Baptism. "An infant should be baptized within the first weeks after birth. If the child is in danger of death, it is to be baptized without delay."[6]

118. Confirmation/Chrismation

As a Sacrament of Initiation, Confirmation (Chrismation) is intimately related to Baptism and the Eucharist. Christians are reborn in Baptism, strengthened by Confirmation, and sustained by the food of Eucharist. Specifically, in Confirmation/Chrismation they are signed with the gift of the Spirit and become more perfect images of their Lord. Confirmation renews and strengthens the Christian's baptismal call to bear witness to Christ before the world and work eagerly for the building up of His body.

Confirmation emphasizes the transformation of life by the outpouring of the Holy Spirit in His fullness. Confirmed Christians claim as fully their own the new life into which they were first initiated at Baptism. The Church community expresses its continued support and concern for the spiritual growth of those confirmed, while the latter promise in turn to help others grow and mature in the Christian life.

119. Catechesis for Confirmation

In the Eastern Churches, Baptism and Chrismation are celebrated together in infancy, and their intimate relationship is apparent. Though the Western Church has for many centuries generally separated the celebration of Baptism from Confirmation, it also recognized that they are intimately related. By emphasizing this relationship in the *Rite of Christian Initiation of Adults*, the Western Church has once again made clear how these two sacramental moments are parts of a unified process of initiation.

Catechesis for adults preparing for Confirmation follows the pattern recommended in the *Rite of Christian Initiation of Adults*.

The revised Rite of Confirmation[7] says episcopal conferences may designate the appropriate age for Confirmation. Practice in this matter now varies so much among the dioceses of the United States, that it is impossible to prescribe a single catechesis for this sacrament. A few years ago young people were generally confirmed around the age of 10 or 12. More recently, emphasis upon Confirmation as the sacrament of Christian commitment has led to postponement until the recipients are 12, 14, or, in some dioceses, 17 or older. Appropriate catechesis for these ages is being given. Among the elements of such catechesis in various places are performance standards for Church membership and community service; requiring a specified minimum number of hours of service to qualify for Confirmation; a letter of request for Confirmation; formational programs of catechesis extending over two or three years; and the use of adult advisors.

As with Baptism, catechesis for this sacrament takes place within the parish community, which has an obligation to participate in the catechetical preparation of those to be confirmed. The parish is the faith community into whose life of prayer and worship they will be more fully initiated. It also embodies the message to which they are to respond and gives witness, in service, to the faith they profess. The parish should strive to catechize on behalf of "obedience to Christ" and "loyal testimony to him" through the power of the Spirit.[8]

As the primary educators of their children, parents, along with sponsors, are to be intimately involved in catechesis for Confirmation. This will help them renew and strengthen their own faith, besides enabling them to set a better example for their children or godchildren. The parental program is an important element in planning for Confirmation for children and young people.

120. The Eucharist[9]

Initiated into the Christian mystery by Baptism and Confirmation (Chrismation), Christians are fully joined to the Body of Christ in the Eucharist. The Eucharist is the center and heart of Christian life for both the universal and local Church and for each Christian. All that belongs to Christian life leads to the eucharistic celebration or flows from it.

It is a traditional theme of both the Eastern and Western Churches that Eucharist forms Church. Eucharist and Church are the basic realities, bearing the same names: communion and Body of Christ. The Eucharist increases charity within the visible community. The other mysteries (sacraments) dispose people to participate fruitfully in the central mystery of the Eucharist. The Eucharist is also seen as the chief source of divinization and maintains the pledge of immortality.

NC Photo by Todd Tarbox

NC Photo by Vern Bartos

The Eucharist is a memorial of the Lord's passion, death, and resurrection. This holy sacrifice is both a commemoration of a past event and a celebration of it here and now. Through, with, and in the Church, Christ's sacrifice on the cross and the victory of His resurrection become present in every celebration.

The eucharistic celebration is a holy meal which recalls the Last Supper, reminds us of our unity with one another in Christ, and anticipates the banquet of God's kingdom. In the Eucharist, Christ the Lord nourishes Christians, not only with His word but especially with His body and blood, effecting a transformation which impels them toward greater love of God and neighbor.

"By means of the homily the mysteries of the faith and the guiding principles of the Christian life are expounded from the sacred text during the course of the liturgical year. The homily, therefore, is to be highly esteemed as part of the liturgy itself."[10]

The Eucharist is also a Sacrament of Reconciliation, completing and fulfilling the Sacraments of Initiation. In each Eucharist we reaffirm our conversion from sin, a conversion already real but not yet complete. The Eucharist proclaims and effects our reconciliation with the Father. "Look with favor on your Church's offering, and see the Victim whose death has reconciled us to yourself."[11]

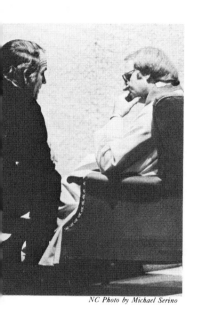

NC Photo by Michael Serino

121. Catechesis for the Eucharist[12]

Catechesis recognizes the Eucharist as the heart of Christian life. It helps people understand that celebration of the Eucharist nourishes the faithful with Christ, the Bread of Life, in order that, filled with the love of God and neighbor, they may become more and more a people acceptable to God and build up the Christian community with the works of charity, service, missionary activity, and witness.[13]

Reflecting upon Christ's life as proclaimed in the Gospels, catechesis considers the Last Supper and the Jewish roots of this covenant meal. It expresses the Church's faith that Christ is present not only in the Christian assembly and in the reading of His word, but in a unique and most excellent way in this sacrament; that the bread and wine are changed, a change traditionally and appropriately expressed by the word transubstantiation, so that, while the appearances of bread and wine remain, the reality is the body and blood of Christ.

Catechesis should also help people understand the importance and significance of the liturgy of the word in the eucharistic celebration.

To encourage reverent and informed participation in the Sacrament of the Eucharist, catechesis gives instruction about the meaning of the ritual, symbols, and parts of the Mass. It also includes instruction and practice in the prayers and rubrics for the laity at Mass.[14] If possible, those catechized should learn to plan eucharistic liturgies, to serve as gift bearers, readers, ushers, etc. Catechesis should make people aware of their obligation to be free of serious sin before receiving Holy Communion. It should also instruct them concerning the time of the eucharistic fast and the conditions under which Holy Communion may be received more than once a day.

Catechesis speaks of the Lord's real and abiding presence in the Blessed Sacrament, and encourages visits and eucharistic devotions. Among the latter is devotion to the Eucharistic Heart of Jesus, a devotion which has among its objectives to call particular attention to Jesus' love in instituting the Eucharist.[15] Catechesis also includes conduct in Church, including appropriate devotional gestures and postures, and how to visit and pray to the eucharistic Lord apart from Mass.

143
89, 143

The preparation of adults for first reception of the Eucharist is an integral part of the catechumenate process.

As for children, their parents, catechists, and pastors are responsible for determining when they are ready to receive First Communion.

Parents have a right and duty to be intimately involved in preparing their children for First Communion. Catechesis aims to help parents grow in understanding and appreciation of the Eucharist and participate readily in catechizing their children.

Catechesis for children seeks to strengthen their awareness of the Father's love, of the call to participate in Christ's sacrifice, and of the gift of the Spirit. Children should be taught that the Holy Eucharist is the real body and blood of Christ, and what appear to be bread and wine are actually His living body. Children around the age of 7 tend to think concretely; they grasp concepts like "unity" and "belonging" from experiences, such as sharing, listening, eating, conversing, giving, thanking, and celebrating. Such experiences, coupled with explanations of the Eucharist adapted to their intellectual capacity and with further efforts to familiarize them with the main events of Jesus' life, help them to participate more meaningfully in the action of the Mass and to receive Christ's body and blood in communion in an informed and reverent manner.

Catechesis for First Communion is conducted separately from introductory catechesis for the Sacrament of Reconciliation, since each sacrament deserves its own concentrated preparation. Continued catechesis is given yearly in all catechetical programs for children, inasmuch as the sacraments require lifelong participation and study. 125

In some Eastern Churches in the United States, First Communion completes an infant's reception of the Sacraments of Initiation and is celebrated in conjunction with Baptism and Chrismation. In this context, eucharistic catechesis follows reception of the sacrament and supports the young Christian's growth into the mystery.

Section II: Sacraments — Mysteries of Reconciliation and Healing

123. Introduction

We are incorporated into Christ's body, the Church, through the Sacraments of Initiation. When we have been weakened by sin or sickness, we are healed and strengthened within that body through the sacraments of Reconciliation and Anointing of the Sick.

124. The Sacrament of Reconciliation

Jesus began His work on earth by calling people to repentance and faith: "Reform your lives and believe in the gospel." (Mk 1,15) Conversion means turning from sin toward Him — present in His Church, in the Eucharist, in His work, and in our neighbor — with love and a desire for reconciliation.

Robert S. Halvey

Jesus began His risen life by giving His apostles power to forgive sins. (Cf. Jn 20,23) The Sacrament of Reconciliation continues His work of forgiving and reconciling. It celebrates the prodigal's return to the eternally merciful Father, renewing the sinner's union with God — and also with the community, inasmuch as our sins harm our brothers and sisters.

The revised ritual offers various forms and options for celebrating this sacrament. Among these are communal celebrations, which more clearly show its ecclesial nature. Penitents have a choice of the customary anonymity or a

Paul S. Conklin

setting face-to-face with the confessor. A choice is also offered among various prayers and readings.

The sacrament's traditional and essential elements are contrition, confession, absolution, and satisfaction. Contrition is heartfelt sorrow and aversion from sin as an offense against God, with the firm intention of sinning no more. It expresses a conversion, "a profound change of the whole person by which one begins to consider, judge and arrange" one's whole life to conform more with Christ's values.[16] Following the revised rite, the penitent, as a sign of conversion, first listens to the priest proclaim God's word calling to conversion. Having earlier reviewed his or her sins, attitudes, failures, etc., the penitent confesses sins, makes an appropriate expression of sorrow, and receives forgiveness and reconciliation from the priest in Christ's name. Afterward the penitent performs the agreed-upon act of satisfaction (penance).

The Sacrament of Reconciliation, including individual and complete confession and absolution, remains the ordinary way of reconciling the faithful with God and with the Church. The Church holds and teaches that this method of receiving the sacrament is necessary and willed by Christ. Individual confession and absolution cannot be easily or ordinarily set aside. Particular, occasional circumstances may render it lawful and even necessary to give general absolution to a number of penitents without their previous individual confession, though the obligation to confess serious sin still remains. The existence of these serious circumstances is identified by the local bishop in consultation with other bishops according to articles 31 and 32 of the Rite of Penance.[17]

Secrecy is essential for safeguarding the sacrament; both penitent and sacrament are protected by the priest's obligation to maintain secrecy. The penitent ought to exercise prudent care in speaking about his or her own confession.

Frequent participation in this sacrament, even though one has not committed a serious sin, is a highly desirable way of celebrating ongoing conversion and making progress in holiness.

AP Photo

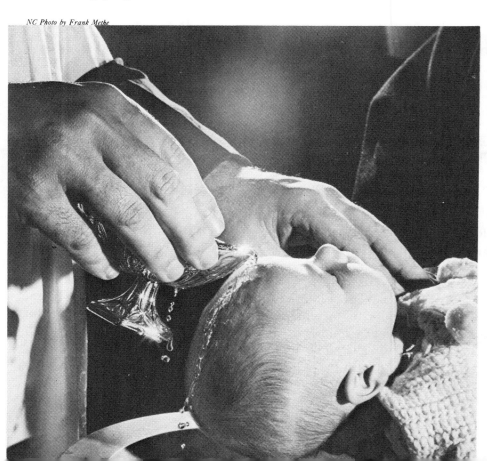

NC Photo by Frank Methe

125. Catechesis for the Sacrament of Reconciliation

An understanding of sin, of oneself as a sinner, and of the conditions requisite for a serious sin are necessary preliminaries in catechesis for this sacrament.

The catechesis itself emphasizes God's mercy and loving forgiveness. It also emphasizes that faith, a gift of God, is a call to conversion from sin.

Catechesis for Reconciliation challenges people to acknowledge the difference between good and evil in the social order, to measure their values and priorities against those of the gospel and the Church, to accept individual and corporate responsibility for their decisions and the consequences of those decisions, and to repent of their participation in evil. A formal examination of conscience, like the one printed in the addenda to the revised ritual, can be useful.

Catechesis prepares the community to celebrate in ritual the realities of repentance, conversion, and reconciliation. Everyone needs this sacrament, for we are all sinners, not just those seriously estranged from God and the Church, and we all find here an opportunity to confront our sinfulness, acknowledge our need for conversion, seek pardon and peace, and celebrate our union with the healing, merciful Christ and His Church. Similarly, we all need to grow in our ability to celebrate this sacrament fruitfully and make good use of the options which are available.

Catechesis calls attention to the obligation to celebrate the sacrament whenever one is in mortal sin and, minimally, to confess such sin within a year. It also notes that, in a world where alienation and loneliness seem to be the norm, it is an expression of one's Christian faith to forgive others and seek forgiveness when necessary.

126. Catechesis of children for Reconciliation

122,178

Catechesis for children must always respect the natural disposition, ability, age, and circumstances of individuals. It seeks, first, to make clear the relationship of the sacrament to the child's life; second, to help the child recognize moral good and evil, repent of wrongdoing, and turn for forgiveness to Christ and the Church; third, to encourage the child to see that, in this sacrament, faith is expressed by being forgiven and forgiving; fourth, to encourage the child to approach the sacrament freely and regularly.

Parents should be involved in the preparation of children for this sacrament.

Catechesis for the Sacrament of Reconciliation is to precede First Communion and must be kept distinct by a clear and unhurried separation. This is to be done so that the specific identity of each sacrament is apparent and so that, before receiving First Communion, the child will be familiar with the revised Rite of Reconciliation and will be at ease with the reception of the sacrament. The Sacrament of Reconciliation normally should be celebrated prior to the reception of First Communion.[18]

Because continuing, lifelong conversion is part of what it means to grow in faith, catechesis for the Sacrament of Reconciliation is ongoing. Children have a right to a fuller catechesis each year. Adults also have a right to continuing catechesis concerning the sacrament. Lent is an especially appropriate season for this.

NC Photo by Joseph Duerr

127. The Anointing of the Sick

Jesus' care and concern for the sick permeate the Gospels. Though primarily concerned with spiritual sickness, He was not indifferent to bodily afflic-

N.C. Photo by Dave Vaughn

tions and seemed often to point to the relationship between the two. To be faithful to Him, the Church must care for those who are sick in body as well as spirit.

The Anointing of the Sick is the special sacrament for Christians dangerously ill as a result of sickness or old age. "As soon as any one of the faithful begins to be in danger of death from sickness or old age, the appropriate time for him to receive this sacrament has certainly already arrived."[19]

The discouragement and anxiety which often accompany illness and suffering can weaken faith; but the Church invites the sick to come to Christ to be healed, to be made whole, to receive peace. (Cf. Jas 5,14f) The Church commends those receiving the sacrament "to the suffering and glorified Lord, that He may raise them up and save them."[20] If physical health is beneficial to salvation, it may be restored. If the sick need forgiveness, their sins will be pardoned.

Communal celebrations of the Anointing of the Sick are recommended. On such occasions the sick, surrounded by the Church in the person of their family and friends, can receive special support and encouragement from the faith community.

While the revised rite for this sacrament emphasizes ministry to the sick, it also treats ministry to the dying. The continuous Rite of Reconciliation, Anointing, and Viaticum (receiving the Eucharist) is provided for the dying.

186,202

128. Catechesis for the Anointing of the Sick

Both catechesis for this sacrament and pastoral care of the sick should examine the meaning of sickness, healing, suffering, and death in the light of faith.

The sacrament is intended for those dangerously ill because of sickness or old age, for patients undergoing surgery on account of dangerous illness, for elderly persons who are in a weak condition, even if they are not dangerously ill, for children who are seriously ill and have sufficient understanding to be comforted by its reception.[21] Since this is a departure in many respects from the Church's practice in the immediate past, catechesis is imperative concerning the Christian interpretation of sickness and healing.

Catechesis encourages the faithful to ask for the anointing and receive it with complete faith and devotion, not delaying its reception. All who care for the sick should be taught the meaning and purpose of anointing.

Catechesis encourages the members of the local parish to visit the sick and express love and concern for them. The faith community should seek out those of its members who have been cut off from it and confined by illness, offering them love and support, praying with them, ministering to their needs. Catechesis points out and provides opportunities for service to the sick, and includes prayer for and with them.

Together with Reconciliation and Viaticum, this sacrament prepares the Christian for death. Catechesis notes that Christians should do more for the dying than wait passively with them. It encourages listening, praying, sharing the word of God, as well as simply being present, or whatever else may make their passage to eternal life peaceful.

Section III: Sacraments — Mysteries of Commitment

129. Introduction

Every Christian's ultimate commitment is to love and serve God revealed in Jesus Christ present in His Church. But individual Christians are called to live out this commitment in various ways. Most do so in the context of marriage and family life, some by serving the faith community as ordained ministers. The sacraments of Matrimony and Holy Orders celebrate these callings, and sanctify and strengthen those who commit themselves to them.

74e),116, 130-133, 170,14), 180b),182

130. The Sacrament of Matrimony

Christian marriage is the union of a baptized man and woman who freely enter into a loving covenant with each other in Christ. The self-giving love of bride and bridegroom is sealed and strengthened by the Lord; the married couple imitates, and in a way represents, Christ's faithful love for His bride, the Church. Thus husbands and wives become signs, in and to the world, of God's steadfast love for His people.

The steadfast and selfless love of husband and wife is beautifully expressed and symbolized in the Eastern tradition by the crowning of the newly married; the marriage ceremony itself is called the "crowning." The ceremony signals the establishment of a new "kingdom," based on mutual love, as a witness to Christ's love for His Church.

The Church proclaims the permanent, exclusive, and binding nature of this loving covenant. In the case of Christian marriage, the man and the woman are themselves the ministers of the sacrament. When either partner in a marriage is Catholic, the couple should be aware of and follow the norms and laws of the Church governing Christian marriage.

Marriage and conjugal love are naturally oriented toward the begetting and education of children. The unitive goal of marriage is also important, for "marriage . . . is not instituted solely for procreation. Rather, its very nature as an unbreakable compact between persons, and the welfare of the children, both demand that the mutual love of the spouses, too, be embodied in a rightly ordered manner, that it grow and ripen. Therefore, marriage persists as a whole manner and communion of life, and maintains its value and indissolubility even when offspring are lacking — despite, rather often, the very intense desire of the couple."[22]

NC Photo by John Keenan

131. Catechesis for Matrimony

The parish community helps people preparing for marriage by providing thorough premarital instructions in which they have opportunity to reflect on the nature of the marriage relationship, the joys and problems of married life, and the responsibilities they will assume toward each other and their children.

Catechesis helps couples understand marriage as a holy relationship, blessed and supported by God for the duration of life itself. Through the Sacrament of Matrimony His grace is constantly available to them.

Catechesis seeks to help couples recognize that only people courageous enough to make promises for life have the love and strength to surmount the inevitable challenges of marriage. Such unselfish love, rooted in faith, is ready to forgive when need arises, and to make the sacrifices demanded to foster the precious and holy marriage relationship. Catechesis stresses that one of the purposes of marriage is this mutual support and growth of love of husband and wife.

Catechesis calls attention to the fact that openness to the procreation and education of children must always be present and is vitally linked to growth in marital and family love.[23]

Catechesis also includes a clear presentation of the Church's teaching concerning moral methods of regulating births, the evil of artificial birth control and of sterilization for that purpose, and the crime of abortion; it should stress

105b),167

the protection due to human life once conceived.

Shared faith is a positive, strengthening element in marriage. While recognizing the sacramental character of interdenominational Christian marriages between the baptized, the Church encourages marriages within the Catholic faith. A Catholic must request a canonical dispensation for an interfaith marriage. Catechesis for those preparing for such marriages should encourage them to engage in honest, open reflection on the special difficulties they will face. The basic unity of belief among Christians should be recognized, along with the differences which will affect the way the couple live out their married life.

177

Catechesis for Matrimony is not limited to the period immediately before marriage. People begin to learn the meaning of married love and to acquire reverence for married life very early in childhood; parents are the primary catechists of their children with respect to such matters. Catechesis on Matrimony, married life, and Christian "parenting" should be given to young people of high school age; and relevant catechesis for adults should be available at all stages of married life. Whenever possible, married couples should be involved in giving catechesis concerning Matrimony.

182,196

At the core of Christian marriage are a radical, permanent commitment and a high ideal of loving fidelity, marital chastity, mutual generosity, fecundity, and personal and social growth. Living up to these demands can be difficult in a secularized, hedonistic, and pluralistic culture in which divorce and remarriage are generally accepted. Concern for those who have suffered the trauma of divorce should be integral to the Catholic community. Spiritual and psychological counseling, in an atmosphere of understanding, is vital for those who have experienced marital failure. Divorced persons and their children should be welcomed by the parish community and made to feel truly a part of parish life. Catechesis on the Church's teaching concerning the consequences of remarriage after divorce is not only necessary but will be supportive for the divorced.

Parish and diocesan catechetical programs which foster supportive interaction between spouses and among couples should be encouraged and made available to all married couples.

132. The Sacrament of Holy Orders

Jesus Christ, the supreme high priest, exercises His salvific work today by extending to all persons the fruits of His death and resurrection, particularly, and in a unique way, in the sacred mystery of the Eucharist. In Holy Orders one is called apart to share in an active and intimate manner the priestly saving action of Jesus Christ in a ministry of sanctifying, teaching, and building the Christian community.[24] All the faithful are participants in this mystery of redemption as they share in Christ's work. Yet ordained priesthood confers the power to act in the person of Christ and in His name and with His power to renew these mysteries, especially the mystery of the eucharistic sacrifice.

Bishops are the successors of the apostles as pastors of souls. Episcopal ordination confers the fullness of the Sacrament of Orders. In the person of the bishop Christ is present in the midst of His people, proclaiming the gospel and preaching the faith to all who believe. During the ceremony of episcopal ordination in the Byzantine rite, the bishop is called to be an imitator of Christ, the true shepherd, who laid down His life for His sheep.[25]

Priests are Christ's ministers. The Church is built up and grows through their ordination to public ministry. In the Byzantine rite, this charge is expressed by the prayer, addressed to Christ, that the new minister may "announce the gospel of your kingdom . . . sanctify the word of your truth . . . offer spiritual sacrifices to you, and . . . renew your people by the washing of rebirth."[26]

NC Photo

Deacons are also called, in Holy Orders, to minister to the Church. They are ordained to serve all people through a threefold ministry "of the Word, of the liturgy and of charity."[27]

133. Catechesis for Holy Orders

Catechesis concerning ordained ministry must be given to all members of the faith community, so that all may share a common vision of the task of these ministers, ordained to the priestly orders.

Catechesis makes it clear that in a special way bishops, priests, and deacons are called — and through ordination empowered — to minister in Christ's name and that of the Church. They do this by proclaiming the word, embodying the gospel in the community of believers, leading the community in worship, healing its divisions, and summoning its members to reconciliation. Public celebration of ordinations and installations calls attention to the intimate link between the community and its ordained members.

Catechesis encourages the people to support bishops, priests, and deacons in their efforts to be faithful to their call and in the exercise of their ministry. It encourages prayer for the Church's ministers and for new vocations to the ordained ministry. It provides opportunities for people to consider the call to ordained ministry as a possible way for them to live out the Christian commitment.

NC Photo by Robert H. Davis

Section IV: The Eucharistic Liturgy for Groups with Special Needs

192-196

134. Introduction

The eucharistic liturgy is the community's central act of worship. Ordinarily, the parish Sunday Mass is the community celebration which reflects and shapes the lives of parishioners.

Occasionally, however, the Eucharist is celebrated by smaller groups whose members are joined by special ties. Masses for such groups can further their growth in faith and in understanding of the Eucharist, by encouraging them to reflect not only upon the particular bonds which bring them together but upon the unity symbolized and effected by eucharistic celebration in the larger community.

Catechists are frequently asked to assist such groups in preparing for their Masses. In doing so, they should take into consideration the nature of the liturgical celebration.[28]

135. Masses for children

139,179
197,199,
229

Children often cannot participate fully in adult liturgies because they do not understand the words and symbols used or understand them only imperfectly.[29] Recognizing this, the Sacred Congregation for Divine Worship issued a *Directory for Masses with Children* in 1973. It sets the framework for catechizing children for eucharistic celebration.

The directory emphasizes the need to integrate liturgical and eucharistic formation with the overall educational experience of children. Catechists should work and plan together to ensure that the children, besides having some idea of God and the supernatural, also have some experience of the human values involved in eucharistic celebration: e.g., acting together as a community, exchanging greetings, the capacity to listen, to forgive and to ask forgiveness, the expression of gratitude, the experience of symbolic actions.[30] Family participation in Masses for children is encouraged on occasion in order to encourage family unity.

136. Masses for youth

For young people to be able to prepare and plan Masses which reflect their faith and feelings, catechesis is needed. It should include study of the Gospels, of the nature of the Church and liturgy, of the way in which the Church celebrates its union with Christ in the Eucharist, and the liturgy's intimate relationship to life, faith, doctrine, and the Church. The meaning of the symbols, of bread, wine, and faith community, is probed. Youth are gradually introduced to the rich liturgical and musical traditions of the Church.

While young people are encouraged to participate actively in celebrating the Mass and to accept the roles open to them, the value of family worship and worship with the larger parish community should also be recognized.

137. Masses for cultural groups

In planning Masses for particular cultural, racial, and ethnic groups it is important to take their needs, preferences, and gifts into account. Preparation for inter-group celebrations should involve mutual planning and effort, so that all may profit from the diverse liturgical heritages.

In liturgical celebrations, homogeneous cultural, racial, or ethnic communities have the right to use their own language and cultural expressions of faith in ritual, music, art. However, while diversity enriches the Church and makes it possible for the participants to experience worship more deeply, adaptations must respect the nature of liturgy as the worship of the Church. Not every cultural adaptation will be possible or suitable for liturgical use. More research is needed in this area.

138. Masses for those with handicapping conditions

Masses (and all other sacramental celebrations) for handicapped persons require special adaptations. Each handicapping condition calls for a different approach.

Many mentally handicapped persons, for example, respond profoundly to concrete visual symbols and gesture. Their liturgical celebrations should use color, art, and music, with less emphasis on verbal expressions of faith. Abstract symbols are generally avoided.

To take another example, it should be borne in mind that because most people who are deaf or have severe hearing disabilities live otherwise normal lives, their special needs may go unnoticed. However, provision should be made for Masses and other sacramental celebrations in sign language. If the celebrant himself cannot use this language, qualified interpreters should translate the liturgy into sign language. The use of amplification, good lighting for effective speechreading, and audio-visuals, all in accordance with the specific needs of hearing-impaired persons, should be encouraged.

All adaptations should be designed by qualified specialists and persons who work with the handicapped persons, in consultation, as far as possible, with the handicapped persons themselves. However, specialized liturgies should never entirely replace the integration of handicapped people into the larger worshiping community.

NC Photo by Chris Sheridan

139. Catechetical guidelines for eucharistic celebrations

Since catechists are often called on to prepare people to participate in the liturgy or to direct them in studying and reflecting on it, they themselves should have adequate liturgical preparation, both theoretical and practical. Also, whenever possible, catechists should seek the advice and collaboration of pastors or priests with pastoral experience in addition to formally trained liturgists.

At every level, particularly the national, dialogue between catechists and liturgists should be pursued in order to clarify the relationship between catechesis and liturgy, and to identify areas for cooperation and mutual assistance.

Liturgies for special groups point to the celebration of the parish and the wider Catholic community. Adaptations can be made according to age, maturity, race, cultural or ethnic group, and handicap. Members of the particular group can be involved in liturgical planning and celebration in ways that take the same factors into account. However, the norms and guidelines in the official liturgical books are to be observed.

PART C: PRAYER

140. Introduction

At the very heart of the Christian life lies free self-surrender to the unutterable mystery of God. Prayer, for both individuals and communities, means a deepening awareness of covenanted relationship with God, coupled with the effort to live in total harmony with His will. Private prayer permeates the daily life of the Christian and helps the individual to enter into communal or public prayer. There are four general purposes of prayer: adoration, thanksgiving, petition, and contrition. As a life of prayer matures it becomes more simple, and adoration, thanksgiving, and contrition tend to predominate.

Individuals and communities also pray in word and ritual. This prayer helps people achieve and express the reality of internal self-surrender to God, which lives in the depths of consciousness and flows out into life. Sacramental celebrations are the prayer of the Church, as also is the Liturgy of the Hours.

Whether communal or individual, all strivings in prayer are efforts to associate ourselves as consciously and consistently as possible with the constant activity of the Spirit dwelling within us. He calls us to be open to His inspirations, to cooperate with His initiatives, to remove obstacles to our becoming other Christs. Acknowledging the Spirit's initiative, catechists call upon Him when planning group expressions of prayer and open themselves to His promptings.

141. The Liturgy of the Hours

Since apostolic times, the Christian community has prayed at least twice daily in a structured, public way. Realizing the need for a prayer form transcending the needs and insights of individuals and expressing the worship of the community, the Church turned to the scriptures as the source of its Liturgy of the Hours. This communal prayer is made up of psalms, canticles, readings from scripture and selected Christian writers, hymns, responsories, and intercessory prayers. Its essential pattern is that of a dialogue between God and His people. Through it, local Churches unite themselves with the universal Church to praise God unceasingly with one voice.

The revision of the Liturgy of the Hours has made this prayer accessible once again to the whole People of God. It can be adapted for families, parish groups, and special occasions.

Catechists need to experience the richness and beauty of this prayer in order to appreciate it and be able to introduce it to others. Whenever possible, therefore, leaders in the parish community should provide opportunities for celebration of morning and/or evening prayer.

43,141-145,
177-180,
185,190-
191,206

NC Photo by Robert Strawn

Rick Smolan

NC Photo by Robert Strawn

142. Paraliturgies or scriptural celebrations

Paraliturgies or scriptural celebrations are forms of prayer which appeal to many Catholics today. Generally based on the pattern of the Liturgy of the Hours, they include hymns or songs, psalms, scripture readings, intercessions, responsories or acclamations, and opportunities for silent prayer and reflection.

Because they are flexible in structure, paraliturgies can be designed for special occasions and oriented to particular themes. Although not substitutes for the official liturgy of the Church, they can deepen faith, strengthen community, foster Christian love, lead to more ardent and fruitful participation in sacramental celebration, and intensify the community's commitment to social justice. They offer opportunities for broad participation in planning and leadership. Catechists can foster appreciation of scriptural prayer by planning paraliturgies with those they catechize and providing frequent opportunities for such prayer.

143. Devotions and other forms of prayer

It is difficult to imagine a strong Catholic spiritual life without devotion to particular mysteries or saints. Both the Eastern and the Western Churches have a rich tradition of devotions. Whether private or public, these should harmonize with the liturgy, be in some way derived from it, and lead people toward it.

89-90,
121

In the Western Church devotion to the Blessed Sacrament reserved for adoration has a special place. Holy hours, Benediction, visits of adoration, the 40 Hours Devotions, Corpus Christi processions are all in the Church's tradition. First Friday eucharistic devotions, associated also with the devotion to the Sacred Heart of Jesus, invite many to share in the abiding love of God's presence among His people.

The venerable devotion to the Sacred Heart, based on the symbol of the human heart as a center of love and on the reality of God's love (1 Jn 4,7), considers the heart of Christ as the special meeting place of the divine and the human. Encouraged by several papal documents in this century,[31] devotion to the Sacred Heart has inspired many to respond to Jesus' invitation: "Learn from me, for I am gentle and humble of heart." (Mt 11,29)

Among other devotions, the Way of the Cross is associated especially with the Lenten season, and the rosary of the Blessed Virgin Mary with the months of May and October. In fact, with the multiplicity of ethnic and cultural backgrounds, devotions to the Lord, the virgin and the saints provide a rich tapestry on which is woven the many threads of our ancestry in the faith.

Among the devotions celebrated in Eastern Catholic communities are the Akathistos (praises to our Lord or the Mother of God) and Paraklesis (office of consolation), and Molebens (prayer services), Supplication - Benediction, Lenten services and rosary (privately) in the Byzantine Church, and the Christmas novena, devotion to the cross on the Fridays of Lent, and offices to the saints in the Maronite Church.

43,60a)i

Biblical prayer, involving reading scripture and meditating on it, is highly attractive to many today. Some learn favorite psalms and canticles by heart and base private prayer on them. Others repeat the name of Jesus, either by itself or inserted in brief phrases, such as "Lord Jesus Christ, Son of the living God, have mercy on me a sinner." Intercessory prayer — for oneself, one's family and friends, for the Church and the world — is another way of expressing one's love and confidence toward God. In seeking intimacy with God, silence is necessary; for prayer is a conversation, in which one must listen as well as speak. Meditation and contemplation are highly recommended.

Another contemporary phenomenon is the spread of prayer groups, either in homes or in churches and church-related facilities. Their chief purposes are to praise and thank God for all He has accomplished for us through Jesus in the power of the Holy Spirit, and to lead participants to live more deeply in the presence and power of the Spirit. Catechesis should familiarize people of all ages with this "prayer movement" and may properly encourage and foster participation in these groups.

Singing hymns and religious songs is also a form of prayer. (Cf. Eph 5,19f) Parishes should provide opportunities for people to learn hymns. The rich musical heritage of the Church, including Gregorian chant, should be preserved and made part of the parish musical repertoire.

Sharing common prayers helps people pray together as a community. Thus the great traditional prayers of the Church — such as the Apostles' Creed, the Sign of the Cross, the Lord's Prayer, the Hail Mary, and the Glory to the Father — should be known by all. Everyone should know some form of an act of contrition.

176e)

144. The liturgical year

The Fathers and the tradition of the Catholic Church teach that the historical events by which Christ Jesus won our salvation through His passover are not merely commemorated or recalled in the course of the liturgical year; rather the celebration of the liturgical year exerts "a special sacramental power and influence which strengthens Christian life."[32] "We ourselves believe and profess this same truth."[33]

"The Church celebrates the memory of Christ's saving work on appointed days in the course of the year. Every week the Church celebrates the memorial of the resurrection on Sunday, which is called the Lord's day. This is also celebrated, together with the passion of Jesus, on the great feast of Easter once a year. Throughout the year the entire mystery of Christ is unfolded, and the birthdays (days of death) of the saints are commemorated."[34] "Each day is made holy through the liturgical celebrations of God's people, especially the eucharistic sacrifice and the divine office."[35]

a) Sunday

The Church celebrates the paschal mystery on the first day of the week, the Lord's day or Sunday. "This follows a tradition handed down from the Apostles, which took its origin from the day of Christ's resurrection. Thus Sunday should be considered the original feast day."[36]

b) Other days

The weekdays extend and develop the Sunday celebration. Often "in the course of the year, as the Church celebrates the mystery of Christ, Mary, the Mother of God, is especially honored, and the martyrs and the other saints are proposed as examples for the faithful."[37]

c) The liturgical seasons

The Easter Triduum of the passion and the resurrection of Christ is the "culmination of the entire liturgical year. What Sunday is to the week, the solemnity of Easter is to the year."[38] The fifty days from Easter Sunday to Pentecost are one long feast day, sometimes called "the great Sunday."[39]

The season of Lent is a preparation for Easter. The liturgy prepares adult catechumens "for the celebration of the paschal mystery by the several stages of Christian initiation; it also prepares the faithful, who recall their baptism and do penance."[40]

The Church considers the Christmas season, which celebrates the birth of our Lord and His epiphanies (Magi, Cana, Baptism), "second only to the annual celebration of the Easter mystery."[41]

NC Photo by Robert H. Davis

Manuel Gomez

"The season of Advent has a two-fold character. It is a time of preparation for Christmas when the first coming of God's son to men is recalled." Also it is the "season when minds are directed to Christ's second coming at the end of time. It is thus a season of joyful and spiritual expectation" for the day of the Lord.[42]

"Apart from the seasons of Easter, Lent, Christmas, and Advent . . . there are thirty-three or thirty-four weeks in the course of the year which celebrate no particular aspect of the mystery of Christ. Instead, especially on the last Sundays, the mystery of Christ in all its fullness is celebrated. This period is known as Ordinary Time."[43]

d) Catechesis for the liturgical year

Catechesis for keeping time holy in prayer and the liturgical year is directed to every Christian. "By means of devotional exercises, instruction, prayer, and works of penance and mercy, the Church, according to traditional practices, completes the formation of the faithful during the various seasons of the Church year."[44]

The Commentary on the Revised Liturgical Year and *The General Norms for the Liturgical Year and the Calendar*[45] themselves provide an ample model for catechesis. The many local customs and the multiple ethnic heritages of our people, if properly directed, offer an immense reservoir for parents, teachers, and children to understand better the great loving work of God in Christ.

145. Catechesis for prayer

Inasmuch as it seeks to lead individuals and communities to deeper faith, all catechesis is oriented to prayer and worship. The deepening of faith strengthens the covenant relationship with God and calls Christians to respond in worship and ritual. By the nature of their ministry, catechists are often called to lead the community to prayer.

Catechesis promotes active, conscious participation in the liturgy, helps the faithful to meditate on God's word, and provides opportunities for praying.

177

143

Catechesis for prayer begins very early in childhood by hearing others pray; even small children can learn to call upon the Father, Jesus, and the Holy Spirit. In time, the child will become familiar with the various prayers and prayer forms mentioned earlier and make them part of his or her life. Catechesis encourages daily prayer, family prayer, and prayer at special times, e.g., before and after meals.

Building upon the sense of wonder, catechesis leads people to a sense of the sacred and to recognition of God's presence in their lives. This is the source of both spontaneous and formal prayer.

To lead others to pray, the catechist must be a prayerful person. To lead others to participate fully in liturgical worship, the catechist should have experienced full participation and be familiar with sacramental theology and the principles of liturgical celebration. Whenever possible, dioceses and parishes should provide opportunities for such liturgical catechesis.

PART D: SACRED ART AND SACRAMENTALS

251

146. Sacred art

The fine arts are among the noblest products of human genius. Ideally, their highest manifestation is sacred art. Things used in divine worship "should be truly worthy, becoming, and beautiful, signs and symbols of heavenly realities."[46]

The Western Church has never adopted a particular style or school of art as peculiarly its own, finding virtually all to be suitable instruments for expressing Christian values and truth. "She has admitted fashions from every period according to the talents and circumstances of peoples, and the needs of the various rites."[47] Catechesis should include an introduction to the religious art of the past, such as music, painting, sculpture, mosaics, and frescoes.

In expressing their faith, the Eastern Churches have developed and found great significance in the traditional forms of icons (images). Iconography views redeemed creation as a manifestation of the creator. This art form seeks to express in painting what is divinely mysterious in reality. The composition, perspective, color, and lighting, and the decorative elements of icons all take on a religious sense.

Contemporary art is as suitable for the service of religious worship as the art of past ages, provided it expresses the reverence and honor which are due the sacred. Within the limits set down by the liturgical law of the Church, catechists may make appropriate use of modern literature, dance, drama, mime, music, paintings, sculpture, banners, and audio-visual media in small liturgies, home Masses, and paraliturgies. Catechists should therefore familiarize themselves with liturgical law and official guidelines relating to the liturgy.

147. Sacramentals

Sacramentals are sacred signs which bear a resemblance to the sacraments:[48] they signify effects, particularly of a spiritual kind, which are obtained through the Church's intercession. They remind us of the symbolic nature of all creation, and encourage prayer and attitudes of reverence. Examples of sacramentals are baptismal water, holy oils, blessed ashes, candles, palms, crucifixes, and medals.

In introducing the sacramentals, catechists should discuss their relationship to faith and their function in the Church and in the lives of individuals.

148. Conclusion

Gathered to offer thanks to the Father in Christ through the Holy Spirit, the faith community grows in its sense of unity and its awareness of the Church's mission to the world. The liturgy, heart of the Church's life, leads its members to seek justice, charity, and peace. Both liturgy and catechists call the attention of Christians to what the Lord, the apostles, and the prophets taught concerning these matters. In the next chapter we shall consider the sources and content of catechesis for social ministry directed to the goals of justice, mercy, and peace.

Paul S. Conklin

Carl J. Pfeifer

Chapter VII

Catechesis
for Social Ministry

*On those who inhabit
a land overshadowed by death,
light has arisen.*
Mt 4,16

149. Introduction

Building on what has been said about Christian life, community, doctrine, and worship, this chapter describes the bases of the Church's social ministry; briefly sketches the development of Catholic social teaching and identifies some of its principal themes; and offers guidance for the continued development of a catechesis on behalf of justice, mercy, and peace.

PART A: FOUNDATIONS OF CATHOLIC SOCIAL TEACHING

150. Bases in scripture, moral doctrine, and the mission of the Church

Catholic social teaching is based upon scripture, upon the development of moral doctrine in light of scripture, upon the centuries-old tradition of social teaching and practice, and upon efforts to work out the relationship of social ministry to the Church's overall mission. Catholic social teaching has also been enriched by the contributions of philosophers and thinkers of all ages, including some who predate Christianity itself. With regard to social ministry, the words of the Second Vatican Council should always be kept in mind: "While helping the world and receiving many benefits from it, the Church has a single intention: that God's kingdom may come, and that the salvation of the whole human race may come to pass."[1]

Section I: The Biblical Base

151. Introduction

One finds powerful and compelling bases for the Church's social ministry throughout the Bible, especially in the Old Testament covenants and prophets, and in the Gospels and some epistles in the New Testament. The brief treatment which follows is meant to illustrate these rich sources and their implications with respect to the obligations inherent in the pursuit of justice, mercy, and peace.

Michal Heron

152. Old Testament

The Old Testament contains an urgent, recurring summons to practice justice and mercy — a divine summons based on the precept of love: "You shall love your neighbor as yourself." (Lv 19,18) Love is to lead to justice, equity, and charity. (Cf. Dt 24,6-22)

The Israelites are commanded to respond to the problems of the needy (cf. Dt 15,11), of orphans, widows, and aliens (cf. Dt 10,17ff;24,17), poor neighbors (cf. Ex 22,20-26), debtors, and the enslaved (cf. Dt 15,12-15; Is 58,6). They are admonished to share bread with the hungry, shelter the oppressed and homeless, and clothe the naked (cf. Is 58,7); to be honest "in using measures of length or weight or capacity" (Lv 19,35f; cf. Dt 25,13-16); to refrain from coveting or seizing fields or houses or cheating people of their inheritance (cf. Mi 2,1-13).

Through the prophet Isaiah the Lord commanded His people to pursue justice: "Put away your misdeeds from before my eyes . . . make justice your aim." (Is, 1,16f) Through Amos He commanded: "Let justice surge like water, and goodness like an unfailing stream." (Am 5,24) Earnest conformity to God's moral will is especially incumbent upon leaders and public figures. (Cf. Jer 22,13-16; Prv 8,15; Eccl 5,7f)

The Old Testament is very explicit in warning against mere lip service (cf.

Linda Bartlett

Is 29,13f) and indicating the punishment of evildoers (cf., e.g., Mi 2,1-10). Conversely, it assures the People of Israel that they will be rewarded for doing what is right: "A lasting covenant I will make with them." (Is 61,8)

153. New Testament

The scope of social ministry is broadened and social teaching is refined in the New Testament, especially in the example and words of Jesus. The New Testament expresses the universal kinship of all people, who call on "Our Father in heaven." (Mt 6,9) In God's eyes there does not exist Jew or Greek, slave or freeman, male or female. All are one in Christ Jesus. (Cf. Gal 3,28) Universal human dignity is recalled in the story of Lazarus, the poor man to whom salvation is granted while the rich man who had no mercy on him in life is condemned. (Cf. Lk 16,19-31)

The obligations of charity are movingly described in the parable of the good Samaritan, who showed himself to be neighbor to the man who fell in with robbers (cf. Lk 10,36f), thus doing what was required "to inherit everlasting life" (Lk 10,25). Another dramatic illustration of the need for compassion is the biblical description of the last judgment, at which, we are told, the heirs to the kingdom will be identified as those who showed compassion to the hungry, the thirsty, the stranger, the naked, the ill, and the prisoner: "I assure you, as often as you did it for one of my least brothers, you did it for me." (Mt 25,40) The Gospel also enjoins us to love our enemies, to do good to those who hate us, and to give aid to all who seek it from us; conversely it reminds us that no special credit is to be claimed for doing good to those who do good to us. (Cf. Lk 6,27-34)

John admonishes us to love in deed and in truth "and not merely talk about it." (1 Jn 3,18) Faith without works is as dead as a body without breath (cf. Jas 2,26); it is "thoroughly lifeless" (Jas 2,17).

In fact, God's love cannot survive in people who, possessing a sufficiency of this world's goods, close their hearts to brothers or sisters in need. (Cf. 1 Jn 3,17) Looking after orphans and widows in their distress (and keeping oneself unspotted by the world) is equated with "pure worship." (Jas 1,27)

The New Testament arouses a spirit of mutual concern and formulates principles to insure that people respect one another's rights and perform their duties. It requires forgiveness (cf. Lk 6,37), patience (cf. Rom 2,7), justice (cf. Lk 11,42), and promises peace (cf. Jn 14,27), love (cf. 15,9.12), and union with God (cf. 17,21ff).

154. Example of Jesus

Jesus' obedience to the Father led Him to give Himself fully for the salvation and liberation of others.[2] In the paschal mystery of His living, suffering, dying, and rising Catholic social teaching finds its ultimate ground and source.

Jesus identified Himself as the one who had come to serve, not to be served. He cited His ministry of service as the key to His identity and mission (cf. Lk 4,16ff) and clearly stated that anyone who aspires to follow Him must likewise serve the needs of all (cf. Mt 20,26f; Lk 22,26f).

Jesus not only affirmed the second great commandment — "You shall love your neighbor as yourself" (Lv 19,18; cf. Mk 12,33) — but further specified that this love be like His own: "Love one another as I have loved you." (Jn 15,12) His was an unconditional giving of self to and for others.

Jesus' birth was heralded by the song of angels: "Peace on earth to those on whom his [God's] favor rests." (Lk 2,14) Christ said: "Peace is my farewell to

157

Michal Heron

you, my peace is my gift to you; I do not give it to you as the world gives peace." (Jn 14,27) His coming inaugurated the messianic era of the prince of peace, foretold by Isaiah in the often quoted text, "They shall beat their swords into plowshares and their spears into pruning hooks; One nation shall not raise the sword against another, nor shall they train for war again." (Is, 2,4f)

100,105

Jesus gave many precepts and counsels which teach us how to love in Him and be like Him. Several times He summarized His law in two great commandments of love of God and love of neighbor, and on several occasions He reaffirmed the Ten Commandments. (Cf. Mt 19,17ff; Mk 10,17ff; Lk 18,18ff) He gave us the Sermon on the Mount (cf. Mt 5-7), His discourse at the Last Supper (cf. Jn 14-17), and numerous other indications, in word and example, of how He expects us to live — in Him, for the Father, by the power of the Holy Spirit.

Section II: The Moral Basis

155. Need for systematic development

While the scriptures set forth specific content for social morality in certain instances, for the most part the Bible provides a series of themes which identify social responsibility as an element in Christian life without going into specifics. The systematic investigation and explanation of the meaning of social responsibility in Christian life has been the work of Catholic social teaching.

19,105b), 131,167

156. Dignity of the human person

The fundamental concept in Catholic social teaching is the dignity of the human person. Human dignity and sacredness, present from the moment of conception, are rooted in the fact that every human being is created directly by God in His image and likeness (cf. Gn 1,26) and is destined to be with Him forever. The psalmist of the Old Testament and the evangelists of the New reflect the biblical belief that the person is the pinnacle of God's visible creation, set apart from, and over, the rest of the created order. The same theme is reflected in Preface V for the Sundays in the Ordinary Time of the year (Roman Missal): "All things are of your making, all times and seasons obey your laws, but you chose to create man in your own image, setting him over the whole world in all its wonder."

NC Photo

In Catholic teaching the concept of human dignity implies not only that the person is the steward of creation and cooperates with the creator to perfect it,[3] but that the rest of creation, in its material, social, technological, and economic aspects, should be at the service of the person. Human dignity is secure only when the spiritual, psychological, emotional, and bodily integrity of the person is respected as a fundamental value.

157. *Spectrum of human rights*

Flowing directly from our humanity are certain rights and duties which safeguard and promote human dignity. All human beings have these basic rights and duties, regardless of intelligence, background, contribution to society, race, sex, class, vocation, or nationality. Pope John XXIII gave a systematic catalogue of basic rights in his encyclical *Peace on Earth* (1963).[4] These should be an integral part of catechesis on social ministry.

Rights and duties are complementary: if one person has a right, others have a duty to respect it. The goal is to enable all people more clearly to manifest the divine image present in them.

158. *Persons are social by nature*

Human beings are social by nature. This means that family, state, and society are natural contexts for human life. They are essential for personal development, including the religious dimension.

This emphasis on the social nature of human beings and its implications is a critically important aspect of Catholic social teaching. Since societies are essential to human development, their organization and functioning — legal, political, economic, cultural — raise vitally important moral issues. Catholic social teaching provides principles by which the Church as an institution, and Christians as individuals, can evaluate political, economic, social, and legal structures. As the Church's teaching on personal morality establishes norms of conscience which help us assess issues pertaining to personal character and interpersonal relationships, so its teaching concerning social morality provides norms of conscience for judging social structures and institutional relationships.

NC/KNA Photo

103,190

38,102

159. *Relationship of personal and social morality*

The personal and social spheres of morality are distinct but not separate. All personal actions and human institutions are subject to the judgment of the moral law. Social morality is, however, characterized by the exceptional diversity and complexity of the situations encountered. The Church provides broad guidelines for Christian conscience which must be carefully applied to particular situations, with due recognition given to regional, sociopolitical, and cultural differences. "In the face of such widely varying situations it is difficult for us to utter a unified message and to put forth a solution which has universal validity . . . . It is up to the Christian communities to analyze with objectivity the situation which is proper to their own country, to shed on it the light of the Gospel's unalterable words and to draw principles of reflection, norms of judgment and directives for action from the social teaching of the Church."[5]

Since people of discernment and good will can come to different conclusions in applying principles to particular complex social situations, catechesis should help people anticipate this eventuality and should explain it in a way that avoids reducing social morality to a kind of pragmatism or relativism.

Because of the pressing nature of numerous unresolved social problems today, all the members of the Catholic community are urged to study the

Church's teaching and to become actively involved in seeking solutions according to their roles and responsibilities in society.

Section III: Relationship of the Social Ministry to the Mission of the Church

160. Social ministry within the mission of the Church

Before examining the general development of social teaching and some of its specific content, it is important to specify how social ministry relates to the Church's total mission.

Christ gave His Church no distinct mission in the political, economic, or social order. Rather, its activities in these areas derive from its religious mission. This religious mission is, however, a source of insights and spiritual motivation which can serve to structure and consolidate the human community according to divine law.[6]

The Church shares responsibility for the promotion of justice in the world with many other agencies in society and is to cooperate with people of good will who esteem human values and seek justice, freedom, and the development of peoples.[7]

Throughout its history the Church has catechized concerning the corporal works of mercy. The practice of these corporal works of mercy by Catholics has made the Church more Christlike, more credible before the world. For the past century, furthermore, the systematic development of the Church's moral teaching on social issues has been pursued with particular diligence. Much less systematic attention, however, has been given to the relationship of social ministry to the Church's nature and mission as sign and servant of God's kingdom. How important is social ministry in the mission of the Church?

Building on its teaching in *The Dogmatic Constitution on the Church*, the Second Vatican Council examined, in *The Pastoral Constitution on the Church in the Modern World*, the role and value of Church presence and Christian action in the social, political, economic, and cultural spheres. The treatment of the Church in these two documents taken together points to the conclusion that a rounded view of the Church requires an understanding both of its inner life and of its ministry of service to society. "The expectation of a new earth must not weaken but rather stimulate our concern for cultivating this one."[8]

The Second General Assembly of the Synod of Bishops in 1971[9] further expanded the understanding of the Church's ministry in society. In *Justice in the World*, the bishops said: "Action on behalf of justice and participation in the transformation of the world fully appear to us as a constitutive dimension of the preaching of the Gospel, or, in other words, of the Church's mission for the redemption of the human race and its liberation from every oppressive situation."[10] At the same time, "The Church links human liberation and salvation in Jesus Christ, but she never identifies them."[11] Pope Paul VI has called "the cause of human dignity and of human rights the cause of Christ and his Gospel."[12]

Action on behalf of justice is a significant criterion of the Church's fidelity to its missions. It is not optional, nor is it the work of only a few in the Church. It is something to which all Christians are called according to their vocations, talents, and situations in life.

Any group or institution which ventures to speak to others about justice should itself be just, and should be seen as such. The Church must therefore submit its own policies, programs, and manner of life to continuing review. For example, faith demands a certain frugality in the use of temporal possessions and the Church is obliged to live and to administer its goods in such a way that it

102

162-163

NC Photo by Mark Kiryluk

can authentically proclaim the gospel to the poor; yet the plight of the many millions of hungry people in our world today calls seriously into question the morality of typical life styles and patterns of consumption in our affluent society.[13] We are all — bishops, priests, religious, and laity — called to an ongoing examination of conscience on such matters.

PART B: A BRIEF OVERVIEW OF THE DEVELOPMENT OF CATHOLIC SOCIAL TEACHING

161. *Importance of a historical perspective*

The Church's understanding of and involvement in social ministry have evolved over the centuries. Catechesis should indicate this at the proper time, in a manner suited to the abilities and needs of those being catechized.

162. *Ministry of mercy and charity*

Even as its social teaching was developing, the Church was giving major emphasis to the practice of mercy and charity. (The relationship between charity and justice is described below.) Early writers, such as St. Basil, St. Clement of Alexandria, St. Ambrose, and others,[14] discoursed with eloquence and passion upon the obligations of charity and the rights of the poor. Pope St. Leo the Great (+461) noted in one of his sermons that "where he [God] finds charity with its loving concern, there he recognizes the reflection of his own fatherly care."[15]

Michal Heron

The early monastic orders strove to give Christlike love and attention to the poor, the sick, the traveler, the pilgrim, and others in need. Many saints, canonized men and women, and countless others whose names are not recorded in history, devoted their lives to serving the poor and the needy.

Works of mercy and charity are always incumbent upon the Church and its members, and should involve more than just disbursing superfluous goods.[16] They are carried on with great vitality today by the Catholic Church in the United States and throughout the world. In this country, the Church has founded and maintains many charitable and social service programs and institutions — hospitals, homes for the aged, children's institutions, treatment centers for drug addicts and alcoholics, community houses, refuges for the homeless, recreation programs, and many others. Catholic Charities organizations and similar agencies, as well as volunteer associations (St. Vincent de Paul Society, Ladies of Charity, etc.) have donated hundreds of millions of dollars and hours to the relief of fellow human beings.

NC/KNA Photo

The works of charity performed by the Catholic Church in the United States reach beyond this country. Supported by the generosity of the faithful, missionaries have alleviated all forms of need while proclaiming the good news in other lands. Catholic Relief Services and other agencies have assisted millions throughout the world.

For two millenia, as Pope John XXIII remarked, by teaching and example the Church has held aloft the torch of charity, as Christ instructed it to do.[17] Catechesis relates this story of generosity, identifies its sources, and encourages people to respond generously to Christ's mandate.

163. *Development through the first nineteen centuries*

It was understood from the earliest days that the gospel had social implications. In the Acts of the Apostles we find the Christian community deciding how property should be administered and how "widows and orphans" should be cared for. (Acts 2,44f; 6,1-4)

As the Church grew from a small community living on the edge of the Roman Empire to the principal social institution of medieval Europe, the social implications of the gospel became increasingly imperative in shaping its life. Central to this process were the teachings of the Church Fathers, the writings of medieval canonists and theologians, and the pastoral leadership of bishops and popes.

The development of social teaching was spurred by the great voyages of discovery and subsequent colonization of the New World; by European colonialism in other parts of the globe; by the dislocations and serious human and economic problems created by the Industrial Revolution which began in the 18th century; and by the monumental social problems created by the mass migration of the mid-19th century and later.

It is beyond the scope of this NCD to trace in further detail the development of social teaching from the early Church, through the Middle Ages and the post-Reformation period. More important to understanding Catholic social thought today are developments during the past century.

164. Since the end of the nineteenth century

Since the late 19th century a systematic and organized body of social teaching has developed in the Church, relating gospel teaching and the Catholic tradition to the conditions of modern life. Of central importance are the papal encyclicals, pastoral letters, and conciliar documents, from Pope Leo XIII (*On the Condition of Labor,* 1891) through the writings of Pope Paul VI.[18] Around this central core have developed extensive commentary, preaching, and catechesis.

167-169

This social teaching touches upon a wide variety of topics: education; social and economic justice within nations; the moral analysis of social structures; world order, international justice and peace, and the complex obstacles to their achievement; problems typical of societies with high levels of industrial development and extensive urbanization (e.g., the role of women, the alienation of youth, the impact of the media, labor relations); models of social and economic development and their evaluation; and the political vocation as part of the Christian vocation.

PART C: FACING CONTEMPORARY SOCIAL ISSUES

Section I: Major Concepts

165. Social dimension of morality

It is impossible to grasp or communicate the content of Catholic social teaching without a clear understanding of the social dimension of morality. Here we shall analyze three concepts: social justice, the social consequences of sin, and the relationship of justice and charity. *The Pastoral Constitution on the Church in the Modern World* provides the context: "Let everyone consider it his sacred obligation to count social necessities among the primary duties of modern man, and to pay heed to them. For the more unified the world becomes, the more plainly do the offices of men extend beyond particular groups and spread by degrees to the whole world. But this challenge cannot be met unless individual men and their associations cultivate in themselves the moral and social virtues, and promote them in society."[19]

a) Social justice

This general description of social morality is made more specific in Pope John's teaching that society should be organized and directed by four values: truth, justice, freedom, and love.[20] Each exists and is easily recognized in personal relationships; but, as *Peace on Earth* sought to demonstrate, each also has a social dimension.

Social justice focuses not only on personal relationships but on institutions, structures, and systems of social organization (keeping in mind, however, that these are composed of persons) which foster or impede the common good at the local, national, and international levels. Social justice is the concept by which one evaluates the organization and functioning of the political, economic, social, and cultural life of society. Positively, the Church's social teaching seeks to apply the gospel command of love to and within social systems, structures, and institutions.

The complexity and scope of structural or institutional injustices are commonly such that isolated individuals cannot remedy them by themselves. Some form of political participation, such as voting for candidates who support just laws and policies, is usually required. The close link between political participation (by citizens, groups, and public authority) and social justice is one reason why Paul VI so strongly emphasized the political vocation as part of the Christian vocation today.

Catholic social teaching affirms as fundamental the right of all people to form their own associations, such as labor unions, employer groups, societies for the promotion of culture, recreation, and the like. The Church supports the rights not only of individuals but of groups organized for the pursuit of legitimate ends. It holds that persons should be free to assemble and act peaceably on behalf of human rights.

In summary, social justice affects our personal relations with others; it does so *through* the structures of society; it helps us evaluate our responsibility for the kind of society we are willing to support and share in. The agents of social justice are normally groups working to shape social institutions in the direction of justice, love, truth, and freedom for all.

b) Social consequences of sin

The development of the concept of "social sin"[21] is another example of how the Church seeks to highlight the social dimension of Christian morality. Speaking of how "unjust systems and structures" oppress people, the bishops of the 1971 Synod said: "The hopes and forces which are moving the world in its very foundations are not foreign to the dynamism of the Gospel, which through the power of the Holy Spirit frees men from personal sin and from its consequences in social life."[22]

NC Photo

98

The choice of sin occurs in the human heart, and sin is expressed through personal choices and actions. But it has social consequences. Sin is expressed in some of the structures of human communities. Sinful structures are not simply imperfect human organizations; rather, such structures involve a systematic abuse of the rights of certain groups or individuals. The sinfulness lies in the unjust way in which social relationships are organized. An extreme example is institutionalized racial or ethnic segregation; a less striking example is the absence or inadequacy of minimum wage laws. A very contemporary example is the imbalance in the distribution of the world's goods, which calls for a new international economic order.

Responsibility for correcting a situation of "social sin" rests upon all who participate in the society in question: those whose rights are being systematically denied are called to assert them; others are called to seek to change existing patterns of social relationships.[23]

"Social sin" can affect such large numbers of people that it is almost impossible to identify its causes. It can be so deeply rooted as almost to defy eradication. It can be the fault of so many that no one in particular can be held to blame. But precisely because social injustices are so complex, one must resist the temptation to think that there is no remedy for them.

162

c) Relationship of justice and charity

Some discussions of the social responsibility of Christians tend to set justice and charity in opposition: justice is regarded as a secular idea and obligatory, charity as a Christian concept and optional. In fact, both are part of Christian social responsibility and are complementary.

"Love implies an absolute demand for justice, namely a recognition of the dignity and rights of one's neighbor."[24] Justice is therefore the foundation of charity: i.e., if I love my neighbor, it is absolutely required that I respect his or her rights and meet his or her needs. It is impossible to give of oneself in love without first sharing with others what is due them in justice. This can be expressed very succinctly by saying that justice is love's absolute minimum.

53,66,96

Conversely, justice reaches its fulfillment in charity; once the demands of justice are met, there is still room, in a Christian view of human relationships, to go beyond what is due others by right and share with them in the self-giving manner of Christ. Charity excuses from none of the demands of justice; it calls one to go beyond justice and engage in sacrificial service of others in imitation of Christ, the suffering servant.

Section II: Some Contemporary Problems

166. Introduction

In view of the vast problems facing contemporary society and the speed with which problems and priorities can change, Catholic organizations and institutions at all levels must be constantly alert to society's current and foreseeable needs.

In order to suggest the scope and content of catechesis for social justice, we shall mention here a variety of issues currently of particular concern to the United States, grouping them under three general headings: respect for human life, national problems, and international problems. In categorizing social issues, however, it is important to be aware of their often complex interrelationships in actuality: catechists should avoid treating in isolation social problems which are in fact related.

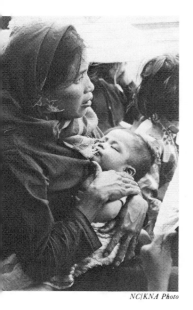

NC/KNA Photo

Since the Catholic Church is concerned with and regularly addresses many social issues, those involved in catechesis for social ministry should keep abreast of the pronouncements of the Holy See, the United States bishops, and other sources in the Church.[25]

19,105b),
131,156

167. Respect for human life

As we have seen, respect and reverence for human life arise from the dignity of the human person made in God's image and likeness. Life is a precious gift from the creator. Through its laws and institutions, society must respect the life of every human being from conception to natural death. Direct attacks on human life — such as abortion, infanticide, euthanasia, and certain forms of fetal experimentation[26] — are gravely immoral.

The right of life touches also upon life's quality. The respect due life is, for example, violated in attempts to hamper another's capacity to live as fully as possible, or to reduce a person to a state of dependency. The authentic meaning of "quality of life" is seriously misconstrued when it is taken to justify such things as the destruction of lives deemed defective because of mental, physical, or social handicaps.

Respect for life should also underlie one's assessment of issues pertaining to warfare and defense policy, as well as the question of capital punishment. These topics have been addressed by the bishops of the United States.

168. National problems

Many other social problems face the United States today. Among the more pressing are: racism; other forms of discrimination, including discrimination against women; encroachments on basic rights by the federal and state governments and courts, reflected in such issues as abortion, pornography, school prayer, etc.; questions of economic justice, including poverty, unemployment, a just price for basic economic goods, and a living wage; problems of refugees and immigrants, particularly those without documentation; various questions pertaining to unionization; farm labor; land ownership; agricultural policy; population issues; bioethical questions arising from the revolution in life sciences; energy policy; ecology; defense policy, military expenditures, and conscientious objection; food and nutrition; housing; health care; the abuse and other problems of the aged and of handicapped persons; family policy and child abuse; alcoholism and drug abuse; capital punishment; inadequacies and abuses in the judicial and prison systems; political and governmental corruption; and threats to personal and corporate privacy and freedom.

In the field of education it is necessary to affirm and vindicate the right of all children and youth to a suitable education free from unjust segregation and unequal treatment; the right of parents to enjoy true freedom in the choice of schools for their children and freedom from unjust financial burdens; and the clear rights of children to their fair share of support by the state.[27]

Many of these questions have been addressed by the bishops of the United States and, in a more global manner, by papal and Roman documents. This body of teaching deserves close study by Catholics actively seeking solutions to contemporary social problems in collaboration with their fellow citizens.

Milt Thomas

169. International issues

c.VII, footnote 18

International issues have received increasing attention from the Church during the pontificates of Popes Pius XII, John XXIII, and Paul VI. On a number of occasions the bishops of the United States have addressed such issues as peace; prisoners of war; immigration; communism; international order and justice; the United Nations; human rights in general and their violation in particular countries and areas of the world; religious persecution; world population; the world food crisis; and social reconstruction.

170. Catechetical guidelines for justice, mercy and peace

Catechesis concerning justice, mercy, and peace should be part of the catechetical process. It should include efforts to motivate people to act on behalf of these values.

1. Catechesis recognizes that the root cause of social injustice, selfishness, and violence reside within the human person: the imbalances of the modern world are linked to a more basic imbalance in the human heart.[28] Injustice, greed, lack of mercy, violence, and war are social consequences of sin.

2. Catechesis for justice, mercy, and peace calls for a renewal of heart based on the recognition of sin in its individual and social manifestations.[29] It seeks to bring people to recognize their individual and collective obligations to

98,165b)

strive to overcome the grave injustices in the world, as well as their inability to do so by their own strength. It points out that all must listen with humble and open hearts to God's word calling attention to new paths of action on behalf of justice, mercy, and peace.

3. Catechesis explains the relationship of personal morality to social morality. It makes clear that the Church provides principles which Christians have a duty to apply carefully to particular situations. Catechists must be careful not to confuse their personal or political opinions with the explicit teaching of the Church on social issues.

4. Catechesis strives to awaken a critical sense, leading to reflection on society and its values and to assessment of the social structures and economic systems which shape human lives.

5. Each Catholic has a responsibility for social action according to his or her circumstances. Because social and economic questions are generally decided in the political order, Catholics should play a responsible role in politics, including fulfilling the duties of informed citizenship and seeking public office.

6. Effective catechesis is based on the sources of the Church's social teaching. Rooted in the Old and New Testaments and uniquely expressed in the ministry of Jesus, social teaching has developed throughout the Church's history. Papal, conciliar, and episcopal documents should be consulted and made part of the content of catechesis, as should the "signs of the times," including manifestations of the interdependence of the world community.

Catechesis also points out that the effectiveness of the Church's social ministry depends largely on the witness which its members give to justice, mercy, and peace in their relationships with one another, as well as upon the witness of the Church's corporate and institutional life.

Linda Bartlett

7. The fundamental concept underlying the social teaching of the Church is the dignity of the person, a dignity rooted in likeness to God and the call to communion with Him. Human rights and the value of human life, from conception to natural death, are emphasized in catechesis. Respect for human life includes appropriate concern for life's quality, as well as its existence and preservation.

8. Catechesis speaks of the works of charity performed by the Church and its members throughout history. It stresses that these works are essential and motivate people — beginning with the very young according to their level of understanding — to give of their time, talents, and earthly goods, even to the point of sacrifice. Catechists also present the lives of saints and other outstanding Catholics who have exemplified the Church's social awareness and desire to help.

9. Catechesis seeks to move people to live justly, mercifully, and peacefully as individuals, to act as the leaven of the gospel in family, school, work, social, and civic life, and to work for appropriate social change.

10. Catechesis includes activities (involving vital contact with the reality of injustice)[30] which empower people to exercise more control over their destinies and bring into being communities where human values are fully respected and fostered.

11. Catechesis for justice, mercy, and peace is a continuing process[31] which concerns every person and every age. It first occurs in the family by word and by example. It is continued in a systematic way by Church institutions, parishes, schools, trade unions, political parties, and the like. This catechesis is an integral part of parish catechetical programs. It should also be an integral part of the curriculum and environment of Catholic schools. It is desirable that courses for children and youth be complemented by programs for parents.

12. The Church and its institutions should seek out and listen to different

points of view on complex social situations. Catechetical materials can reflect different perspectives with respect to justice and peace, showing how these agree with or differ from the Church's teaching.

13. Adult catechesis on social justice and the total biblical concept of stewardship is much needed and should be given priority.

14. Social ministry should be identified as a valid and necessary ministry in the Church and proposed as a possible vocation to those being catechized. Conscious efforts are required to develop leadership in this ministry.

129

15. Catechists should point out the harm which can be done to children's values, attitudes, and behavior by toys and games which make war and its weapons seem glamorous. They should call attention to the damage which excessive exposure to violence and immorality in the mass media, especially television, can do to children and adults.

22,178,
253-258,
261

171. Conclusion

So far this NCD has considered some characteristics of Catholicism in the United States; revelation and the response of faith; the meaning of Church, along with some outstanding elements of its message and its mission to others; the fundamental need for worship and prayer; and social ministry. Next we shall turn to those to be catechized.

AID Photo

Sheila Cassidy

Chapter VIII

Catechesis Toward Maturity in Faith

---

*Let us walk
in the light of the Lord!*
Is 2,5

172. Introduction

This chapter considers the relationship between the life of faith and human development; how people grow in their ability to recognize and respond to God's revelation; conscience formation; sexuality and catechesis; the catechesis of persons with special needs; and certain factors which currently affect the handing-on of the faith in the United States. Revelation, faith, grace, and related matters pertaining to faith are discussed in their own right in Chapter III.

PART A: FAITH AND HUMAN DEVELOPMENT

173. *The developmental character of the life of faith*

c.III

NC Photo by Jim Lackey

Jesus' words, "You are my friends if you do what I command you" (Jn 15,14), point to the fact that the life of faith involves a relationship, a friendship, between persons. As the quality of a friendship between human beings is affected by such things as their maturity and freedom, their knowledge of each other, and the manner and frequency of their communication, so the quality of a friendship with God is affected by the characteristics of the human party. Because people are capable of continual development, so are their relationships with God. Essentially, development in faith is the process by which one's relationship with the Father becomes more like Jesus' (cf. Jn 14,6f): it means becoming more Christlike. This is not just a matter of subjective, psychological change, but involves establishing and nurturing a real relationship to Jesus and the Father in the Holy Spirit, through a vigorous sacramental life, prayer, study, and serving others.

174. *The relationship of growth in faith to human development*

Because the life of faith is related to human development, it passes through stages or levels; furthermore, different people possess aspects of faith to different degrees. This is true, for example, of the comprehensiveness and intensity with which they accept God's word, of their ability to explain it, and of their ability to apply it to life.[1] Catechesis is meant to help at each stage of human development and lead ultimately to full identification with Jesus.

175. *The role of the behavioral sciences*

The Church encourages the use of the biological, social, and psychological sciences in pastoral care.[2] "The catechetical movement will in no way be able to advance without scientific study."[3] Manuals for catechists should take into account psychological and pedagogical insights, as well as suggestions about methods.[4]

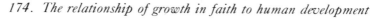

The behavioral sciences cause neither faith nor growth in faith; but for that matter, neither does the catechist. Faith is from God: "This is not your own doing, it is God's gift." (Eph 2,8)

These sciences do, however, help us understand how people grow in their capacity for responding in faith to God's grace. They can, therefore, make a significant contribution to catechesis. At the same time, catechists should not be uncritical in their approach to these sciences, in which new discoveries are constantly being made while old theories are frequently modified or even discarded. There are different schools of psychology and sociology which do not agree in all respects; nor are all developments of equal merit. Catechists should not imagine that any one school or theory has all the answers. Finally,

33,54,57-
58,84,98,
188,213

behavioral sciences do not supply the doctrinal and moral content of catechetical programs. Their discoveries and developments must be constantly and carefully evaluated by competent persons before being integrated into catechetics.

The framework used here to describe the stages of human development is one of a number that could be used. Other models offer valuable insights. One's understanding of catechesis should not be linked exclusively to a single explanation of the stages of human development and its implications for growth in faith.

176. Elements of methodology

a) A new methodology

In the covenant of the Old Testament, God announced His plan of salvation prophetically and by means of types. He revealed the truth about Himself gradually over centuries.

Now, in the fullness of time when revelation has been consummated in Christ, the Church uses a pedagogy adapted to the final age of salvation history, one in which the message is presented in its entirety while also being expressed according to the circumstances and ability of those being catechized. The principal elements of the Christian message (cf. Chapter V) must be central in all Catholic catechesis; they must never be overlooked or minimized, and must receive adequate and frequent emphasis.

47,73,
181,12)
229

b) No single methodology

Catechesis is not limited to one methodology. Although certain norms or criteria apply to all catechesis, they do not determine a fixed methodology, nor even an order for presenting the truths of faith. For instance, catechesis can begin with God and proceed to Christ, or do the reverse; it can proceed from God to humanity, or from humanity to God; and so on.

47

Whatever the method, catechists are responsible for choosing and creating conditions which will encourage people to seek and accept the Christian message and integrate it more fully in their living out of the faith.

c) Induction and deduction

All methods used in catechesis employ both induction and deduction, each with a different emphasis. The inductive approach proceeds from the sensible, visible, tangible experiences of the person, and leads, with the help of the Holy Spirit, to more general conclusions and principles. The deductive approach proceeds in the opposite manner, beginning with general principles, such as a commandment, whether from the decalogue or the Sermon on the Mount, and applying it to the real world of the person being catechized. The deductive approach produces its fullest impact when preceded by the inductive.[5]

d) Experience

Experience is of great importance in catechesis. Experiential learning, which can be considered a form of inductive methodology, gives rise to concerns and questions, hopes and anxieties, reflections and judgments, which increase one's desire to penetrate more deeply into life's meaning. Experience can also increase the intelligibility of the Christian message, by providing illustrations and examples which shed light on the truths of revelation. At the same time, experience itself should be interpreted in the light of revelation.

The experiential approach is not easy, but it can be of considerable value to catechesis.[6] Catechists should encourage people to reflect on their significant experiences and respond to God's presence there. Sometimes they will provide appropriate experiences. They should seek to reach the whole person, using both cognitive (intellectual) and affective (emotional) techniques.

Lou Niznik

e) Formulations[7]

In every age and culture Christianity has commended certain prayers, formulas, and practices to all members of the faith community, even the youngest. While catechesis cannot be limited to the repetition of formulas and it is essential that formulas and facts pertaining to faith be understood, memorization has nevertheless had a special place in the handing-on of the faith throughout the ages and should continue to have such a place today, especially in catechetical programs for the young. It should be adapted to the level and ability of the child and introduced in a gradual manner, through a process which, begun early, continues gradually, flexibly, and never slavishly. In this way certain elements of Catholic faith, tradition, and practice are learned for a lifetime and can contribute to the individual's continued growth in understanding and living the faith.

140-143,
145,177-
180,181,8)
51,52,
60a)i.

Among these are the following:

1. Prayers such as the Sign of the Cross, Lord's Prayer, Hail Mary, Apostles' Creed, Acts of Faith, Hope and Charity, Act of Contrition.

2. Factual information contributing to an appreciation of the place of the word of God in the Church and the life of the Christian through an awareness and understanding of: the key themes of the history of salvation; the major personalities of the Old and New Testaments; and certain biblical texts expressive of God's love and care.

c.VI

3. Formulas providing factual information regarding worship, the Church Year, and major practices in the devotional life of Christians including the parts of the Mass, the list of the sacraments, the liturgical seasons, the holy days of obligation, the major feasts of our Lord and our Lady, the various eucharistic devotions, the mysteries of the rosary of the Blessed Virgin Mary, and the Stations of the Cross.

100,105,
154,
Appendices
A and B

4. Formulas and practices dealing with the moral life of Christians including the commandments, the beatitudes, the gifts of the Holy Spirit, the theological and moral virtues, the precepts of the Church, and the examination of conscience.

PART B: CATECHESIS AND HUMAN DEVELOPMENT

Section I: The Stages of Human Development

26-27,
197,226,
230

177. Infancy and early childhood (birth to age 5)[8]

Life's beginning stages are of critical importance to individual growth and development. Here foundations are laid which influence the ability to accept self, relate to others, and respond effectively to the environment. Upon these foundations rests the formation of the basic human and Christian personality — and so also one's human capacity for relating to God.

Healthy growth is most likely in a positive, nurturing environment — normally, the immediate family. Family relationships and interaction provide young children with their most powerful models for developing attitudes, values, and ways of responding to external influences which foster or hinder Christian and human growth.

131

God's love is communicated to infants and young children primarily through parents. Their faith, their confidence in human potential, and their loving and trusting attitude toward God and human beings strongly influence the child's faith. Parents are best prepared for this role by prior education for parenthood and by prenatal and pre-baptismal catechesis concerning the religious upbringing of children. During this stage in the lives of children, catechesis is directed primarily to their parents, to help them in their task. This also contributes to strengthening the conjugal bond and deepening their Christian commitment.

Parents and others in intimate contact with infants and small children should speak naturally and simply about God and their faith, as they do about other matters they want the children to understand and appreciate. Catechesis for prayer, accommodated to age and understanding, is part of this religious formation; it encourages the child to call upon God who loves and protects us, upon Jesus, God's Son and our brother, who leads us to the Father, and upon the Holy Spirit who dwells in our hearts. The child is also encouraged to pray to Mary, Jesus' mother and ours, and to the saints.[9] Parental example, including the practice of prayer, is particularly important.

145

Catechetical programs for preschool children seek to foster their growth in a wider faith community. While they should build upon and reinforce everything positive in the family and home environment, they can also be of particular importance for children who lack certain opportunities at home, children in one-parent families, and those whose parents do not spend much time with them, either because they both work outside the home or for some other reason.

25

26-28, 197,199

Early childhood catechetical programs allow 3- to 5-year-olds to develop at their own pace, in ways suited to their age, circumstances, and learning abilities. They encourage appropriate attitudes toward worship and provide occasions of natural celebration with other children and adults, including religious and clergy. They seek, by deepening the child's sense of wonder and awe, to develop the capacity for spontaneous prayer and prayerful silence.

In formal catechetical programs for young children, groups should be small and at least one adult should work with the children of each level. The staff should be composed of parents and other adults, and should include persons with training in such areas as theology, scripture, early childhood growth and development, and methodology.

The learning of young children can also be fostered through coordinated courses for the entire family, which help parents become active, confident, and competent in encouraging their children's emerging faith.

226

Dick Swartz

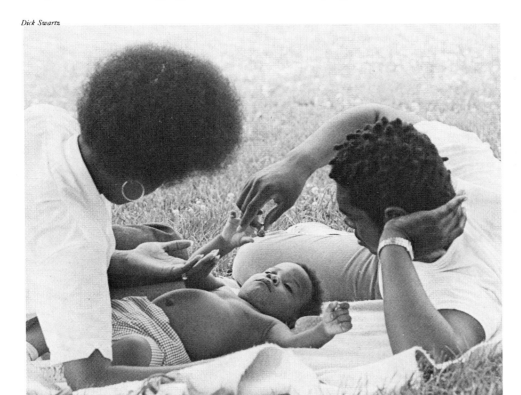

NC Photo by Phillip A. Stack

178. Childhood (ages 6-10)

Emotional development at this age is mainly a matter of growing in the capacity for satisfactory relationships with a wider circle of children and adults. Self-acceptance, trust, and personal freedom undergo significant changes, with acceptance of self coming to involve an awareness of specific talents (or their absence), unqualified trust of others giving way to a qualified trust which excludes some people and situations, and the expression of personal freedom being modified by recognition that other people, too, have rights and freedom.

Intellectual capacity gradually expands. Before, the world was viewed in very concrete terms drawn from direct personal experiences; now, the ability to form abstract ideas or concepts based on experience increases.

Catechesis calls attention to God's self-revelation and His invitation to us to be His children and friends; it points out that the revelation, the invitation, and the capacity to respond are all supernatural gifts. How children understand these realities still depends largely on analogous experiences in their relationships with other people. But "other people" now include a community much larger than the immediate family, notably the community to which children are exposed through media, particularly television which occupies so much of most children's time. TV should be evaluated in relation not only to the behavior it may encourage but that which it prevents — for instance, conversations, games, family festivities, and other activities which foster learning and character development.

The immediate environment, normally the home, remains the principal setting in which children experience a relationship with God. But now the support of the larger community becomes highly important to education in the faith, and its absence a more serious matter. Children accustomed to seeing others give witness to their faith are more likely to be ready for a fuller, more systematic presentation of concepts, forms of liturgical expression, and religious practices.

The child's first serious experience of work, usually in school, is relevant to catechesis. It serves as an introduction to values important in both the secular and religious spheres of life: the joy of doing things well, cooperation with others, and discipline experienced as something understandable and reasonable.[10]

Michal Heron

NC Photo

Catechesis seeks to help children make an increasingly personal response to God's word and gifts. This response is not just a matter of external expressions, however useful they may be, but is truly heartfelt and prayerful. Catechesis approaches young persons with reverence and aids them in discovering and developing their unique, God-given gifts with the help of the gospel.

In presenting the values and teachings of Jesus, catechesis takes note of children's experience and encourages them to apply the same teachings and values to their lives.

At this stage significant changes occur in the ability to learn and understand. Certain prayer formulas become more intelligible. Stories like the parables take on deeper meaning. Practices like sharing and helping others make a great deal more sense. Memorization can be used very effectively, provided the child has a clear understanding of what is memorized and it is expressed in familiar language. *176e)*

In the Western Church and in most Eastern Churches in the United States, catechesis is ordinarily provided at this stage for the sacraments of Reconciliation and Eucharist. Preparation for the reception of these sacraments is discussed in articles 122 and 126. *122,126*

179. *Pre-adolescence and puberty (ages 10-13)*
27,145, 191,197-199,226, 229

Important physical changes have a direct bearing on how pre-adolescents perceive other people and relate to them. Young people at this stage face the task of coming to terms with themselves and others as sexual beings. While the foundations for doing so are laid in infancy, the effort now becomes conscious. They need to accept themselves precisely as male or female and to acquire a whole new way of relating to others. Usually, too, this involves some confusion, uncertainty, curiosity, awkwardness, and experimentation, as young people "try on" different patterns of behavior while searching for their unique identity. Puberty also adds a new dimension to the practice of personal freedom: increased responsibility for directing one's actions, together with increased readiness to accept their consequences.

Now more than ever interests extend beyond the home to the peer group, which exercises an increasing influence on attitudes, values, and behavior. Sensitivity toward others is growing, and efforts to develop a sense of community and of membership in the Church should continue.

While each child develops at his or her own rate, girls are generally more advanced than boys of the same age. The characteristics typical of this stage will be more or less intense according to an individual's physical and emotional attributes, home influences, previous experiences, and cultural background.

Catechesis should make use of all aspects of the pre-adolescent's experience, including the needs generated by rapid, radical change. The example of living faith given by others — at home and in the larger community — remains highly important and catechetically effective.

Topics like the nature of scripture, the Church, the sacraments, and the reasons which underlie moral norms can be discussed in greater depth than before. Reading and lectures can be used more effectively. But the life of faith is still best presented through concrete experiences which afford the pre-adolescent opportunities to incorporate Christian values into his or her life. *176d)* These experiences are a point of departure for presenting the deeper aspects of the faith and its mysteries. Audio-visuals, projects, and field trips can be effective catechetical tools for this purpose. This is the age of hero worship, and it is helpful to present — in a manner which appeals to contemporary youth — the lives and deeds of the saints and other outstanding persons,[11] and especially the words and example of Jesus.

Growing more aware of themselves as individuals, pre-adolescents become better able to experience faith as a personal relationship with God. Prayer and service to others can become more meaningful. However, while it is possible for pre-adolescents, with the help of grace, to commit themselves to God, their faith is not that of fully mature persons.

Participation in the Mass, sacraments, and other rituals of the adult community can also become more meaningful. Young people can take a greater part in planning, preparing, and celebrating the liturgy.

As the sense of personal responsibility for behavior comes into sharper focus, specific Christian principles of conduct become more important, and the Sacrament of Reconciliation takes on deeper meaning.

Crises of faith, particularly relating to identification with the Church, occur among some pre-adolescents today. It is therefore extremely important that catechists with appropriate theoretical and practical expertise design catechetical programs which anticipate and ease such crises.

180. *Adolescence*

a) No specific age bracket

There are generally accepted age brackets for earlier stages, but not for adolescence. Different cultural, racial, and ethnic groups have their own standards for determining the length of time between puberty and adulthood.

b) Development of conscious spiritual life

The transition from childhood can be marked by an experience of emptiness. The self-awareness, relationship with others, sense of personal freedom, and intellectual understanding of reality achieved in childhood no longer suffice, but there is often nothing at hand to take their place. Now — and later, too — many have profound lack of self-confidence, magnified by life's complexity and ambiguity. The Church's ministry of service and healing richly equips it to respond to their need for interior reconciliation.

Lou Niznik

Interior turmoil and self-doubt are often expressed in external symptoms popularly associated with adolescence: boredom, frustration, sharp changes in mood, withdrawal, rebelliousness, apathy toward religion. Adolescents should be encouraged to understand that these symptoms are typical of many maturing persons and to be patient with themselves even while seeking to acquire the skills which will enable them to deal with their problems. Unfortunately, at precisely this time many experience difficulty in articulating their feelings, particularly to their parents.

Yet adolescents also commonly manifest increasing spiritual insight into themselves, other people, and life in general. A growing self-awareness and self-acceptance and a resultant greater capacity for authentic love of others begin to emerge, as well as increasing ability to respond with a mature faith.

A new sense of responsibility matching their expanded capacity for independent action often leads adolescents to reject, or seem to reject, laws and rules which they regard as arbitrary, external restrictions on their personal freedom. Many substitute a kind of inner law or norm of behavior based on personal ideals.

As idealism grows, so does the desire for continuous growth, even perfection, in the life of faith — or at least the ability to appreciate its value. Adolescents are increasingly critical of real or imagined imperfections in the Church and the adult faith community. The example of the adult community is extremely important at this time, although the direct influence of family and parents generally declines. For good or evil, peers exert the strongest influence of all; thus the need for developing strong youth ministry programs. School and media, especially television, also exert strong influences.

As they become more intellectually competent, adolescents need more intellectual stimulation and growth. At this time catechesis seeks to make clear the inner coherence of the truths of faith, their relation to one another and to humanity's final end. Careful attention must be given to the rational bases for faith; the intellectual investigation and articulation of religious belief are not "merely a kind of addition," but should be "counted as an essential need for the life of faith."[12] Appropriate experiences, involving participation by adolescents, provide a context in which doctrine can be systematically presented and reflected upon most effectively.

176d)

While the foundations of vocations — to marriage, the single life, priesthood and religious life, etc. — are laid and nurtured from early childhood on, vocational choices are imminent in adolescence. Now is the time to address the question directly and study the possibilities open to individuals, taking into account such things as youthful idealism, God's call, and the grace of the Holy Spirit. Catechists should be aware, however, that more and more young people are today delaying vocational and career choices until later in life.

74e),116, 129-133, 170,14), 182

Private prayer tends to become more personal and reflective now, while ritualized prayer often loses its attraction. Young people who see no point to prayer and meditation should be introduced — or reintroduced — to the idea that it is personal communication with Jesus and, through and in Him, with the Father. This can help make prayer an attractive reality in their lives. Prayer in all forms should be an integral and appealing part of catechesis for this age group.

140-145

Most people pass through adolescence during their teens, but in some cases the transition is delayed. The awakening of a conscious spiritual life is normally an impetus to move to the next stage of development, adulthood.

Michal Heron

181. *Some guidelines for the catechesis of children and youth*

Norms and guidelines for the catechesis of children and youth are indicated throughout this chapter, as well as in other parts of the NCD. The most important task of such catechesis is to provide, through the witness of adults, an environment in which young people can grow in faith.

The following guidelines offer supplementary assistance to catechists.

1. In order to understand children and youth and communicate with them one must listen to them with respect, be sensitive to their circumstances, and be aware of their current values.

2. Both in the Church and in human society, children and young people have a dignity of their own. They are important not only for what they will do in the future, but for what they are here and now — for their intrinsic value and their value in relation to the common good.

3. Through catechesis all should be encouraged to know and respect other cultural, racial, and ethnic groups. Catechetical materials should be adapted to accommodate cultural, racial, and ethnic pluralism, the concerns of particular groups, and persons with special needs, as described in Part C of this chapter.

194

4. Effective catechesis takes into account the fact that the child's comprehension and other powers develop gradually. Religious truths are presented in greater depth, and more mature challenges are proposed, as the capacity for understanding and growth in faith increases.

5. Catechesis also provides experiences to live faith and apply the message of salvation to real-life situations. It encourages the use of imagination, as well as intelligence and memory. It stimulates not only exterior but interior activity — a prayerful response from the heart. Fostering a sense of community is also an important part of education for social life.

176d) 176e)

6. As children mature, catechesis does more to help them observe, explore,

interpret, and judge their experiences, ascribe a Christian meaning to their lives, and act according to the norms of faith and love.[13] The presence in today's society of many conflicting values makes it all the more important to help young people to interiorize authentic values.

7. Catechesis emphasizes that growth in faith includes growth in the desire for a deeper, more mature knowledge of the truths of faith.

8. Private prayer is presented as an instrument of individual reflection and personal communication with God.

9. As the adolescent grows in intellectual ability, catechesis fosters insight into the interrelationship of religious truths and their relationship to the individual's final end. Especially in view of the contemporary emphasis on scientific criteria and methods, it also carefully establishes the rational foundations of faith.

176c)

10. Because adolescents are better able to reason deductively, it is possible to make more use of systematic, formal methods of instruction and study. However, deductive reasoning and methodology are more effective when preceded by induction. Sound methodology therefore includes providing continued opportunities for concrete experiences of lived faith, in which the message of salvation is applied to specific situations. Such things as field trips, meaningful social action, weekend retreats and programs, group dynamics of a sound and tested nature, simulation games, audio-visuals, and similar techniques can be very helpful. Constructive interaction and personal involvement are extremely important, and are present in gospel-based value clarification, group discussions, programs for the development of communication skills, and group prayer.

176d)

11. A correct understanding of experiential learning includes recognition that the entire faith community is an important part of the experience of children and youth: parents, catechists, and community all have roles in the catechesis of the young.

12. Catechetical materials are adapted to the stages of intellectual, spiritual, emotional, and physical development. Properly sequenced programs present the Christian message, and the history of the Church's response to it, in a manner appropriate to each age level. Particular truths receive the emphasis appropriate to their significance in the total body of revealed truth. Multi-year programs are best evaluated in their totality. Using appropriate media and methodology, these programs should give satisfactory emphasis to doctrine and moral content, to efforts to develop community, to worship, and to service of the faith community and society at large.

47,73,
176a),
229

13. Research, experimentation, and professional competence are required in the continued development of catechetical programs which respect the developmental character of human maturation and growth in faith. Ideally, national, regional, and diocesan agencies and private institutions should cooperate with one another and with publishers of catechetical materials to produce such programs.

201,227,
243

182. Early adulthood

The point of transition from adolescence to early adulthood varies considerably from one individual to another. Here we are considering young adults as those between the ages of 18 and 35, although not everyone has reached psychological, emotional, and spiritual maturity even by the latter age.

There are many subgroups with overlapping membership within the young adult population (e.g., high school students, members of the military, veterans, college, university, and technical school students, blue-collar workers and professionals, unemployed persons, members of particular cultural, racial, and ethnic groups). Young adults may be single, married with children, unmarried with children, married without children, separated, divorced, or widowed. Some are physically handicapped, emotionally disturbed, or mentally retarded. Obviously, no single catechetical approach will suffice for all.

Young adults are among the most likely to sever contact with organized religion.[14] This is unfortunate for many reasons, not least because this is the period during which critical decisions are generally made concerning state of life, choice of partner, and career.[15] It must be recognized that many in this age group are alienated from the institutional Church and may be lost if greater emphasis is not placed on their evangelization and catechesis.

24,201b)

183. *The making of life decisions*

Near the end of adolescence or in early adulthood it becomes necessary to translate one's ideals into a personal way of life. Long-term choices and decisions must be made concerning vocation, career, and even religious affiliation. Such choices condition future growth. Prolonged unwillingness to make any choices of this kind prevents continued growth and is usually a sign that, regardless of age, the individual is still at an earlier stage of maturity.

Catechesis seeks to help people make the crucial decisions of this period in accord with God's will. It invites young adults to commit themselves to the living of full Christian lives and to engage in ministry within and for the Church community.

Catechesis also continues to present scripture and encourage reflection on it. While experience and personal interaction remain helpful for learning, reading and disciplined study are even more important than before. Catechesis seeks to encourage faith-inspired decisions and close identification with the adult faith community, including its liturgical life and mission. At this age level, catechesis, particularly of those continuing their education in college, will include courses in Christian philosophy and theology.

Michal Heron

184. *Middle adulthood*

At present there is no generally accepted theory of life stages in adulthood that satisfies stringent scientific criteria. The middle years seem to resist categories. In fact, middle age itself is a relatively new concept: before 1900, when average life expectancy in the United States was less than 50, old age was thought to set in around 40. Catechists, nevertheless, will find many helpful insights in the new and increasingly numerous studies on the stages of adult life.

Typically, an individual enters the adult years with optimism and enthusiasm. Ideals are dominant. High goals are set. Ambition is strong. Challenges are eagerly accepted. Self-confidence is undimmed.

Crises of limits arise when people are defeated and disappointed in their efforts to achieve major goals in life: for example, through the experience of incompatibility and disillusionment in marriage; divorce; job dissatisfaction or job loss; the uncertainties associated with deciding on a second career; severe financial problems; difficulty in maintaining friendships; inability to undertake or sustain commitments; severe illness; the death of a loved one and its consequences; serious problems with offspring; inability to express deep emotions; profound loss of self-esteem; fear of failure; fear of success.

Linda Bartlett

As a result, many people experience increasing boredom and loneliness, a sense of routine, fatigue, discouragement in facing decisions and their consequences. Ideals suffer in confrontation with hard reality. Hopes for ultimate success are dimmed by failure and the experience of personal weakness. The first signs of physical aging begin to appear. Eventually, a kind of spiritual crisis is likely. Before, the limitations of being human were to a great extent either not apparent or not part of one's personal experience; now they are inescapable realities in one's own life.

Several options are possible: escape — literal, physical flight or retreat into fantasies; change — new life decisions which may or may not succeed; rebellion, resentment, and hostility; or acceptance of one's limitations and, thereby, of one's humanity. Escape delays or prevents further growth; change may further growth or be another kind of escape; hostility is generally self-destructive. Positive acceptance means moving to a new stage of maturity, which can be a basis for spiritual growth. With grace and the use of Christian wisdom,[16] it is possible to deepen one's relationship with God and other people. One can also exercise a more truly personal freedom, for many obstacles to the exercise of responsible freedom have been removed and one is better able to place oneself wholly at God's disposal and to love without expecting anything in return, either from God or other people.

Linda Bartlett

Catechesis can help adults live out their life decisions; prepare them for the crises of life; and assist them through these crises.

185. Some guidelines for the catechesis of adults

A number of catechetical norms and guidelines for adult catechesis have already been mentioned in this chapter. Others are noted elsewhere. What follows is intended to offer further assistance with regard to the Christian message as it pertains to adults, as well as to methodology.

a) The Christian message

The content of adult catechesis is as comprehensive and diverse as the Church's mission. It should include those universally relevant elements which are basic to the formation of an intelligent and active Catholic Christian and also catechesis pertaining to the particular needs which adults identify themselves as having.

47,73,176a)

The following description of content is not exhaustive.[17] Its elements have been selected either because of their relationship to the fundamental objectives of catechesis or their relevance to the present social scene in the United States.

Adult catechesis includes the study of scripture, tradition, liturgy, theology, morality, and the Church's teaching authority and life.[18] Church history is important for placing events in proper perspective.

Adult catechesis seeks to present the Church in all its dimensions, including its missionary nature, its role as sign or sacrament of Christ's presence in the world, its ecumenical commitment, and its mandate to communicate the whole truth of Christ to all persons in all times. (Cf. Mt 28,20)

Because Christ commissioned the apostles to teach people to observe everything He had commanded (cf. Mt 28,20), catechesis includes "not only those things which are to be believed, but also those things which are to be done."[19] Adult catechesis seeks to make adults keenly aware that an authentically Christian moral life is one guided and informed by the grace and gifts of the Holy Spirit, and that decisions of conscience should be based on study, consultation, prayer, and understanding of the Church's teaching.

38,102-105

103,190

Adult catechesis gives parents and guardians additional instruction to help them in carrying out their particular responsibilities. It also provides similar instruction, at least of a general kind, to all adults, since the entire community has obligations toward the young.

It addresses the Church's mission to promote justice, mercy, and peace, including the vindication of religious, human, and civil rights which are violated.

c.VII

Adult catechesis offers education for change, including the skills essential for dealing with the rapid changes typical of life today.

Adult catechesis gives special attention to spiritual life and prayer.

140-145

b) The methods

Adults should play a central role in their own education. They should identify their needs, plan ways to meet them, and take part in the evaluation of programs and activities.

Catechesis for adults respects and makes use of their experiences, their cultural, racial, and ethnic heritages, their personal skills, and the other resources they bring to catechetical programs. Whenever possible, adults should teach and learn from one another.

Much effective learning comes from reflecting upon one's experiences in the light of faith. Adults must be helped to translate such reflection into practical steps to meet their responsibilities in a Christian manner. Where

176d)

appropriate experiences have not been part of a person's life, the catechetical process attempts to provide them, to the extent possible. This suggests the use of discussion techniques, especially in small groups, and the cultivation of communication skills.

257, 265b)

Other methods of adult catechesis include reading, lectures, workshops, seminars, the use of the media, the Catholic press and other publications, and audio-visuals: in fact, all methods available to sound secular education. Specifically religious experiences — retreats, prayer meetings, and the like — provide extremely valuable opportunities for people to pause and reflect on their lives.

221-222

All catechetical programs, including those for adults, should be evaluated periodically.

202

186. Later adulthood

As people mature, their increased knowledge and proper love of self make it possible for them to enter more readily into self-giving relationships with others. Their courage, honesty, and concern increase. Their practical experience grows. They come to enjoy higher levels of personal freedom. Properly used, these can be the most creative and fruitful years. The attitudes, example, and experience of mature persons make them invaluable educators in and of the faith community.

It would be a mistake, however, to suppose that as people grow older they automatically grow more religious or more mature in their faith. Generally speaking, pastoral ministry has paid too little attention to old age.[20] The needs of this age group have seldom been addressed by catechesis. Everyone needs to be confirmed in supernatural hope and prepared for the coming passage from this life to eternal happiness with God.

108-110
127-128

Death should be depicted for what it is, the final opportunity to assent to the divine will and give oneself freely to God. Several stages have been identified in the process by which an individual typically comes to terms with the fact that he or she will die: denial, anger, bargaining with God, depression, and finally acceptance. Impending or anticipated death provides an opportunity to catechize the elderly and their families on the meaning of Christian death as a sharing in the paschal mystery, a personal sharing in Christ's death so that one may share also in His resurrection, as well as on the steps by which one prepares oneself spiritually for death. So the aged become signs of God's presence, of the sacredness of earthly life, of eternal life, and of the resurrection to come.[21]

187. Some recommendations for catechesis in later adulthood

Rick Smolan

Aging is a natural process with positive and negative aspects. Besides continuing the emphases of adult catechesis, catechesis for the aging seeks to give them physical, emotional, intellectual, and spiritual support so that they can make fruitful use of leisure time, understand and accept the increasing limitations imposed by age, and grow in faith even as they grow in years.

Catechesis notes the significant contributions which the aged make to the entire community through their work and witness.

Catechists and all others who deal with the aged should make use of the growing body of research in geriatrics and related subjects. This area, relatively unexplored, is one where the Church could usefully initiate research, develop creative new programs, and disseminate information about effective programs which already exist.

Elderly people themselves can provide some of the most effective catechesis for the aged. They should receive preparation for this work and should have the opportunity not only to participate in programs but direct them.

188. *The importance of adult catechesis*

The act of faith is a free response to God's grace; and maximum human freedom only comes with the self-possession and responsibility of adulthood. This is one of the principal reasons for regarding adult catechesis as the chief form of catechesis. To assign primacy to adult catechesis does not mean sacrificing catechesis at other age levels; it means making sure that what is done earlier is carried to its culmination in adulthood.

Rapid changes in society and the Church make adult catechesis especially important today. Adults need help in dealing with their problems and communicating their faith to the young. Adult catechesis is also relevant to the Church's mission on behalf of justice, mercy, peace, and respect for human life — a mission which depends heavily upon informed and motivated lay people.[22] Adults need to learn and practice the gospel demands of stewardship: God gives everyone a measure of personal time, talent, and treasure to use for His glory and the service of neighbor.

Because of its importance and because all other forms of catechesis are oriented in some way to it, the catechesis of adults must have high priority at all levels of the Church. The success of programs for children and youth depends to a significant extent upon the words, attitudes, and actions of the adult community, especially parents, family, and guardians.

33,40,54,57-58,84,98, 175,212-213,225

45,70, 102,156, 170,8),13) 221b)

189. *Motivation for adult catechesis*

There are many ways of motivating people to become involved in adult catechesis; here we shall mention only a few. Today, when perhaps more adults than ever before are participating in continuing education courses of all kinds, there is every reason to think many can be attracted to appealing catechetical programs.

The best inducement to participate is an excellent program. People are drawn by the testimony of satisfied participants, as well as by personal invitations from friends and Church leaders.

The total learning environment of the parish is also an important factor in motivating adults. This includes the quality of the liturgies, the extent of shared decision making, the priorities in the parish budget, the degree of commitment to social justice, the quality of the other catechetical programs. Programs for adults should confront people's real questions and problems honestly and openly. As far as possible, they should offer positive reinforcements and rewards; the learning environment should be attractive and comfortable; adults should be encouraged to realize their potential for becoming religiously mature — or more mature — persons. Good publicity in the media, religious and secular, is also very helpful.

Section II: Conscience Formation

190. *The process of conscience formation*

Conscience is discussed in articles 101-105. Here we consider formation of conscience. Both sections should be consulted in catechesis dealing with conscience.[23]

An individual's conscience should develop as he or she matures. Many

NC Photo by Kati Ritchie

psychologists trace a series of stages of growth in the faculty and process by which moral judgments are made. Knowledge of these stages can be helpful when interpreted in a Christian context.

Conscience formation is influenced by such human factors as level of education, emotional stability, self-knowledge, and the ability for clear objective judgment. It is also influenced by external factors: attitudes in the communities to which an individual belongs and cultural and social conditions, particularly as reflected in parents and family.

The central factor in the formation of conscience and sound moral judgment should be Christ's role in one's life. (Cf. Jn 14,6ff; 12,46-50) His ideals, precepts, and example are present and accessible in scripture and the tradition of the Church. To have a truly Christian conscience, one must faithfully communicate with the Lord in every phase of one's life, above all through personal prayer and through participation in the sacramental life and prayer of the Church. All other aspects of conscience formation are based on this.

Catholics should always measure their moral judgments by the magisterium, given by Christ and the Holy Spirit to express Christ's teaching on moral questions and matters of belief and so enlighten personal conscience.[24]

The process of conscience formation should be adapted to age, understanding, and circumstances of life. People should not only be taught Christian moral principles and norms, but encouraged and supported in making responsible decisions consistent with them. The community's example of Christian love is one of the best sources of such encouragement and support.

101

The Church is "a force for freedom and is freedom's home."[25] Taking into account the age and maturity of the learner, freedom must be respected in conscience formation as in all catechesis. "When grace infuses human liberty, it makes freedom fully free and raises it to its highest perfection in the freedom of the Spirit."[26]

It is a task of catechesis to elicit assent to all that the Church teaches, for the Church is the indispensable guide to the complete richness of what Jesus teaches. When faced with questions which pertain to dissent from non-infallible teachings of the Church, it is important for catechists to keep in mind that the presumption is always in favor of the magisterium.[27]

16,41,47,
59,60c),69,
74f),93,
104,181,12)
208,264

16,60c),
206,212

Conscience, though inviolable, is not a law unto itself; it is a practical dictate, not a teacher of doctrine. Doctrine is taught by the Church, whose members have a serious obligation to know what it teaches and adhere to it loyally. In performing their catechetical functions, catechists should present the authentic teaching of the Church.

Section III: Sexuality and Catechesis

191. *Sexuality and catechesis*[28]

According to the Second Vatican Council, "As they [children and young people] advance in years, they should be given positive and prudent sexual education."[29] Education in sexuality includes all dimensions of the topic: moral, spiritual, psychological, emotional, and physical. Its goal is training in chastity in accord with the teaching of Christ and the Church, to be lived in a wholesome manner in marriage, the single state, the priesthood, and religious life. Sexuality is an important element of the human personality, an integral part of one's overall consciousness. It is both a central aspect of one's self-understanding (i.e., as male or female) and a crucial factor in one's relationships with others.

Many experiences have some potential bearing, positive or negative, upon education in sexuality; and virtually all catechists and educators have at least some potential responsibility in this regard, whether or not they ever deal directly with the matter.

Education in sexuality must always be given with reverence and respect, which extend to the language used. More than that, all have a need for catechesis in sexuality in the context of religious values. The God-given dignity and beauty of sex and the sanctity of marriage and family life should be emphasized. Christ's love for the Church is the model for the love between husband and wife. (Cf. Eph 5,25) To abuse the sanctity of love and marriage is anti-sexual, contrary to a proper understanding of sexuality, and in violation of God's will and command. Catechesis calls particular attention to the role of self-control, self-discipline, prayer, the reception of the sacraments, and devotion to the Blessed Mother, model of chastity, as elements in developing a Christian approach to sexuality.

Catechesis should call attention simultaneously to the essential equality of men and women and to the respect due the uniqueness and complementarity of the two sexes.

Education which helps people understand and accept their sexuality begins in infancy and continues in adulthood. The best catechesis for children comes from the wholesome example of their parents and other adults.

However, many parents need assistance in catechizing their children on this subject.[30] The Church can be of great help in this matter. Parents will find help in suitable reading materials and audio-visuals, in family life education and other instructional programs. Appropriate materials can be used by parents in giving instruction to their children. Catechesis should help parents in giving instruction to their children. Catechesis should help parents be competent and at ease with respect to content and methodology. Catechists themselves need suitable preparation.

In recent years education in sexuality has been introduced under different titles into public school systems as well as many Catholic schools and parish catechetical programs. Some courses and programs treat sexuality in a comprehensive manner, including its physical aspects along with the rest; but others deal almost exclusively with physical aspects without reference to values or ethics. This is unfortunate, for human sexuality involves much more besides the physical. Education in sexuality should be given in an integral manner.

NC Photo by Robert Strawn

212

The primacy of the parental right in education obviously extends to children's formation in relation to sexuality. Blessed with the grace of their state in life, parents are presumed to know and understand their children better than anyone else. Parents — especially those with some special familiarity with education in sexuality — should be invited to take part in planning, presenting, and evaluating programs. They should be involved in developing or assessing the philosophy and objectives of such courses and should have opportunities to examine proposed curricula and materials before they are introduced into the classroom.

It is helpful for parents to become acquainted with the teachers who will instruct their children. Also, when possible, parents themselves should participate in the instruction, either regularly or occasionally.

Parents have a right and duty to protest programs which violate their moral and religious convictions. If protests based on well-founded convictions and accurate information are unsuccessful, they have a right to remove their children from the classes, taking care to cause as little embarrassment to the children as possible.

Even after their reasonable requirements and specifications have been met, however, some parents may remain anxious about education in sexuality. They should not let their feelings express themselves in indiscriminate opposition to all classroom instruction in sexuality, for that would not be consistent with the position of the Second Vatican Council[31] and the bishops of the United States. Furthermore, to the extent such opposition might impede or disrupt responsible efforts along these lines, it would violate the rights of other, no less conscientious parents who desire such instruction for their children.[32]

PART C: CATECHESIS FOR PERSONS WITH SPECIAL NEEDS

192. *Introduction*

Articles 134-139 consider the liturgical needs of various special groups. Now we consider their catechetical needs.

193. *Adapting catechesis to a pluralistic society*

Catechesis is prepared to accommodate all social and cultural differences in harmony with the message of salvation. Within the fundamental unity of faith, the Church recognizes diversity, the essential equality of all, and the need for charity and mutual respect among all groups in a pluralistic Church and society.

Guidelines for catechesis by geographical area can easily be inferred from what follows concerning the catechesis of cultural, racial, and ethnic groups. Catechetical guidelines concerning the Catholic Church's relationship to other religious traditions are discussed in articles 75-79.

194. *Catechesis of cultural, racial, and ethnic groups*

At one time or another almost every cultural, racial, and ethnic group in the United States has held minority status in society and in the Church. Many still do. "Minority" can be understood either numerically or as referring to a group whose members are hindered in their efforts to obtain, keep, or exercise their rights.

In some cases, it is important that catechesis distinguish among subgroups within larger groups. For example, the Spanish-speaking, while sharing a common language, include Mexican-Americans, Puerto Ricans, Cubans, and others, each group with its distinct cultural characteristics, customs, needs, and potential. The same is true of various tribes and nations of Native Americans, Afro-Americans, and others.

The preparation of catechists is of the greatest importance. Ideally, the catechist will be a member of the particular racial, cultural, or ethnic group. Those who are not should understand and empathize with the group, besides having adequate catechetical formation.

The language of the particular group should be used in the catechesis of its members: not just its vocabulary, but its thought patterns, cultural idioms, customs, and symbols. Catechetical materials should suit its characteristics and needs. Rather than simply translating or adapting materials prepared for others, it is generally necessary to develop new materials. To be appropriate, even adaptations must involve more than translations and picture changes. Catechetical materials should affirm the identity and dignity of the members of the particular group, using findings of the behavioral sciences for this purpose.

Catechesis takes into account the educational and economic circumstances of diverse groups, avoiding unrealistic demands on time, physical resources, and finances and making adjustments which correspond to the educational level of those being catechized.

NC Photo by Anne Bingham

13,16,39,
47,51,72c),
137,139,
236,242a)

Catechesis takes into account a group's special needs in relation to justice and peace, and prepares its members to assume their responsibility for achieving its just goals.

181,3)

Even in culturally homogeneous areas and parishes catechesis should be multi-cultural, in the sense that all should be educated to know and respect other cultural, racial, and ethnic groups. Minority group members should be invited and encouraged to participate in religious and social functions.

The Church at all levels must make a special commitment to provide funds, research, materials, and personnel for catechesis directed to minority groups. Parishes in which there are no members of such groups have an obligation to help provide funds and personnel. Dioceses with many minority group members should be assisted by dioceses in which there are few or none. Parochial,

John Troha

NC Photo

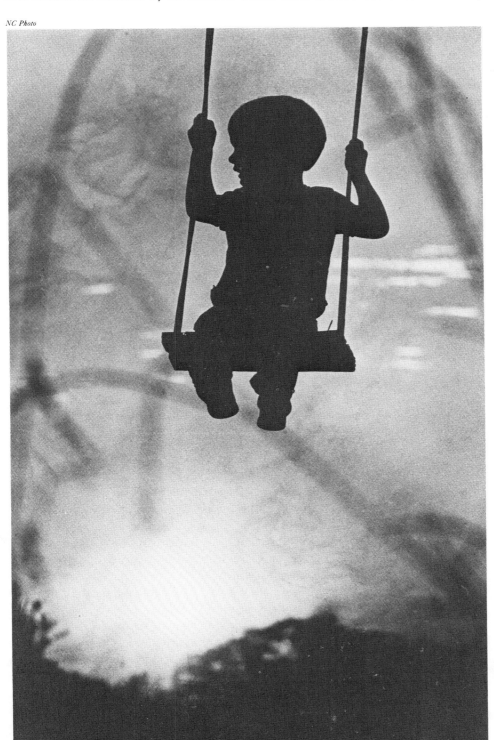

regional, and national leadership and coordination are needed.

At the same time, the leaders of minority groups should support catechesis, especially by engaging in broad consultation to ascertain their people's catechetical needs. Community leaders can stimulate catechetical research, planning, and promotion, and participate in actual catechesis.

At all times catechesis must respect the personal dignity of minority group members, avoiding condescension and patronizing attitudes. The ultimate goal is that minority groups be able to provide for their own catechetical needs, while remaining closely united in faith and charity with the rest of the Church. This unity can be fostered in many ways, including the educational and informational efforts of mission agencies and missionaries.

138,231

Robert Hollis

195. *Persons with handicapping conditions*

Handicapped persons, approximately 12.5 percent of the total population of the United States, include the mentally retarded, those with learning disabilities, the emotionally disturbed, the physically handicapped, the hard of hearing, the deaf, the visually impaired, the blind, and others. Many handicapped persons are in isolating conditions which tend to cut them off from learning. Each handicapped person has special needs — including a need for catechesis — which must be recognized and met.

Catechetical programs should not segregate the handicapped from the rest of the community excessively or unnecessarily.

Catechesis for certain groups (e.g., the deaf, the blind, the mentally retarded) often requires specialized materials, training, and skills (such as the ability to sign). The entire Church has a responsibility for providing training and research; leadership preparation and funding are needed at the national, diocesan, and local levels. On the diocesan and parish levels, sharing of resources and personnel and collaboration in the preparation and sponsorship of programs are appropriate; the possibility of ecumenically sponsored and conducted programs should also be investigated.

It is particularly important for the families of the handicapped persons to be involved in their catechesis. Supportive participation by family members helps them better understand handicapped individuals.

The goal is to present Christ's love and teaching to each handicapped person in as full and rich a manner as he or she can assimilate.

196. *Other persons with special needs*

The list of groups with special needs is almost endless: the aged — often among the socially and economically disadvantaged; the illiterate and educationally deprived; young single people in college or vocational programs; young single workers; military personnel; unmarried people with children; young married couples with or without children; couples in mixed marriages; the divorced; the divorced and remarried; middle-aged singles; the widowed; the imprisoned; persons with a homosexual orientation; etc.

Catechesis is also needed by people in the "caring" professions — such as doctors, nurses, and social workers — who have their own special requirements along with many opportunities for witness and for catechizing in their dealings with the deprived, the sick, and the dying.

The Church is seriously obliged to provide catechesis suited to the special needs of these and other groups. Some were overlooked in the past, but in several cases these special needs are of relatively recent origin: for example, those of the aged, whose current difficulties are largely associated with increased longevity and the decline of the extended family; and those of young single people, whose needs are related to the recent emergence of new life styles.

Catechesis is part of a total pastoral ministry to people with special needs. It emphasizes aspects of the Church's teaching and practice which will help them make personal, faith-filled responses to their special circumstances. Sensitivity and careful planning are essential.

Catechetical programs should, whenever possible, be developed in consultation with representatives of those for whom they are intended. The aim should be to help them overcome the obstacles they face and achieve as much integration as they can into the larger community of faith.

PART D: SOME SIGNIFICANT FACTORS AFFECTING CATECHESIS IN THE UNITED STATES

10,c.1

197. Isolation of infants, children, and youth

Interaction between parents and children in all spheres has decreased significantly in the United States in the past twenty-five years. (This is caused, to a considerable extent, by factors mentioned in articles 24-28.) Children begin to be segregated from their parents in the first years of life, and this isolation continues through preschool, elementary school, high school, and college.

As adults give less time to parenting, young people respond by creating a youth subculture, whose values and attitudes are dictated largely by television and peers instead of by parents and teachers.

In view of the intrinsic importance of parents and family in transmitting cultural and religious attitudes and values, this isolation of infants, children, and youth poses major problems for catechesis. Comprehensive solutions require a major reorganization of social institutions, beyond the scope of this NCD to prescribe. Catechists can, however, at least make parents aware of the problem and its consequences, and encourage as much interaction as possible between them and their children. Of special importance is family catechesis, where young people can spend "quality time" with parents or guardians.

25

198. Children and youth not attending school

According to census figures, nearly 3 percent of the children aged 7 to 10 in the United States and over 10 percent of those 16 and 17 receive no formal schooling. Migration is one of the causes of nonattendance at school. Efforts are needed to locate these children and youth and persuade them to participate in catechetical programs. Their nonattendance may also reflect other problems — e.g., illiteracy, a handicap — which must be dealt with before formal catechesis is possible. Parental involvement is extremely important.

199. Children and youth from religiously indifferent families

As noted in article 24 and elsewhere, the number of religiously indifferent parents seems to have grown in the United States in recent years. The causes of this phenomenon must be identified if catechetical programs oriented to evangelization are to have an impact on them and their children.

Parish members should seek out such families and invite them to take part in parish activities: e.g., services for the sick, the elderly, the poor, and others who are in need. Efforts should be made to include them in such things as weekend retreats and days of prayer. Home visitations by parishioners and priests may also help motivate them to become religiously active.

John Troha

Although contemporary youth culture changes rapidly, it is helpful to describe some of its current traits with particular significance for catechesis.

a) Population trends

Over the next several years the number of school-age children and youth in the United States will decrease, while the proportion belonging to racial, cultural, and ethnic minorities increases.

The number of children and youth in Catholic elementary and secondary schools has been declining since 1965, although there have been recent signs of stabilization. At the same time, large numbers of young Catholics receive no formal catechesis.[33] Research into this problem, particularly its causes and effects, is badly needed.

179-180,
200

b) Age of religious crisis

Between 12 and 18 many young people either begin to abandon the faith of their childhood or become more deeply committed to it.

There is a tendency for young people around age 13 to regard much previous teaching about religion as childish, in the erroneous belief that there is no coherent and mature explanation for what they have learned earlier. Resolution of the conflict between faith and reason, formerly thought to take place by age 20, now appears to be occurring earlier.[34] These developments must be taken into account in preparing catechetical programs and materials for young people facing or about to face a crisis of faith.

c) Traditional beliefs and religious practice[35]

There is ample evidence of a contemporary decline in traditional beliefs and religious practices. For instance, fewer youths than in the past believe in a personal God, divine revelation, life after death, and the Bible as God's word. Sunday and holy day Mass attendance has decreased, as has the practice of daily prayer.

There is a more permissive attitude with regard to sexual morality and greater use of alcohol, marijuana, and other drugs. While crimes of assault have declined, truancy, running away from home, and theft have increased. The suicide rate among young people rose 250 percent between 1954 and 1973 (10.9 per 100,000); in a recent poll 23 percent said they believe that in some circumstances it is not wrong to take one's life.

Many experts attribute these phenomena to isolation and loneliness. Others hold that society burdens young people with awesome pressures and responsibilities which they are not ready to handle alone.

d) Positive aspects

While some young people are moving away from organized religion, others remain firmly committed. A few never attend religious services or say prayer is of little importance to them. But a clear majority of those 13 to 18 believe that, in some way, the Church and religious authorities represent God, and about one-fourth of Catholic youth claim to be active in Church-sponsored activities. For the most part, young people are searching for direction to help them become what God has created them to be. A large majority are satisfied with their country, families, and schools. Adolescents are also strongly interested in the practical dimensions of life.

In general, young people mirror the values and standards of society. Their problems tend to be essentially symptoms of malaise in the larger community; they are more the victims than the source of religious and social ills. Most are conscientious persons growing toward maturity, really concerned about their mistakes and interested in their fellow human beings. Such qualities offer a starting point for effective catechesis.

NC Photo by Sigmund J. Mikolajczyk

e) Some observations and recommendations

The "personal-experiential" dimension of religion (closeness to God, frequency of prayer, and the importance of religion in one's life) is least affected as the person grows older. This indicates that for many adolescents a personal relationship with Jesus Christ is not bound up with formal religious practice or traditional beliefs.

Thus there seems to be no inherent reason why young people should become more prone to lose their faith as they grow older. They are more exposed to competing world views and value systems, but catechesis can and should be adapted to mental age and to the social context and other circumstances.

It is significant that many adolescents apparently stop thinking about religion long before they consciously reject it. Various reasons are suggested: boredom with religion as they know it; the association of religion with fairy tales ("science has proved religion isn't true"); religion's apparent remoteness from life; confusion concerning the language and thought of the Bible. To the extent that these explanations are valid, the answer seems to lie in adapting catechesis to the mental age of young people, and allowing them to question, discuss, and explore religious beliefs. The young insist on dialogue, as opposed to what they consider religious indoctrination. If such steps as these are taken; if young people are provided with models of faith which they perceive as credible and relevant; if they are challenged to confront the fullness of religious truth — then there is reason to hope that, as they grow older, adolescents will progress in faith and religious practice and suffer no delay in the process of religious maturation.

All this indicates that adolescents are more like adults than children in relation to faith. Catechesis must reflect this fact.

John Troha

Catechists should be aware that, with God's grace, many factors can help foster religiousness in youth. Operating in varying ways and to varying degrees are age, sex, social class, city size, parental education, parental religious practice, parental affection-support, parent approval of friends, attendance at religion classes, etc. The two most important factors are parental religious practice and the current study of religion. In addition, parental affection and support have a positive effect, especially on social morality.[36] These considerations point to priorities in youth catechesis, including the active involvement of parents. Furthermore, by creating a sense of community, religion can probably help relieve some of the tensions created by changing attitudes toward sex, religion, politics, and social relationships.

Lou Niznik

201. Some characteristics of young adults

a) College students[37]

College students, close to half of the 18 to 21 age group, differ in many respects from other young adults.

Many studies have been made of their religious attitudes and values. Because of rapid changes, it is quite possible that data gathered a few years ago no longer reflect current attitudes. However, there are certain long-term trends of which catechists and campus ministers should be aware.

Research on college students over the past fifty years shows that: they now have more freedom and personal responsibility than ever before; there have been changes in moral orientations, including greater tolerance regarding the specifics of moral codes; a distinct conscious youth culture has emerged.

In recent years, living a moral life, the importance of religion, and patriotism have all receded in importance for students. In all areas related to sexual morality (premarital and extramarital sex, relations between consenting homosexuals, having an abortion, etc.) deviations from traditional norms find greater acceptance. Along with the desire for greater sexual freedom, there is less regard for authority and for hard work.

Many conclude that the emphasis on individualism, autonomy, and personal fulfillment will continue in the years ahead, while positive attitudes toward authority, personal sacrifice, and traditional sexual morality will grow progressively weaker. It has been observed that there is even a considerable difference in religious beliefs and practices between freshmen and seniors, with first-year students more traditional than fourth-year ones.

Religious belief and practice have declined among Catholics on both secular and Catholic campuses. While more trend studies are needed to ascertain the current situation, it appears that students in some Catholic colleges are becoming increasingly like students in other colleges in the United States as far as religion is concerned.

180,200a)

Further study is also needed concerning the finding that, between 1948 and 1974, the percentage of college students reacting wholly or partly against beliefs taught them at home rose from 57 percent to 79 percent. At the same time, the median age for the onset of doubt fell to 14.4 (from 16.4 in 1948), indicating that the crucial time for religious development is in high school, not college. Another part of the picture is the alarming rate at which college-educated persons leave the Church (discussed in article 24).

25

Several factors appear to have influenced religious changes among students. For example, the surveys reflect some rural-urban difference; and students who are more "cosmopolitan" (acquainted with and accepting of different cultural settings) tend to be a bit weaker in religious commitment. The most important factor, however, seems to be the amount of religious influence in the home. Students who are closer to their parents have more ties to traditional religion and the Church. To a large extent, attitudes toward the Church seem to be extensions of attitudes toward the family and thus to reflect interpersonal and social factors.

Linda Bartlett

There is some evidence that, while the roles of both mother and father are important, they are different. For example, conflict with the mother appears to contribute more to later rejection of her religious values.

b) Non-college young adults[38]

While in the past college education generally tended to exert a secularizing influence on religious practice and belief, among Catholics it was related positively to orthodoxy and religious practice. In regard to both orthodoxy and moral values, however, the difference has been narrowing in recent years.

College youth attend Mass more frequently and appear to be more orthodox in doctrinal matters, but non-college youth are more traditional on moral issues (e.g., sexual freedom, abortion, the need to live a moral life). On the specific issue of acceptance of papal authority, the decline has been greatest among college males and the least among non-college males. Women experienced an intermediate degree of impact, with the college-educated reporting more questioning than non-college women.

24,182

Non-college youth pray more frequently and are more inclined to regard religion as an important value in life. The apostasy rate (leaving the Church) is also somewhat lower among youth under 30 who did not attend college.

c) Some observations and recommendations

The younger, more affluent, and more closely aligned with the national culture a person is, the more subject he or she is to short-range changes in religious commitment.

Religious disaffection may be linked to a general mentality of independence; sociopolitical changes have apparently been accompanied by disillusionment with many social institutions, including organized religion. Religious commitments are closely related to other important commitments, and when social changes take place, religious commitments also change. Apparently religious commitment is determined not only by clergy, church, and school, but even more by family, community, and nation. The extensive social changes in the United States in recent years must be taken seriously into account in preparing catechetical programs for college students and all others.[39]

The general decline in orthodoxy, moral values, religious devotion, and acceptance of ecclesiastical authority has been most precipitous among young people. But the majority have not defected from the Church, even though their participation is sometimes peripheral. This strongly suggests that the young generation, including young adults, are waiting for the Church to address itself more specifically and forcefully to the new forces and values shaping society.

202. *Some characteristics of later adulthood*

186

The number of persons 65 or older is increasing rather rapidly in the United States. It is expected to rise from 22.8 million in 1976 to approximately 30 million in 1990.

Because women tend to live longer than men, there are now 143 women for every 100 men over 65 in this country. Women, on the average, can expect to live more than 20 years with their husbands after the children leave home, and about eight years as widows.

The vast majority of persons over 65 are not employed, but are in good health (although perhaps with some chronic, non-disabling condition). Perhaps no more than 10 percent need nursing home care, and half of these are receiving such care.

Pastoral ministers should know how many elderly people are present within parish or diocesan boundaries. This information is needed in developing catechetical programs.

203. *Conclusion*

We have described in broad terms how a human being grows and changes from birth to death, and pointed to the relationship between this process and growth in the life of faith. Catechists recognize, however, that another, mysterious, uniquely powerful action is taking place: the work of the Holy Spirit in each person, in the Church, and in the world.

Having considered those who are catechized, we shall next consider those who do the catechizing — catechetical personnel.

Michal Heron

Chapter IX

Catechetical Personnel

There was a man named John
sent by God,
who came as a witness
to testify to the light,
so that through him
all men might believe. . . .

Jn 1,6f

204. Introduction

In this NCD the term catechist is used in a broad sense to designate anyone who participates formally or informally in catechetical ministry. All members of a community of believers are called to share in this ministry by being witnesses to the faith. Some, however, are called to more specific catechetical roles. Parents, teachers, and principals in Catholic schools, parish catechists, coordinators or directors of religious education, those who work in diocesan and national catechetical offices, deacons, priests, and bishops — all are catechists with distinct roles. Here we shall describe ideal qualities, for which all catechists should strive, and discuss the various roles and the educational preparation required for them.

PART A: IDEAL QUALITIES OF CATECHISTS

205. An ideal and a challenge

Because it points to an ideal, what follows is meant to be a challenge as well as a guide. This ideal should not discourage present or prospective catechists. On the contrary, as they participate in the catechetical ministry their religious lives will be intensified and they will find themselves growing in the qualities needed for successful ministry to others. It is these human and Christian qualities of catechists, more than their methods and tools, upon which the success of catechesis depends.

206. Response to a call

As important as it is that a catechist have a clear understanding of the teaching of Christ and His Church, this is not enough. He or she must also receive and respond to a ministerial call, which comes from the Lord and is articulated in the local Church by the bishop. The response to this call includes willingness to give time and talent, not only to catechizing others, but to one's own continued growth in faith and understanding.

207. Witness to the gospel

For catechesis to be effective, the catechist must be fully committed to Jesus Christ. Faith must be shared with conviction, joy, love, enthusiasm, and hope. "The summit and center of catechetical formation lies in an aptitude and ability to communicate the Gospel message."[1] This is possible only when the catechist believes in the gospel and its power to transform lives. To give witness to the gospel, the catechist must establish a living, ever-deepening relationship with the Lord. He or she must be a person of prayer, one who frequently reflects on the scriptures and whose Christlike living testifies to deep faith. Only men and women of faith can share faith with others, preparing the setting within which people can respond in faith to God's grace.

208. Commitment to the Church

One who exercises the ministry of the word represents the Church, to which the word has been entrusted. The catechist believes in the Church and is aware that, as a pilgrim people, it is in constant need of renewal. Committed to this visible community, the catechist strives to be an instrument of the Lord's power and a sign of the Spirit's presence.

The catechist realizes that it is Christ's message which he or she is called to proclaim. To insure fidelity to that message, catechists test and validate their

16,60c),
190,212

60a)i,143

68,93

understanding and insights in the light of the gospel message as presented by the teaching authority of the Church.

209. Sharer in community

70,94

The catechist is called to foster community as one who has "learned the meaning of community by experiencing it."[2] Community is formed in many ways. Beginning with acceptance of individual strengths and weaknesses, it progresses to relationships based on shared goals and values. It grows through discussion, recreation, cooperation on projects, and the like.

Yet it does not always grow easily; patience and skill are frequently required. Even conflict, if creatively handled, can be growth-producing, and Christian reconciliation is an effective means of fostering community. Many people have had little experience of parish community and must be gradually prepared for it.

Christian community is fostered especially by the Eucharist, "which is at once sign of community and cause of its growth."[3] The catechist needs to experience this unity through frequent participation in the celebration of the Eucharist with other catechists and with those being catechized. Awareness of membership in a Christian community leads to awareness of the many other communities in the world which stand in need of service. The catechist seeks to cooperate with other parish leaders in making the parish a focal point of community in the Church.

60d),224

210. Servant of the community

66,96

Authentic experience of Christian community leads one to the service of others. The catechist is committed to serving the Christian community, particularly in the parish, and the community-at-large. Such service means not only responding to needs when asked, but taking the initiative in seeking out the needs of individuals and communities, and encouraging students to do the same.

Sensitive to the community's efforts to find solutions to "a host of complex problems such as war, poverty, racism, and environmental pollution, which undermine community within and among nations,"[4] the catechist educates to peace and justice, and supports social action when appropriate. The Church often becomes involved in efforts to solve global problems through missionaries, who also carry out in a special way its mission of universal evangelization. The catechist should show how support for missionary endeavors is not only required by the Church's missionary nature but is an expression of solidarity within the human community.

c.VII

Linda Bartlett

USCC Creative Services

John Troha

211. Knowledge, skills, and abilities

Although even the best preparation for catechetical ministry will have little effect without the action of the Holy Spirit in the hearts of catechists and those being catechized, catechists should certainly seek to acquire the knowledge, skills, and abilities needed to communicate the gospel message effectively. They must have a solid grasp of Catholic doctrine and worship; familiarity with scripture; communication skills; the ability to use various methodologies; understanding of how people grow and mature and of how persons of different ages and circumstances learn.

PART B: CATECHETICAL ROLES AND PREPARATION

117,119,
122,126,
170,11),
177,191,
226,229-
230

212. Parents as catechists

Parents are the first and foremost catechists of their children.[5] They catechize informally but powerfully by example and instruction. They communicate values and attitudes by showing love for Christ and His Church and for each other, by reverently receiving the Eucharist and living in its spirit, and by fostering justice and love in all their relationships. Their active involvement in the parish, their readiness to seek opportunities to serve others, and their practice of frequent and spontaneous prayer, all make meaningful their professions of belief. Parents nurture faith in their children by showing them the richness and beauty of lived faith. Parents should frequently be reminded of their obligation to see to it that their children participate in catechetical programs sponsored by the Church.

117

When children are baptized the Church community promises to help parents foster their faith. It keeps this promise, first of all, by its own witness as a worshiping, believing, serving community; and also by providing formal catechesis for adults, youth, and children. Adult catechesis, which deepens the faith of parents, helps them nurture faith in their children.

The Church community also keeps its promise to parents by providing programs intended specifically to help them in their catechetical role. Such programs focus on the task of parents in relation to particular moments or issues in the child's religious life, such as sacramental preparation and moral development. They also seek to familiarize parents with the stages in children's growth and the relevance these have for catechesis.

16,60c),190,
206

When formally participating in the catechesis of their children, parents must be mindful of the pre-eminent right of the Church to specify the content of authentic catechesis. They always have an obligation to catechize according to the teaching authority of the Church.[6]

Parish and diocesan personnel should collaborate in planning and presenting programs for parents, including the parents of handicapped children. Parents themselves should have a direct role in planning such programs.

213. Parish catechists

117

Parish catechists, many of whom are volunteers, may be engaged in catechizing adults, young people, children, or those with special needs. Theirs is a particular way of carrying out the promise which the Church makes at every Baptism: to support, pray for, and instruct the baptized and foster their growth in faith.

The fundamental tasks of catechists are to proclaim Christ's message, to participate in efforts to develop community, to lead people to worship and prayer, and to motivate them to serve others. To accomplish all this, catechists must identify and create "suitable conditions which are necessary for the Christian message to be sought, accepted, and more profoundly investigated."[7] They recognize, however, that faith is a gift and that it is not ultimately their efforts but the interaction of God's grace and human freedom which lead people to accept faith and respond to it.

33,54,57-58,84,98, 175,188

Parish and diocesan personnel and others involved in catechetical ministry should help catechists develop the qualities outlined here. Because catechists approach their task with varying degrees of competence, programs should be designed to help individuals acquire the particular knowledge and skills they need. Catechists typically participate in a variety of teaching and learning programs, liturgical experiences, classes, retreats, service programs, study clubs, and similar activities. They carry on their ministry in parish catechetical programs, Catholic schools, and other settings. Their training should equip them to make effective use of the resources available for catechesis and to adapt materials to the age, capacity, and culture of those they seek to reach.

Men and women from all walks of life volunteer for parish catechetical programs. Parish and diocesan programs for the preparation and in-service training of volunteers should include the following elements.

1. Basic orientation and preparation, including instruction in theology, scripture, psychology, and catechetical techniques. They should be shown how to identify goals and achieve them in their particular circumstances.

2. Opportunities for liturgical celebrations, prayer, retreats, and other experiences of Christian community with others engaged in this ministry.

3. Continuing in-service educational opportunities.

4. Regular assistance, from more experienced persons, in planning and evaluating their performance.

5. Opportunities to evaluate not only their performance but the programs in which they are involved.

6. More specialized training for those who will work with physically or mentally handicapped persons.

7. Cultivation of a sense of community among the catechists during the entire formation process.

8. Some form of commissioning ceremony which expresses the faith community's call and the catechists' dedicated response.

Kati Ritchie

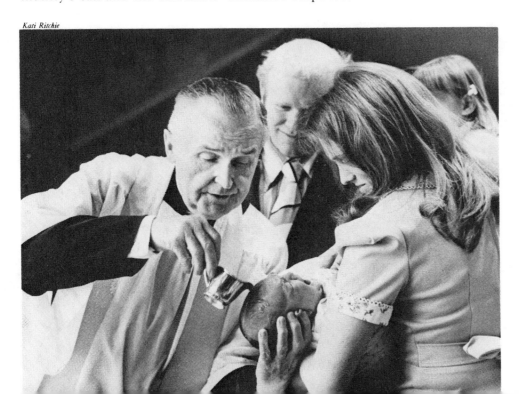

U.S. Bureau of Indian Affairs Photo by Donald J. Morrow

129

214. *Directors and coordinators of religious education*

As awareness has grown of the need for continuing, comprehensive catechesis for all, an increasing number of men and women have assumed positions as parish or inter-parish directors and coordinators of religious education. Such positions vary in their specific functions, depending on factors like size of staff, scope of program, and parish size.

Two basic roles seem to be emerging, together with variations on them. In one, the individual is responsible for overall direction of the parish's catechetical programs. This includes working with the pastor, other ministers, and appropriate committees, boards, or councils involved in setting policy and planning; designing catechetical programs; assisting in liturgical planning; conducting sacramental preparation workshops; and providing opportunities for staff development. Appropriate preparation includes studies in theology, scripture, liturgy, psychology, educational theory, and administration, as well as practical experience with children and adults.

The other role involves responsibility for administration of a parish's catechetical program on a particular level or for a particular group or groups. Functions include working with the pastor, the director, and other staff members in recruiting catechists; and being responsible for the general day-to-day operation of the program. For this work, a good background in catechetics, administration, and communication skills is needed, together with parish experience.

Both roles are generally designated by the title Director, Minister, or Coordinator of Religious Education; but the title varies from place to place.

People who hold such positions need to continue their education in order to bring fresh insights to their ministry. They should participate in diocesan programs of in-service education. Parishes are encouraged to provide funds to help them attend catechetical institutes, conventions, retreats, and accredited summer school programs.

Pastors or parish boards which hire directors or coordinators must formulate clear and specific agreements with them concerning their duties, in line with diocesan policies. These agreements should also specify the spiritual, psychological, and financial support to be provided by the parish.

Dick Swartz

NC Photo by Carolyn Wells

215. School principals

8,232-233

The Catholic school principal plays a critical role in realizing the goals of Catholic education. While specifics of this role vary according to circumstances, certain functions relating to catechesis are basic.

Recognizing that all faculty members share in catechetical ministry,[8] principals recruit teachers with appropriate qualifications in view of the Catholic school's apostolic goals and character. They provide opportunities for ongoing catechesis for faculty members by which they can deepen their faith and grow in the ability to integrate in their teaching the fourfold dimensions of Catholic education: message, community, worship, and service. In collaboration with the faculty, principals see to it that the curriculum reflects these dimensions.

Principals foster community among faculty and students. They understand the Catholic school as a part of larger communities, religious and secular. They collaborate with parish, area, or diocesan personnel in planning and implementing programs for a total, integrated approach to catechesis. They also establish norms and procedures of accountability and evaluation within the school, and in relation to the larger community.

216. Permanent deacons

93,132-133

Permanent deacons are ordained to a ministry of service and participate in the catechetical ministry of the Church. Commissioned as ministers of word as well as sacrament, they exercise this ministry in teaching and preaching. Among their duties are preparing others for the sacraments; ministering in hospitals, prisons, and other institutions; directing or participating in parish or diocesan catechetical programs; serving as campus ministers.

The preparation of permanent deacons should include studies in theology, scripture, communication skills, and catechetical formation for their particular area of catechetical ministry. As part of their training, candidates for the diaconate and the priesthood should have supervised catechetical experiences in parishes, hospitals, or other institutional settings.

Linda Bartlett

217. Pastors and priest associates

Priests exercise a uniquely important role and have a special responsibility for the success of the catechetical ministry. They are a source of leadership, cooperation, and support for all involved in this ministry. As leaders in developing a faith community under the guidance of the Holy Spirit, they perform indispensable catechetical functions: encouraging catechists, praying with them, teaching and learning with them, supporting them. The preaching ministry of the priest is one of his most important catechetical functions. His liturgical-sacramental ministry is also a central factor in the catechesis of the Christian community. The priest gives active support to catechetical programs by participating in planning, by catechizing, by providing liturgical celebrations for classes or groups, and by other expressions of interest and concern.

120,225

The pastor is primarily responsible for seeing to it that the catechetical needs, goals, and priorities of the parish are identified, articulated, and met. In planning and carrying out the catechetical ministry, he works with his priest associates, parish council, board of education or analogous body, directors and coordinators, principals, teachers, parents, and others. He respects the organizational principles mentioned in articles 221-223 and attempts to make as much use as possible of team ministry in catechetical efforts.

47

It is imperative that priests continue their education after ordination. This can be done to some degree through reading, participating in discussions, and attending lectures. However, dioceses, in collaboration with colleges, universities, and seminaries, should provide ongoing clergy education programs, in theology, scripture, and other subjects according to need. This is particularly important because of the rapid changes in society and in many fields of knowledge. By study, reading, and prayer a priest enriches his ministry and also encourages parishioners to take seriously their own obligation to grow in faith.

218. Diocesan catechetical personnel

47,69

a) The bishop

The bishop, chief catechist in the diocese (cf. Acts 20,28), is responsible for seeing to it that sound catechesis is provided for all its people. He should not only "devote himself personally to the work of the Gospel," but should "supervise the entire ministry of the word in regards to the flock committed to his care."[9]

221-223

In carrying out his responsibility the bishop ensures that catechetical goals and priorities are established by the Christian community, that the necessary structures exist, and that appropriate programs are designed, carried out, and evaluated. He takes every opportunity to preach and teach personally. He summons his people to faith and strengthens them in it, using such means as parish visits, pastoral letters, and the communications media.

The bishop does not work alone. He is assisted by parents, catechists, directors and coordinators, religious, deacons, and priests. He is responsible for choosing qualified leaders for the catechetical ministry; for ensuring that catechists are adequately prepared for their work; and for seeing to it that all involved in this ministry receive continuing catechetical formation. He is also mindful of his own need for continuing education.

b) Diocesan staff

The bishop directs catechesis through the diocesan offices responsible for catechetical activities. These serve parishes in many ways.

"The extent and diversity of the problems which must be handled demand that the responsibilities be divided among a number of truly skilled people."[10] Although catechetical needs and priorities vary from one diocese to another, diocesan offices should in general perform the following functions.

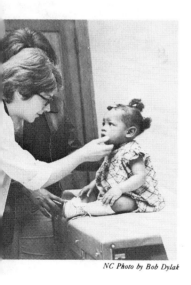

NC Photo by Bob Dylak

1. Encourage and motivate catechists on every level by visits, in-service training, newsletters, diocesan institutes, etc.

2. Propose alternative models of educational priorities which can be adapted to the needs of particular areas, parishes, or schools.

3. Supply guidelines for parish organization, programs of sacramental preparation, and other programs to help parishes provide comprehensive catechesis.

4. Recommend catechetical curricula and textbooks.

5. Provide in-service training and formation opportunities for parish and regional catechetical leaders.

6. Provide prior training and continuing education for catechists, by establishing permanent centers for catechetical training or cooperating with Catholic colleges or universities in setting up such programs.

7. Keep catechetical personnel informed concerning important Church documents and recommendations which pertain to catechesis.

8. Provide access to catechetical resources, including textbooks and instructional aids.

9. Provide personnel and resources to meet the needs of the physically and mentally handicapped.

10. Conduct regular surveys to determine the number of adults, youth, children, preschoolers, physically or mentally handicapped persons, etc. re-

ceiving formal catechetical instruction; the number who are not receiving instruction at each level; the availability of training and continuing education of personnel; the kinds of programs in use and their effectiveness; the number of hours of instruction being given; the service and worship components of programs; costs; etc.

11. Establish norms for accrediting catechists, including directors and coordinators, catechists in parish programs, Catholic school personnel, etc. These norms should require demonstrated competence and should not be based solely on "paper credentials."

12. Integrate catechesis with the diocese's total plan for Catholic education and prepare parish catechetical personnel to do the same.

13. Establish and provide instruments for evaluating programs, including both their cognitive and affective dimensions.

222

14. Keep the diocese mindful of its mission to evangelize.

Diocesan personnel should have previous catechetical experience in parishes or schools, as well as formation comparable to that required for parish directors, coordinators, and teachers in Catholic schools.

Frequent participation in celebrating the Eucharist together is highly desirable for the staff members of diocesan offices. In this way they foster community among themselves, grow in their ability to proclaim the message in truth, intensify their prayer life, and make their work truly a service of the Lord.

219. Conclusion

This chapter has discussed the ideal personal qualities of catechists, as well as the training and skills required by particular catechetical roles. Next we turn to organizational principles and structure.

Rick Smolan

Michal Heron

Chapter X

Organization for Catechesis

For God who said,
"Let light shine out of darkness,"
has shone in our hearts,
that we in turn might make known
the glory of God
shining on the face of Christ.
2 Cor 4,6

220. Introduction

One can hardly emphasize too strongly the catechetical importance of the witness to faith given by individuals living according to their Christian beliefs and values. But organizational structures are also needed to achieve the goals and ideals set forth in this NCD. Appropriate structures can help ensure opportunities for the entire Christian community to grow in faith.

Some topics treated in this chapter have already been discussed in Chapter VIII in relation to faith and human development; here they are examined from the point of view of organization.

PART A: GENERAL ORGANIZATIONAL GUIDELINES

222

221. Organizational principles

The following principles are important to catechetical organization.

a) Effective planning is person-centered. It does not propose structures without reference to the people involved. It sets growth in faith as the goal and recognizes the Christian family as the basic community within which faith is nurtured.

b) Each of its members has a responsibility for the whole Church. Each has a duty to foster a living, conscious, active faith community. Laity, religious, and clergy alike are called to participate in those aspects of catechesis — organization, implementation, evaluation — with respect to which they are interested and qualified. Recognizing that they are stewards of God's gifts, they should be generous in supporting the catechetical effort. Shared responsibility implies the development and use of such structures as councils and boards.

c) Planning groups should make a clear statement of their philosophy, their goals, and the basic beliefs underlying the goals. (Cf. next article.)

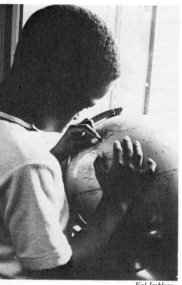

Val Imbleau

d) Higher-level planning groups should not try to do what can be done as well, or better, by groups at lower levels. For example, diocesan bodies ought not to set policies or make decisions which deprive parishes of authority concerning matters they are able to handle. Respect for local decision making encourages initiative, while freeing larger units to concentrate on needs which only they can meet, or which require coordination or a common approach. Groups should seek outside help only when needs clearly exceed local capabilities.

e) At all levels it is essential that overall plans make provision for communication and accountability.

f) Administrators in each local community are responsible for the equitable allocation of available services, opportunities, and resources. Strong central leadership is needed to ensure that resources are used for the good of all. Communities in need should have opportunities equal to those enjoyed by more favored communities.

g) Structures should flow from need and be suited to the achievement of the stated goals.

h) Goal setting, planning, implementation, accountability, and evaluation are continuing processes.

221

222. Planning and evaluation

a) Planning

Planning is an essential part of any serious organizational effort. There are many planning processes; catechists involved in organization should be exposed to several and familiar with at least one.

Certain elements are common to all planning systems:

    i) a clear understanding of the essential mission and major objectives;

    ii) assessment of needs, as well as current and potential resources;

    iii) identification of long- and short-range goals;

    iv) identification of concrete activities to reach the goals, rated according to priority;

    v) establishment of a budget which reflects available resources;

    vi) establishment of favorable conditions for carrying out the activities which have been decided upon;

    vii) periodic review and evaluation;

    viii) restatement of goals and activities when necessary.

It is important that planning for catechetical programs at the parish, diocesan, and national levels be part of a total pastoral plan. Such a plan, which takes into consideration the Church's entire mission, is best developed by representatives of the various ministries in the Church.[1] Urgent demands upon limited resources require cooperation among all pastoral ministries.

Planning is a continuous process. The associated skills develop with experience. Good planning enriches decision making and forestalls crisis-oriented decisions.

NC Photo by Robert Strawn

266

b) Evaluation

Catechetical programs should be subjected to regular evaluation. The evaluation should be made in light of established goals and objectives, which themselves should be evaluated periodically.

There is a need to develop instruments for evaluating catechetical programs. The United States Catholic Conference, National Conference of Diocesan Directors of Religious Education-CCD, National Catholic Educational Association, and other representative agencies should collaborate in meeting this need. The norms and guidelines set forth throughout this NCD provide criteria for evaluation.

223. Research

Rapid developments in the Church, society, and education underline the great need for research related to catechesis. Wherever possible, dioceses and parishes ought to examine themselves in order to ascertain their requirements and make plans for meeting them.

Diocesan, regional, and national groups are responsible for developing research instruments and projecting and testing models for local use. It is the responsibility of the religious education representative of the USCC Department of Education to coordinate efforts on the various levels and disseminate the results of research to diocesan offices and other interested parties. The other offices of the Department of Education, the departments of the United States Catholic Conference, and the agencies of the National Conference of Catholic Bishops provide the same services to their constituents, with regard to the catechetical components of their ministries.

The Office of Research, Policy and Program Development of the USCC Department of Education has the following functions: to maintain a listing of current and completed research in Catholic education, including catechetics; to help identify present and future research needs; to make a continuing study of trends in Catholic education, including projections for the immediate and distant futures. The staff works closely with Catholic colleges, universities, learned societies, and research groups in performing these functions.

Associated with the Office of Research, Policy and Program Development is the United States Center for the Catholic Biblical Apostolate. In relation to

25,29,
181,13),182,
186-187,194-
195,200a),
201a),222b),
226,242,
261

catechesis its pastoral purpose is to ascertain the needs of the dioceses with respect to Bible study programs, especially in adult education, and to promote popular biblical publications as well as wide distribution of the scriptures.[2]

It is highly desirable that catechists at all levels know and use the results of research. Useful research at any level should be shared as widely as possible with the rest of the Church.

PART B: THE PARISH

60d)

Bob Fitzgerald

224. *The parish community*

The parish is the basic structure within which most Catholics express and experience faith. Ordinarily, a parish is made up of the people within a defined territorial area, for whose care and service a priest has been assigned by the bishop. There are other parishes for Catholics of a particular ethnic group or particular rite; and there are some parishes which do not have fixed boundaries but are made up of persons linked by common social bonds.[3]

Catholics have a right to look to their parishes to carry out Christ's mission by being centers of worship, preaching, witness, community, and service. At the same time, parishioners have reciprocal duties of involvement and support toward their parishes. Maturity of faith obviously rules out the neglect of one's duties as a parish member.

Every parish needs a coherent, well-integrated catechetical plan which provides opportunities for all parishioners to encounter the gospel message and respond by fostering community and giving service.

The parish and its catechetical program take into account that the whole Church is missionary and that evangelization is a basic duty of God's people.[4]

A single representative board, responsible for the total educational program, should be involved in catechetical planning in every parish. Different circumstances will require different organizational forms. The board can be a separate body, a committee of the parish council, or some other entity, elected or appointed. Its members should receive training and pastoral formation to help them share a vision of the Church's global mission, of the overall parish goals, and of catechetical priorities in the context of those goals.

As far as possible, parish catechetical programs are to be established, financed, staffed, and evaluated in light of the goal of meeting the needs of everyone in the parish. Particular concern will be directed to the handicapped, the neglected, those unable to speak up effectively on behalf of their own rights and interests, and minority cultural, racial, and ethnic groups.

Parish catechetical efforts should be related to the catechetical undertakings of neighboring parishes and other religious groups. They should take into account the schedules and programs of public and parochial schools. Interparochial cooperation is particularly necessary to make resources available to poor or otherwise disadvantaged communities.

Parish bulletins and other publications should be utilized in catechesis.

32,40,115,
117,170,13),
182-189,196,
201-202,
226-227

225. *Adults*

Through a parish catechetical board, a committee, or a chairperson of adult catechesis, the pastor should see to it that catechetical programs are available for adults as part of the total catechetical program.

The form adult catechesis takes will depend on a variety of factors: size and makeup of parish, community stability, cultural and educational background of parishioners, etc. There are a number of appropriate models: small group discussions, lectures with questions and discussion, retreat programs, sacramental programs, dialogues between adults and young people, adult catechumenate.

Parish planning groups should be creative in designing ways to reach and motivate adults to participate.

189

Priests should be mindful that the Sunday homily, based on the scriptures of the day, is a notable opportunity to nurture the faith of the adult community through the ministry of the word.

120,217

226. *Family ministry*

25,177-180

Family ministry involves announcing the good news to those within the immediate family circle first of all. However, family members should in turn be aware of the Christian family's authentic mission to evangelize the wider community. "In a family which is conscious of this mission, all the members evangelize and are evangelized. The parents not only communicate the Gospel to their children, but from their children they can themselves receive the same Gospel as deeply lived by them. And such a family becomes the evangelizer of many other families, and of the neighborhood of which it forms part."[5]

As the Church in miniature, the family is called to serve the needs of its own members, other persons and families, and the larger community. In it evangelization, worship, catechesis, and Christian service are vitally present.

Many parishes offer family-centered catechetical programs. These are intended to bring families together — to learn, experience, and celebrate some aspect of Catholic belief or living — and help them carry out their responsibilities in and to the Church's catechetical mission.

Some family programs center upon the liturgy, using themes of the liturgical year as the starting point. Participants separate according to age (preschool, primary, intermediate, junior and senior high school, and adult levels) to discuss the theme and then come back together for a common activity and celebration. Suggestions for home activities may also be given. Other programs, such as "family evenings," focus on the family in the home setting. Each family examines the designated theme in relation to its own circumstances, in order better to understand and carry out its mission in the world. Some family programs have a more elaborate design and aim at total catechesis.

144

While family-centered catechesis is to be encouraged, peer group catechetical experience should also be part of a total catechetical program.

Michal Heron

Within families there is need and opportunity for spouses to catechize each other and for parents to catechize children. There are several possibilities: e.g., parents can catechize their children directly, which is the ideal; they can participate in parish catechetical programs which serve their children; spouses can catechize each other by trustingly and openly sharing their insights concerning the gospel's relevance to their lives.

Since the Christian family is a "domestic Church," prayer and worship are central to it. Christian family life involves prayerful celebration within the family, as well as liturgical celebration in the parish community of which it is an integral, active part.

Another component of authentic family ministry and an important goal of family catechesis is the rendering of Christlike service. Sensitized to others' needs by the imperatives of Christian love and justice, the individual family seeks, according to its ability and opportunities, to minister to the spiritual, psychological, and physical needs of the whole human family.

Family ministry is a vital source of strength for the catechetical process in the home and in the parish.

More research is needed concerning the influence of the home on family members. This would help catechists and people engaged in family ministries to develop more effective forms of home- and family-oriented catechesis.

NC Photo by Robert S. Halvey

182-183,
201,243

227. Young adult ministry

This is a "catechetical moment of the gospel" with respect to young adults (18-35), for all practical purposes a newly identified population in U.S. society, many of whose members are engaged in an intense search for spirituality and values.

Church-sponsored young adult programs should respond to the expressed needs of participants while reflecting the four interrelated purposes of catechesis: to proclaim the mysteries of the faith; to foster community; to encourage worship and prayer; and to motivate service to others.

115,117

The gradual manner of God's self-revelation, manifested in scripture, provides a model for catechetical efforts directed to young adults, as does the catechesis recommended in the revised *Rite of Christian Initiation of Adults*. Program content includes psychological and sociological matters considered in the light of faith, questions of faith and moral issues, and similar matters pertaining to human experience.

Catechists not only instruct young adults but learn from them; they will be heard by young adults only if they listen to them. Young adult ministries must be developed and conducted in ways which emphasize self-direction, dialogue, and mutual responsibility. The Church should encourage young adults to minister to one another, to listen to God's word in community, and to serve other members of the faith community and the world community. It should offer leadership in developing new ministries, alternative community experiences, and instruments of effective catechesis, for this purpose using the talents of young adults who are willing to collaborate.

136,180-
181,200,
226

228. Youth ministry

a) Description of youth ministry

Youth catechesis is most effective within a total youth ministry. Such ministry requires the collaboration of many people with different kinds of expertise.

It is *to* youth that it seeks to respond to adolescents' unique needs. It is *with* youth in that it is shared. It is *by* youth in that they participate in directing it. It is *for* youth in that it attempts to interpret the concerns of youth and be an advocate for them.

Total ministry to youth includes catechetical activities in which the message is proclaimed, community is fostered, service is offered, and worship is celebrated. There is need for a variety of models integrating message, community, service, and worship and corresponding to the stages of development and levels of perception of the young. Guidance and healing, involvement of youth in ministry, and interpretation and advocacy of their legitimate interests and concerns also have catechetical dimensions.

The need for a variety of approaches should be taken into consideration in preparing social, recreational, and apostolic programs, as well as retreats and other spiritual development activities.

b) Parish catechetical programs for youth

Parish and community programs designed to meet the needs of Catholic students who do not attend Catholic high schools provide settings for formal catechesis for many Catholic young people in the United States. Participation in such programs is voluntary, and they are usually less structured than school programs and open to a number of alternative models.

Professional advice, local initiative, and consultation with young people themselves should all go into the planning of these programs. Local circumstances should determine such decisions as whether to make them parish- or home-centered, whether they should have a formal "classroom" or informal "group" format, whether they should be scheduled weekly over an extended period of time or concentrated in a shorter time span, or whether some particular mixture of formats and schedules should be employed.

200a)

Catechetical planners should know the number of young people of high school age in the community and how many are not being reached by the catechetical ministry of school or parish.

Adequate personnel, professional services, and budget are essential. Programs broad enough to appeal to all the young people of a community are usually most effective.

The study of scripture, the Church, the sacraments, and morality should be part of the overall program. In a comprehensive ministerial program such instruction will flow from and lead to service, liturgy, and community.

The community dimension will usually be expressed in a preference for small groups within which relationships can develop. Weekend prayer, "search," encounter, or retreat experiences provide liturgical experiences in a communal setting of acceptance and exchange.

Carl J. Pfeifer

Linda Bartlett

Service opportunities (e.g., visiting the aged or shut-ins, assisting catechists who teach handicapped children, working with community action programs) should also be part of programs for youth. They help develop lasting motivation for service to others.

Catechesis consistently speaks of the Church's missionary nature and the obligation of all its members to share in some way in its missionary activity. It discusses religious vocations (priesthood, diaconate, brotherhood, and sisterhood) and encourages students to be open to the call of the Holy Spirit. Lay ministries are also presented as a form of direct involvement in the mission of the Church. In particular, catechesis should remind parents of the need to extend a prudent but positive invitation to their children to consider a religious vocation as a way of living out their Christian commitment.

26-27,122, 126,135, 145,178- 179,181, 197-199, 226

229. *Catechetical programs for children*

While giving increased emphasis to adult catechesis, the faith community must also strive continually to provide parish programs of high quality for children.

Primary, intermediate, and junior high school catechesis are specialized fields requiring specialized training. They are grouped here to emphasize the need for sequence and coordination.

Though the influence of peers and of adult catechists is important, catechetical programs are not intended to supplant parents as the primary educators of their children. Parental involvement in catechetical programs is essential.

Adequately staffed and budgeted parish catechetical programs at every level should be provided for children who do not attend Catholic schools. The limited time available for these programs makes it absolutely necessary to set priorities and to give them active support.

47,73,176a), 181,12)

Curricula should be properly sequenced, presenting essential truths in a manner appropriate to the abilities of the age group. Whether a curriculum's content is sufficiently comprehensive is determined by judging the curriculum as a whole. As the ability to understand develops, more important truths should be reinforced and treated in greater depth. Religious learning should relate to the child's general experience of learning.

135,142

It is essential that a parish elementary catechetical program include opportunities for participants to experience community. Children grow in their understanding and appreciation of what a worshiping community is through participating in class or group prayer and in liturgies which have been carefully planned together by students and teachers.

The concept of service has limited application on the elementary level, especially in the early years. Parents play an important role in its development by sensitively prompting their children to perform acts of kindness and compassion in the home and neighborhood. Service-oriented class projects can be introduced in the intermediate grades. By junior high school, service projects similar to those mentioned above in the discussion of youth ministry are appropriate.

Catechesis introduces children to the idea that the Church's mission is the mission of Jesus and of the Holy Spirit. It describes this work of the Church and explains the notion of vocation.

26-27,145, 177,197,226

230. *Catechesis for preschool children*

Preschool programs should focus mainly on parents, providing them with opportunities to deepen their faith and become more adept at helping their children "form a foundation of that life of faith which will gradually develop and manifest itself."[6] However, programs for preschool children themselves are also desirable, in accordance with the guidance given in article 177.

231. *Special catechesis* 138,195

Catechetical programs for people with mental, emotional, or physical handicaps should be provided on the parochial, regional, or diocesan level. Each handicap requires its own approach, and separate programs are therefore required for each category of handicapped persons. Those involved in special catechetical programs should receive the training needed to perform their particular duties.

The parish community should be informed about the needs of its handicapped members and encouraged to support them with love and concern. The faith witness of handicapped persons can be a model and stimulus to growth in faith on the part of parishioners generally.

The families of the handicapped also need care and concern, including assistance directed to helping them participate with competence and confidence in the catechesis of their handicapped members.

232. *Catholic schools* 215,233

Catholic schools are unique expressions of the Church's effort to achieve the purposes of Catholic education among the young. They "are the most effective means available to the Church for the education of children and young people."[7]

Catholic schools may be part of the parish structure, interparochial or regional, diocesan or private. Growth in faith is central to their purpose.

As a community and an institution, the school necessarily has an independent life of its own. But a parochial school is also a community within the wider community, contributing to the parish upon which it depends and integrated into its life. Integration and interdependence are major matters of parish concern; each program in a total catechetical effort should complement the others.[8]

Similarly, regional, diocesan, and private schools should work in close collaboration with neighboring parishes. The experience of community in the schools can benefit and be benefited by the parishes.

Teachers in Catholic schools are expected to accept and live the Christian message and to strive to instill a Christian spirit in their students. As catechists, they will meet standards equivalent to those set for other disciplines and possess the qualities described in Chapter IX, Part A.

The school should have a set religion curriculum, with established goals and objectives, open to review and evaluation by parish boards and diocesan supervisory teams. It is recommended that an integrated curriculum provide options for catechists and students by offering electives along with the core curriculum.

It is desirable that Catholic high schools in a diocese work together to share resources, provide opportunities for teacher training and development, and cooperate in establishing program guidelines.

The school's principal and faculty are responsible for making clear the importance of religion. The quality of the catechetical experience in the school and the importance attached to religious instruction, including the amount of time spent on it, can influence students to perceive religion as either highly important or of little importance.

Its nature as a Christian educational community, the scope of its teaching, and the effort to integrate all learning with faith distinguish the Catholic school

Dave Vaughn

John Neubauer

from other forms of the Church's educational ministry to youth and give it special impact. In Catholic schools children and young people "can experience learning and living fully integrated in the light of faith,"[9] because such schools strive "to relate all human culture eventually to the news of salvation, so that the life of faith will illumine the knowledge which students gradually gain of the world, of life and of mankind."[10] Cooperative teaching which cuts across the lines of particular disciplines, interdisciplinary curricula, team teaching, and the like help to foster these goals of Catholic education.

136,142

"Building and living community must be prime, explicit goals of the contemporary Catholic school."[11] Principal and faculty members have a responsibility to help foster community among themselves and the students. Creative paraliturgies and sacramental celebrations for particular age groups can strengthen the faith community within the school.

Catholic school students should be introduced gradually to the idea and practice of Christian service. In early years, efforts to instill a sense of mission and concern for others help lay a foundation for later service projects, as does study of the lives of the saints and outstanding contemporaries.

Junior and senior high school programs should foster a social conscience sensitive to the needs of all. Familiarity with the Church's social encyclicals and its teaching on respect for human life will be part of this formation. (Cf. Chapter VII) Opportunities for field and community experiences are highly desirable. Teachers, administrators, parents, and students should be involved in planning service projects. One measure of a school's success is its ability to foster a sense of vocation, of eagerness to live out the basic baptismal commitment to service, whether this is done as a lay person, religious, deacon, or priest.

Michal Heron

Catechesis speaks of the missionary nature of the Church. It points out that all Christians are responsible for missionary activity by reason of the love of God, which prompts in them a desire to share with everyone the spiritual goods of this life and the life to come. Catholic schools provide opportunities for participation in missionary projects through the Holy Childhood Association, the Society for the Propagation of the Faith, etc. They also provide students with opportunities to search for the gifts that the Holy Spirit offers them for this ministry.

Through a carefully planned process, the entire school community — parents, students, faculty, administrators, pastors, and others — needs to be involved in the development of its goals, philosophy, and programs.

8,215,232

233. Catholic schools and the disadvantaged

The Second Vatican Council urged bishops and all Catholics to "spare no sacrifice" in helping Catholic schools to fulfill their functions more perfectly, and especially to care for "the needs of those who are poor in the goods of this world or who are deprived of the assistance and affection of a family or who are strangers to the gift of faith."[12]

In many places in the United States the Church has responded with an extremely large human and economic investment in schools whose pupils are for the most part disadvantaged children in the poverty areas of large cities. An increasing number of parents in poverty areas are making heroic personal sacrifices to send their children to Catholic schools, convinced that the education provided there affords a realistic and hopeful opportunity for breaking out of "the hellish cycle of poverty"[13] and moving into the social and economic mainstream. These schools serve a critical human and social need, while also providing a complete education which includes catechesis and guidance. In urban areas the Catholic school has a special role of giving witness and fostering evangelization.

234. Religion and public education

In a series of decisions concerning prayer and Bible reading during the 1960s, the United States Supreme Court in effect excluded specific efforts to inculcate religious values from the public schools.[14]

Efforts have been made to fill the vacuum created by these decisions by introducing into public schools courses and programs which in one way or another bear upon religion and values. The objective study of religion, whatever form it takes, seeks to convey information about religion or to foster appreciation of its nonreligious contributions, but not to advocate religious belief and values; while courses in sex education, psychology, and sociology, along with "sensitivity" and value clarification programs, deal directly with values.

Many believe it is not possible to produce neutral textbooks on religion and values, much less to teach in a truly neutral way about such matters. Some ask whether "neutrality" about religion and values is appropriate, even supposing it were possible. Many, particularly parents and Church leaders, believe so-called neutrality of this kind weakens young people's religious and moral beliefs and leads to relativism and indifference.

In order to remedy the situation, parents and community leaders, including representatives of churches and synagogues, should become involved in the planning, development, implementation, and evaluation of courses and programs dealing with religion and values. Issues of a highly controversial nature should be treated with extreme sensitivity. Teachers and administrators should be conscious of their responsibility to deal respectfully with pupils from diverse backgrounds and value systems, and should be adequately trained to do so. When young people or their parents object to a program on religious or moral grounds, the public schools should exempt such pupils from participation without embarrassing them.

Michal Heron

It is important that parish planners be aware of such courses and programs in public schools and be prepared to address the issues and questions they raise in parish catechetical programs.

235. Released time

The laws of some states provide for releasing students from public school during regular school hours so that they can attend catechetical programs off the school premises.[15]

Some states make an hour or more available each week for catechetical instruction. Others provide for "staggered" time, releasing students on an individual or group basis at different hours and days throughout the week. While a number of places have reported good success with these forms of released time, others have complained that scheduling and transportation present serious practical difficulties; they have also noted the bad effect of compartmentalizing religion and relegating catechesis to a small and inadequate portion of the child's or youth's total school time.

Linda Bartlett

More satisfactory results have been reported in a few places which make available a block of time for catechesis — several hours, a whole day, or even several consecutive days.

Good results have been achieved in both released time programs and after-school catechesis by catechetical centers established adjacent to public schools.

Released time programs are more effective when part of a broader parish catechetical program.

Dioceses and state Catholic conferences will find it helpful to appraise the local situation and seek viable released time programs, if these are desired. As this is an issue that interests many, a cooperative approach with other churches is advantageous.

Parishes, individually or collectively, should seek out viable alternatives to released time in cooperation with educational administrators in the public sector.

13,16,39, 47,51,72c), 137,139, 193-194, 242a)

236. *Ethnic parishes*

Revived interest in ethnicity, based on recognition of the major contribution made by ethnic groups to the nation's cultural richness, has stimulated interest in ethnic parishes. They provide significant liturgical and cultural experiences for many people. While "ethnic" forms of religious expression are to be encouraged, means should also be sought for sharing their values with the Church at large, including neighboring geographical parishes.

Representatives of national parishes and of cultural and ethnic groups should be the prime movers in planning and organizing catechetical programs for themselves.

237. *Military parishes*

The special needs of military personnel and their families must be recognized by both diocesan and military chaplaincy administrators. Military and diocesan parishes should cooperate. Diocesan catechetical offices should relate to and serve military parishes.

Because of the mobility and, at times, the isolation of military life, it is important to give priority to standard procedures for procuring catechetical materials, and to the development of parental and lay leadership. The need for professional catechists and coordinators, especially on large bases or posts, is as urgent as in any civilian parish.

Military parishes provide good opportunities for ecumenical efforts, since places of worship and educational facilities are frequently shared by all denominations.

PART C: THE DIOCESE

238. *Diocesan structures*

The chief elements of the diocesan administrative structure directly related to catechesis are as follows:

a) Diocesan pastoral council

In fulfilling his duties as pastor and chief teacher of the diocese, the bishop consults with the diocesan pastoral council where one exists.[16] Its consultative function extends to everything which is part of the bishop's pastoral responsibility.

The council assists in establishing a broad pastoral plan for the diocese. In relation to catechesis, it works with the bishop to identify the values, philosophy, needs, and goals of the Christian community, both in general and with specific reference to catechesis. It also consults with other diocesan bodies, such as the diocesan council of the laity, priests' senate, sisters' council, etc.

b) Diocesan catechetical/education board

The diocesan board has the responsibility of developing policy, thus giving

NC Photo by Robert Strawn

218a),221- 222

unified leadership to the various concerns reflected in the total catechetical ministry.

Its tasks are to identify, define, and set priorities among catechetical/educational objectives related to the goals specified by the pastoral council; to specify broad programs to achieve the goals; and to make decisions concerning implementation. Periodically the board should evaluate itself and its performance. A diocesan board is most effective when it is broadly representative of all the people of the diocese. In choosing members, cultural, racial, and ethnic groups, geographic regions, and the like should be considered. Its members should include people of faith active in catechesis and related educational and pastoral fields. When possible, it is advantageous for the membership to include specialists of various kinds, parents, youth, and public educators. The board should seek advice from other boards and similar bodies in the local Church and from individuals who can assist the catechetical ministry.

c) Diocesan catechetical office

The *General Catechetical Directory* refers to the "Catechetical Office" which is "part of the diocesan curia" and "the means which the bishop as head of the community and teacher of doctrine utilizes to direct and moderate all of the catechetical activities of the diocese."[17]

No single model can be recommended here for a diocesan administrative structure to direct catechetical activities. The size, needs, administrative style, and resources of a particular diocese affect this decision. However, a number of workable models or structures have been developed during the past decade.

NC Photo

In large dioceses with complex problems, a chief diocesan administrator of Catholic education, representing the bishop, is responsible for and coordinates the entire catechetical/educational mission through a Department of Education. All offices — which may include a School Office, Office of Religious Education (CCD), Adult Education Office, Campus and Young Adult Ministry Office, and Family Life Ministry Office — report directly to this chief administrator. Frequent collaboration among staff of the various offices fosters the coordination of catechetical efforts and facilitates interdisciplinary projects and programs.

In some dioceses, the Office of Religious Education is responsible for administering diocesan catechetical policy. Where this structure exists as the "catechetical office," personnel should be available to administer and service adult, youth, elementary, preschool, and special catechetical programs.

In other dioceses there is an Office for Christian Formation, with a vicar or secretary responsible for administering catechetical policy and coordinating the catechetical functions with other aspects of pastoral ministry: education, liturgy, ecumenism, etc.

Whatever its structure, the Diocesan Catechetical Office should have sufficient professional personnel to serve as resources to parishes, areas, or regions in relation to all aspects of catechesis. It should engage in regular collaboration and cooperation with other diocesan offices which have a catechetical dimension: i.e., offices for continuing education of the clergy, liturgy, ecumenism, communications, social justice, etc.

Manuel Gomez

PART D: PROVINCES, REGIONS, THE NATIONAL OFFICE

239. Regional and provincial cooperation

Regional and provincial cooperation is desirable to coordinate diocesan efforts, provide a common voice in consultation, and broaden the insights and experiences of all involved. Such cooperation should involve bishops, diocesan catechetical personnel, pastors, priests, deacons, religious, and laity, especially parents. Planned coordination promotes mutual assistance and the sharing of programs and personnel, and fosters people's growth in faith through action. Liaison should be established and maintained with state Catholic conferences, where they exist, and with ecumenical groups involved in catechetical or religious education work.

240. National catechetical office

The *General Catechetical Directory* states that a conference of bishops should have a permanent structure to promote catechetics on the national level.[18] The Department of Education of the United States Catholic Conference, through its religious education component, has the mission of carrying out the catechetical policies of the bishops of the United States.

Through its coordinator and specialists in catechetics, the department is to keep informed of catechetical developments, evaluate them, identify needs, specify directions for the future, and determine strategies of implementation. It is to disseminate information and provide consultation, especially with regional groupings, while undertaking only those activities that cannot be done, or done as well, at the local, diocesan, or regional levels. The department also is to collaborate with national professional associations.

It is desirable that the United States Catholic Conference include specialists from the Eastern Churches on the staff of its Department of Education or, at least, establish liaison with the corresponding entities of the Eastern Churches in order to insure catholicity in catechetical programs.

Before national policy decisions are made, the department is to consult with various advocacy groups and with the USCC Committee on Education, which is a representative group responsible for formulating and recommending policy. Policy itself is established by the USCC Administrative Board and the General Assembly of Bishops.

To the extent possible, the Department of Education is to maintain liaison and exchange information with the national catechetical offices of other countries.

NC Photo by Tom Salyer

PART E: HIGHER EDUCATION

241. Seminaries

Seminarians in college or the theologate need a clear understanding of the roles they will have in the catechetical programs of the parishes and institutions to which they will be assigned as priests.

"In addition to having an accurate knowledge of Sacred Scripture and systematic theology, the seminarian should learn those special skills of pedagogy needed to communicate the Gospel message in a clear, precise and well-organized way."[19] It is also necessary that seminarians come to understand the process of human growth and development so that they can give catechesis adapted to the age and ability of those being catechized. They should have an opportunity to acquire the skills necessary to organize and direct a catechetical program on the parish level.

The catechetical preparation of seminarians should be carried on in collaboration with the personnel of the diocesan catechetical office. Training includes in-service experiences, catechetical workshops, and congresses.

Seminaries serve the local Church by making their faculties and facilities as available as far as possible to the diocese and the community-at-large.

a) Graduate programs in religious studies

Graduate departments of religious education offer a variety of programs for people preparing for professional careers in catechetical ministry. Such programs establish academic qualifications for professional leadership, serve as centers for research and development, and convene appropriate seminars. They should be interdisciplinary, offering advanced courses in theology, scripture, liturgy, catechetics, communications, parish administration, and related sacred and human sciences.

Graduate schools of religious studies, through their own national organizations and in cooperation with the USCC Department of Education, are invited to establish uniform standards for candidates for advanced degrees in catechetics.

Graduate programs should make special provisions to meet the needs of cultural, racial, and ethnic groups or individuals with special catechetical requirements: for example, through research, placement of student catechists, and pilot programs directed to such groups.

Graduate schools are encouraged to offer courses and programs in the theologies, liturgies, and forms of spirituality of the Eastern Churches. In doing so, they will be taking advantage of and helping to make more widely known an often neglected source of enrichment for the Church.

Within their financial means, graduate schools can meet a great need by providing scholarships to poor but talented persons, representatives of minority groups, and those who wish to dedicate themselves to some aspect of special education but are unable to pay for their training.

Graduate departments should seek to know and collaborate with local pastoral personnel. Whenever possible, they should cooperate with diocesan catechetical offices in arranging field experiences for their students in local pastoral settings (parishes, schools, institutions, etc.). Catechetical offices and graduate schools can also serve the Church by cooperating in other training efforts related to adult catechesis.

Rick Smolan

b) Undergraduate programs

Catholic colleges are encouraged to offer undergraduate degree programs in catechetics and theology, both for those who wish to pursue graduate studies and become full-time catechetical workers and for those who may assume other leadership roles in the Church. The requirements for such degrees should be as demanding as those for any other academic discipline.

It is important that Catholic institutions of higher learning maintain strong programs in theology and religious studies. Besides being centers of authentic Catholic theology, they should, as far as possible, offer courses in other theologies to meet the needs of an ecumenical age.

The cooperation of Catholic colleges with diocesan catechetical offices, neighboring parishes, and other institutions which require the services of catechists is highly desirable. The college faculty should be available to help ascertain local pastoral needs and provide supervised in-service training in catechetics or theology programs.

NC Photo

243. Campus ministry

182, 201, 227

Campus ministry is the Church's presence on the college and university campus. It views the milieu of post-secondary education as a creative center of society, where ideas germinate and are tested, leadership is formed, and the future of society is often determined.

Campus ministry involves pastoral service to the entire campus community: students, administrators, faculty, and staff. In every institution, regardless of size and character, campus ministry confronts a range of concerns which reflect in microcosm the catechetical concerns facing the entire Church.

Especially on the nonsectarian, non-Catholic campus, today's student often receives uncritical exposure to modern ideologies and philosophies, to crucial questions concerning faith, ethical behavior, and human life, and to a multiplicity of cults and new religious movements. Campus ministry must create, in an atmosphere of freedom and reverence, an alternative forum for theological and philosophical inquiry. This includes classes on Catholic thought, scripture seminars, opportunities for different forms of prayer, workshops or lectures in social justice, and opportunities to share on various levels with other recognized religious groups. Formal and informal counseling relating to spiritual, social, and psychological concerns should also be offered to help people integrate the gospel into their lives.

Pastoral service on the campus is to emphasize worship, community, and tradition through the development of a community of faith. It should offer enriching exposure to modern and traditional liturgical forms, not only in the liturgy itself but through paraliturgical services emphasizing the communal aspects of sacramental life.

Finally, campus ministry should seek to serve the university institution itself. It should work for responsible governance on the part of the academic institution and for the maintenance of high standards and values. Campus ministers must be concerned with the institution's programs, policies, and research, and with how these promote or hinder human development. This affords them opportunities to deepen understanding of social justice and be of service to the broader community.

Since these various modes of service are expanding and becoming more complex, campus ministry must have adequate personnel. Today's ministry staff is, typically, composed not only of priests, but increasingly of religious and lay persons, faculty, and graduate students, each with special areas of concern and often working as a team to develop a community of faith. As part of the diocese's mission and responsibility, campus ministry should be carried on in cooperation with local parish communities.

PART F: OTHER CATECHETICAL SETTINGS

244. Residential facilities

Catechesis takes place in a variety of comprehensive but specialized settings, such as convalescent or nursing homes, child-care institutions, residential facilities for the mentally handicapped, and schools for the deaf. People in such facilities have a right to live as normally as possible.

Chaplains in such facilities should be trained for their specific tasks, including catechetical approaches suited to particular groups.

Professional or nonprofessional catechists with appropriate experience work with chaplains by visiting the residents regularly and catechizing, either formally or informally.

Parish, diocesan, and other Church structures and agencies must take the needs of persons in residential facilities into consideration in their planning. As far as possible, they should be incorporated into the life of the parish community, with steps taken to accommodate their special needs.

245. Specialized groupings

A number of movements in the United States bring together men and

Michal Heron

women who are seeking to deepen their faith. Groups which join for prayer, worship, and the sharing of insights provide catechetical settings. Their members should be encouraged to participate actively in their parishes. Priests, religious, and lay people need to become involved with such groups, and diocesan and parish catechetical offices should assist them as much as possible.

246. Chaplaincies

Hospitals, professional groups, police and fire departments, fraternities, prisons, and juvenile homes provide settings for adult catechesis and reflection. Chaplains to such groups and institutions should take advantage of these opportunities. Diocesan and parish catechetical personnel should assist the chaplains as much as possible, particularly by offering standards for catechesis in these settings.

247. Other ministerial training centers

Ministerial training centers, such as formation centers for religious men and women or lay people, should provide quality programs in catechesis, appropriate to the particular ministry for which the students are preparing.

Catechesis encourages the development of new ministries in and for the life of the Church. The concept of the priesthood of the laity calls for the development of new ministries to supplement the pastoral office in the Church. This would include ministries in the liturgical, catechetical, teaching, service, and administrative fields.

248. Conclusion

At all levels high priority must be given to providing structures within and through which the total catechesis of God's people can be accomplished. In providing such structures, national, regional, diocesan, and parish planning groups should apply the principles set forth in this chapter. Next we turn to the resources which catechists have available for their work.

Thomas C. Krieger

Rich Smolan

PILGRIM PASTOR
The Story of Paul VI

Chapter XI

Catechetical Resources

Men do not light a lamp
and then put it
under a bushel basket.
They set it on a stand
where it gives light
to all in the house.

Mt 5,15

249. Introduction

The quality of catechists is more important than the quality of their tools. But good tools in the hands of skilled catechists can do much to foster growth in faith. Catechetical "tools" are many and varied. They include human and organizational resources, the communications media, textbooks, and audio-visual materials.

PART A: RESOURCES IN GENERAL

250. Organizational resources

There are many organizational resources which provide catechetical information and services. A partial list includes the committees and offices of the National Conference of Catholic Bishops, the United States Catholic Conference, and related bodies (e.g., the NCCB Committee for Pro-Life Activities, the Campaign for Human Development, etc.); the National Conference of Diocesan Directors of Religious Education-CCD (NCDD); the National Catholic Educational Association (NCEA); other national Catholic organizations; colleges and universities, catechetical institutes and schools; publishers; diocesan offices; professional organizations associated with other churches; the educational components of local, state, and federal agencies; libraries and data banks; religious orders; and retreat houses. Catechetical agencies are encouraged to compile and maintain inventories of such resources, lest valuable sources of assistance be overlooked.

251. Historical use of communications media in catechesis

146

The collaboration of catechesis and the arts and media deserves close attention and encouragement. From the very beginning, the Church has used the arts to communicate Christ's message and fix it in people's minds and hearts. Biblical stories, saints' lives, and religious themes of all sorts have been depicted in stained glass, mosaics, painting, and sculpture. Music, poetry, dance, drama, architecture, and other art forms have also served catechetical purposes. Contemporary media such as television, films, photography, filmstrips, slides, and tapes do so today.

22

252. Impact of communications media in catechesis

The communications revolution has had a profound impact on our world, with implications as great for religion as for any other area of life. Contemporary media offer marvelous new opportunities for catechesis, but they also present serious challenges and problems. They can unite people, foster the sharing of ideas, promote mutual help, justice, and peace, and carry the gospel to those who otherwise might never hear it.

There are at least three different ways of thinking of the communications media in relation to catechesis: as shapers of the environment in which it takes place; as useful catechetical tools; and as appropriate subject matter. Not all catechists can or need be media specialists, but all should have some understanding of the implications of media for their work. The media are relevant to every level of catechesis; they help foster human development and are capable of contributing to growth in theological understanding and to faith experience itself.

Although media are instruments for transmitting messages, they also possess inherent capabilities and potentialities.[1] Every medium has its own integrity and special genius requiring specific skills of interpretation on the part of

Lou Niznik

both communicators and audiences. There is an intrinsic connection between medium and message, between the "how" and "what" of communication. In using and evaluating media, catechists should be aware that a concept concretized in a medium is no longer simply an abstract idea but an event. Communication is not just the delivering of messages but an experience of sharing among human beings.

PART B: RADIO AND TELEVISION

253. *Instruments of catechesis*

Broadcast media present special opportunities and challenges to the creativity of catechists. Radio and television can be direct instruments of catechesis. Catechists who plan to use them for this purpose should either acquire specialized media training or collaborate with others experienced in broadcast production. It may be appropriate for them to seek positions as consultants or advisors to producers of programs dealing with religious matters within their competence.

Lou Niznik

254. *Accountability of broadcast media*

The broadcast media should be encouraged and supported when they promote human values and called to task when they air unworthy, degrading presentations. This points to the need to make people familiar with the criteria and procedures which local television and radio stations are legally required to observe in order to obtain and keep their operating licenses. Individuals should be made aware that they have a right and duty to state their views to broadcasters.

Rick Smolan

255. *Audience*

Knowledge of the audience is as important to successful broadcast production as familiarity with media technology. Producers must understand people's attitudes and values. Religious and catechetical programming should be professionally excellent and responsive to the interests and needs of viewers and listeners.

Broadcast media can be particularly helpful in meeting special catechetical needs and problems. They can, for instance, be the most effective means of communicating with people in isolated and rural areas, as well as with such groups as the aged and shut-ins. Radio and television also offer opportunities for ecumenical collaboration and so, potentially, for reaching larger audiences.

256. *Air time*

As a condition of licensing, local radio and television stations are required to make public service time available free of charge to eligible groups. Catechists, generally in cooperation with diocesan communications offices, should investigate the possibility of applying for this air time to present programs. They should realize, though, that public service time is generally not available at peak viewing and listening hours. Free air time is also offered (often at better hours) for TV and radio spot announcements; and many excellent spots of a religious or value-oriented nature are available from Catholic and other religious producers. Though cost and other factors may generally rule out the purchase of air time, the possibility is worth investigating in particular situations.

257. *Collaboration in use of resources*

More pooling of local, diocesan, and national talent and funds is essential to upgrade the amount and quality of religious and catechetical programming. The Catholic Television Network (CTN), an organization formed by the U.S. dioceses with their own instructional television capabilities, is one such effort. The Office of Film and Broadcasting and the Office of Promotion and Training in the United States Catholic Conference's Department of Communication are also sources of information about the electronic media and of material of possible use to catechists.

258. *Ongoing technological developments*

People concerned with the religious and catechetical potential of media need to be alert to significant changes in technology, organizational structure, and policy now occurring or anticipated in the broadcasting industry. Cable television, for example, may bring about major changes in the foreseeable future, including a great increase in the number and variety of programs. Catechists and Church-related communicators at the diocesan and national levels should be informed participants in these developments. It is important that the Church have an active role in the planning and licensing process which precedes the inauguration of cable TV in a community, besides monitoring and taking early advantage of other media developments as they occur.

185b)

PART C: THE PRESS

259. *Catholic press*

Rick Smolan

Despite the emergence of electronic data, print media of many different kinds continue to reach daily into virtually every home and place of work in the country.

The Catholic press has long been central to the Church's communication effort in the United States. It is the least expensive way of regularly bringing comprehensive religious news and instructional features to a large number of Catholics. It helps foster the sense of Christian community among its readers. It serves as a forum, providing the people of the Church with opportunities for discussion and the exchange of ideas.

Catholic newspapers, magazines, books, pamphlets, and parish bulletins can be useful catechetical tools, especially in adult programs. Editors and publishers should provide appealing publications which help contemporary Catholics evaluate their experience in the light of Christian values, foster their growth in faith, and promote community among them. Minority cultural, racial, and ethnic groups should have access to and make use of Catholic publications which are in their languages and reflect their special cultural values and concerns.

Lou Niznik

There is need for continuing dialogue and cooperation between catechetical leaders and the editors and publishers of Catholic publications at the diocesan and national levels. The aim is to exchange ideas and information about catechetical needs and about the effective use of the Catholic press for catechetical purposes. Catechists and catechetical offices at all levels should provide the Catholic press with news releases and photographs which reflect newsworthy aspects of catechesis — trends, programs, meetings, personalities. They should also offer suggestions for interpretive features and columns of a catechetical nature, and should be prepared to supply these when asked. As opportunities arise, they should collaborate with the Catholic press as planners, consultants, and writers.

260. Secular press

The secular press also offers opportunities to catechists, although it would generally be unrealistic to consider it a vehicle for direct catechesis.

Either through a diocesan (or other) communications office or directly, catechists should provide secular publications with accurate and interesting information on catechetical matters. Typically, this is done by news releases. Catechesis ought to be prepared to respond to press inquiries and to spend time when necessary discussing questions and issues with journalists. Secular publications are usually willing to entertain suggestions for articles and features on catechetical topics, provided these are of general interest. Community-oriented newspapers, many of them published weekly or biweekly, offer perhaps the best opportunities; but there may also be occasional opportunities in large daily newspapers and even national publications. Particularly when approaching the secular press on the latter levels, catechists are advised to work with diocesan or national communications offices.

PART D: MEDIA LITERACY

261. Training media producers

All who use the communications media in their work "have a duty in conscience to make themselves competent in the art of social communication,"[2] and this applies in particular to people with educational responsibilities, including catechists. Theory, technique, and research are part of media training. In line with what has been said above, catechists should learn how to take media into account as a crucial part of the cultural background and experience of those being catechized; how to use media in catechesis; and how to help their students understand and evaluate media in the light of religious values.

Lou Niznik

22

22,170,15),
178,253-258

262. Training media users

Catechetical instruction concerning media should help people become knowledgeable viewers, listeners, and readers. Such training is necessary for them "to benefit to the full from what the instruments of social communications have to offer."[3] It is also required if they are to seek to improve the quality of media, either by advocacy directed at professional communicators, or by pursuing careers in media.

Because television occupies so much of the time of so many people in the United States, catechesis should seek to foster critical understanding of this medium in particular. Viewers need to know, for example, how programs are planned and produced; techniques used by advertisers and others to influence and persuade; whether and to what degree TV gives a true picture of life or distorts reality; and the role of profit motives in determining policy in commercial television.

Because people grow in maturity and because there are frequent changes in the media, continuing education is necessary to keep abreast of the changes.

Lou Niznik

PART E: OTHER CATECHETICAL MATERIALS

263. Introduction

Designers of catechetical curricula should take written materials and materials in other media into consideration as elements in a total plan. The classroom learning situation itself is only one element in total catechesis.

Section I: Textbooks

264. Textbooks

Textbooks are guides for learning, summary statements of course content, and ready instruments of review. They must present the authentic and complete message of Christ and His Church, adapted to the capacity of the learners, with balanced emphasis proportionate to the importance of particular truths. Modern texts do more than present information. Their graphics, for example, can foster learning and stimulate — or discourage — interest. The graphics in catechetical texts must be in the best tradition of Christian art, chosen with sensitivity to the age, psychological development, intellectual capacity, and background of learners.

Teachers' manuals are essential components of any textbook series. They should contain "an explanation of the message of salvation (constant references must be made to the sources, and a clear distinction must be kept between those things which pertain to faith and to the doctrine that must be held, and those things which are mere opinions of theologians); psychological and pedagogical advice; suggestions about methods."[4] Manuals or developed notes for parents should accompany any materials designed for children. Wherever possible, special manuals for use in catechesis of the handicapped should be developed, by professionals in special education.

Textbooks must avoid racism, sexism, and narrow provincialism of all kinds, and must take special care to represent other religious traditions fairly. They should provide for variety in worship and service. In catechizing older children, youth, and adults, the Bible should be used as a text for study along with other textbooks.

The various regional, cultural, economic, and religious characteristics in the United States are to be taken into account in the preparation and evaluation of textbooks and other materials. Some of these are identified in Chapter I and Chapter VIII, Part D.

Section II: Other Instructional Materials

265. Other instructional materials

a) Correspondence courses

Correspondence courses, using print or electronic media, can be helpful in supplementing catechetical programs for everyone. They are of particular importance in the catechesis of families and individuals in isolated areas, the sick, the elderly, people with irregular working hours, those who wish to study the faith privately, and any others who find it difficult to participate in organized catechetical programs. In special circumstances, correspondence courses can be used for training teachers, helping parents in the catechesis of their children, etc.

b) Other media

Today most people, especially the young, are accustomed and even expect to experience much of their learning through sophisticated media presentations. The Church needs to make creative use of these tools in communicating with them.

Instructional media are of many kinds, both print and nonprint, and include activities such as arts, crafts, dramatics, mime, dance, role playing, simulation or instructional games, music, storytelling, visuals such as posters and charts, videotapes, films, filmstrips, slides, cassette tapes, and overhead transparencies. All instructional materials used in catechesis should be artistically sensi-

146

*16,41,47,
59,60c),
69,93,
104,190,
208*

USCC Creative Services

tive and technically competent. They should also be theologically accurate and should reflect the insights derived from good catechetical research.

It is essential that all catechists be trained in the use of media. Training will cover such things as the language of film and television and the characteristics of different media,[5] and will include opportunities to learn how to operate audio-visual equipment.

Media centers, established on a diocesan or regional basis, can provide consulting services for catechists in the use of media. Typically, these centers will include libraries of media materials available free or on a rental basis, provide in-service training programs, and offer production facilities to supplement those available from commercial sources. In some areas bookmobiles can provide an extension of the services of the media center.

Section III: Preparation and Evaluation of Catechetical Materials

266. Preparation and evaluation

222b)

All catechetical textbooks and other materials are to be prepared according to the criteria and guidelines contained in this NCD. It is also fully expected that all such texts and materials will be evaluated by those responsible for catechesis in light of these criteria and guidelines. The appropriate offices of the United States Catholic Conference will assist publishers, producers, and others in this regard.

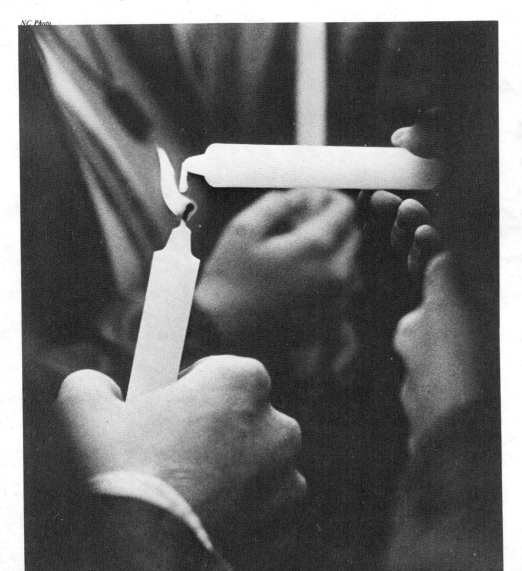

NC Photo

John Willig

159

Conclusion

Effective catechesis is always a gift of God. "I planted the seed and Apollos watered it, but God made it grow." (1 Cor 3,6) It is important, therefore, to pray for this gift. Catechesis goes forward in the light of the risen Christ, energized by the love of the Holy Spirit, drawing creativity from the power of the Father.

Yet effective catechesis also depends a great deal on human effort: on planning, performance, and evaluation, on personal qualities and commitment. Especially does it depend upon the faith, hope, and love of catechists, responding to God's grace by growing in these virtues and ministering to others. The person of the catechist is the medium in which the message of the faith is incarnated. Whether catechists be parents, teachers, religious, priests, bishops, or any other of God's people, their witness to faith plays a pivotal role in catechesis.

St. Frances Xavier Cabrini, St. Elizabeth Ann Seton, and St. John Neumann are luminous figures in the history of the Catholic Church in the United States who exercised fruitful ministries because they were heroic in their goodness. Their example should be imitated and their intercession sought by those striving, like them, to share with others the light of faith and the love of Christ.

Finally, therefore, the guidelines in this NCD are meant not simply to provide a framework for programs and activities, but to foster hope and confidence in the work of catechesis. Writing under the sign of the rainbow and in the spirit of the brightening dawn of Easter, we seek to lead people, and to be led, ever more fully into the light.

The night shall be no more.
They will need no light from lamps
or the sun,
for the Lord God shall give them light,
and they shall reign forever.
Rv 22, 5

Appendices

APPENDIX A

100, 105, 154

The Ten Commandments of God are of special importance in teaching specifics of morality. The Old Testament, the New Testament, and the long tradition of the Church testify to this. A summary presentation of the Ten Commandments of God taken from the New American Bible translation[1] is:

1. I, the Lord, am your God. You shall not have other gods besides me.

2. You shall not take the name of the Lord, your God, in vain.

3. Remember to keep holy the sabbath day.

4. Honor your father and your mother.

5. You shall not kill.

6. You shall not commit adultery.

7. You shall not steal.

8. You shall not bear false witness against your neighbor.

9. You shall not covet your neighbor's wife.

10. You shall not covet anything that belongs to your neighbor.

APPENDIX B

From time to time the Church has listed certain specific duties of Catholics.[1] Among those expected of Catholic Christians today are the following:

1. To keep holy the day of the Lord's resurrection; to worship God by participating in Mass every Sunday and holy day of obligation; to avoid those activities that would hinder renewal of soul and body on the sabbath (e.g., needless work and business activities, unnecessary shopping, etc.).

2. To lead a sacramental life; to receive Holy Communion frequently and the Sacrament of Reconciliation regularly — minimally, to receive the Sacrament of Reconciliation at least once a year (annual confession is obligatory only if serious sin is involved); minimally also, to receive Holy Communion at least once a year, between the First Sunday of Lent and Trinity Sunday.

3. To study Catholic teaching in preparation for the Sacrament of Confirmation, to be confirmed, and then to continue to study and advance the cause of Christ.

4. To observe the marriage laws of the Church; to give religious training, by example and word, to one's children; to use parish schools and catechetical programs.

5. To strengthen and support the Church — one's own parish community and parish priests, the worldwide Church and the pope.

6. To do penance, including abstaining from meat and fasting from food on the appointed days.

7. To join in the missionary spirit and apostolate of the Church.

Notes

Preface

1. Cf. Bishops, 14. Chapter II discusses catechetics.
2. *Ibid.*, 44.
3. Cf. *Paths of the Church* (Paul VI, 1964), 113-114, 78-112; cf. also Ecumenism and Non-Christian Religions of the Second Vatican Council.
4. Cf. GCD, 134.
5. Cf. *Ibid.*, Foreword.
6. Such small communities exist more or less everywhere throughout the Church. They often spring from a desire to live the Church's life more intensely, or from the desire and search for religious experience on a more "human" scale than some feel large ecclesial communities can easily offer. Cf. *On Evangelization* (Paul VI, 1975), 58.
7. *Paths of the Church* (Paul VI, 1964), 117.

Chapter I

1. In 1973-74, 15% of Catholics in the United States had been born outside the United States; 39% had fathers born outside the United States; 36% had mothers who were not native-born; 55% had all grandparents born abroad. Only 20% had all grandparents born in this country. Cf. *Catholic Schools in a Declining Church* (1976), p. 40.
2. Cf. "Evangelizing the 80,000,000 Unchurched Americans," George Gallup Jr., report given at the Marriottsville Spiritual Center, Marriottsville, Md., November 12, 1975, p. 2.
3. This section reflects the text of *The Theological Formation of Future Priests*. Sacred Congregation for Catholic Education, February 22, 1976. United States Catholic Conference, 1976, 64-68. Cf. also Ecumenism, 4.
4. Cf. *On Evangelization* (Paul VI, 1975), 65.
5. Modern World, 82.
6. There are 276 such metropolitan areas in the United States. They are found in every state except Vermont and Wyoming.
7. Cf. Gallup, *op. cit.*, pp. 2-3.

8. Cf. *Catholic Schools in a Declining Church* (1976), pp. 32, 35-36. Similar results have been obtained in other surveys.
9. Cf. *Ibid.*, pp. 29-30.
10. Cf. *Ibid.*, p. 32.
11. Cf. *Ibid.*, pp. 145-146.
12. Cf. *Religion in America*, 1976. The Gallup Poll Opinion Index, Report 130, p. 14.
13. In this connection, the words of Pope Paul VI need to be kept in mind: "While being clothed with the outward forms proper to each people, and made explicit by theological expression which takes account of different cultural, social and even racial milieux, it must remain the content of the Catholic faith just exactly as the ecclesial magisterium has received it and transmits it." *On Evangelization* (Paul VI, 1975), 65.
14. The principal goal of adult catechesis is growth in the faith of the adult.

Chapter II

1. Cf. GCD, 17.
2. Cf. Lk 1,2; Acts 6,4; Rom 12,7; Eph 4,11f.
3. Cf. Rom 15,16; Heb 8,1f.6; 1 Pt 2,5.9.
4. Cf. Mt 25,33-40; Rom 12,6ff; 2 Cor 9,12f; 1 Pt 4,10f.
5. Bishops, 14.
6. Cf. GCD, 20.
7. *Ibid.*, 29.
8. *Ibid.*, 22.
9. Cf. *Ibid.*, 23.
10. *Ibid.*, 24; Eph 1,9f.
11. Cf. GCD, 25.
12. *Ibid.*, 26; cf. Modern World, 62.
13. Cf. GCD, 28; Church, 1.
14. GCD, 30.
15. *Ibid.*, 17.
16. *On Evangelization* (Paul VI, 1975), 18.
17. *Ibid.*; cf. Rom 12,2.
18. GCD, 22.
19. *Ibid.*, 25.
20. Cf. *Ibid.*, 31.
21. Cf. *Ibid.*, 20.
22. Cf. TJD, 43.
23. Cf. GCD, 45.
24. *Ibid.*

25. *Ibid.*, 11.
26. Liturgy, 8.
27. GCD, 13; Revelation, 8.
28. "A Message to the People of God," Fourth General Assembly of the Synod of Bishops, October 29, 1977, 8.
29. Cf. Modern World, 4.
30. Cf. GCD, 26; cf. Modern World, 62.
31. Cf. GCD, 97.
32. Cf. *Ibid.*, 37-44.
33. "A Message to the People of God," October 29, 1977, *op. cit.*, 7.
34. GCD, 43.
35. Cf. *Ibid.*
36. *Ibid.*, 44.
37. *Ibid.*, 38.

Chapter III

1. Revelation, 3.
2. Cf. *Ibid.*
3. God's self-manifestation through creation is often referred to as natural revelation.
4. Non-Christian Religions, 2.
5. Cf. *Ibid.*; Modern World, 58.
6. St. Ephrem, *Nisibene Hymns*, 3,3; 48,7, etc.
7. Revelation, 4.
8. *Ibid.*, 8.
9. Church, 25.
10. General audience, January 19, 1972. Cf. Denzinger-Schönmetzer, 3421.
11. Cf. *Ibid.*; GCD 11, 13, 26, 44.
12. GCD, 36.
13. *Ibid.*
14. Revelation, 5; Second Council of Orange, Denzinger-Schönmetzer, 377; First Vatican Council, Denzinger-Schönmetzer, 3010.
15. Religious Liberty, 10.
16. Revelation, 10.
17. *Ibid.*, 9.
18. *Ibid.*, 8.
19. Cf. *Declaration in Defense of the Catholic Doctrine on the Church Against Certain Errors of the Present Day.* Sacred Congregation for the Doctrine of the Faith, June 24, 1973. No. 5.
20. *Ibid.*
21. St. Jerome, *Commentary on Isaiah, Prol.*, quoted in Revelation, 25.
22. The sign that a Bible has been approved for Catholic use is the "imprimatur" or preliminary statement that the translation has been checked for accuracy and authorized by a Catholic bishop.
23. Revelation, 12.
24. "Instruction on the Historical Truth of the Gospels." Pontifical Biblical Commission, 1964. In *Catholic Biblical Quarterly*, Vol. 26, July 1964, pp. 299-304.
25. GCD, 44.
26. An example of doctrinal development is noted in Religious Freedom, 1: "In taking up the matter of religious freedom this sacred Synod intends to develop the doctrine of recent Popes on the inviolable rights of the human person and on the constitutional order of society."
27. "Judgment as to their [charisms'] genuineness and proper use belongs to those who preside over the Church, and to whose special competence it belongs, not indeed to extinguish the Spirit, but to test all things and hold fast to that which is good." (Cf. 1 Th 5,12.19ff); Church, 12.

Chapter IV

1. *The Documents of Vatican II*, Abbott and Gallagher, p. 14, from Pope Paul VI's opening allocution at the second session (September 19, 1963).
2. For example, Rom 12,5; 1 Cor 12,13; 1 Cor 12,27; Eph 4,4; Col 1,18.
3. Church, 8.
4. Cf. Eastern Churches, 9.
5. Cf. Church, 22.
6. Missionary Activity, 2.
7. Church, 23.
8. *Ibid.*, 24.
9. Eastern Churches, 2.
10. Cf. *Ibid.*, 5.
11. Ecumenism, 15.
12. *Ibid.*, 17.
13. Cf. *Ibid.*, 19.
14. In addition to Ecumenism, cf. *Directory Concerning Ecumenical Matters: Part One*, May 14, 1967, and *Part Two: Ecumenism in Higher Education*, April 16, 1970. Secretariat for Promoting Christian Unity.
15. Cf. Ecumenism, 14-18.
16. Non-Christian Religions, 4.
17. In addition to Non-Christian Religions, 4, cf. *Guidelines on Religious Relations with the Jews* (N. 4), December 1, 1974, Commission for Religious Relations with the Jews; and *Statement on Catholic-Jewish Relations on the Occasion of the Celebration of the Tenth*

Anniversary of Nostra Aetate (N. 4), November 20, 1975, National Conference of Catholic Bishops. Additional information may be obtained from the Secretariat for Catholic-Jewish Relations, National Conference of Catholic Bishops, 1312 Massachusetts Avenue, N.W., Washington, D.C. 20005.

18. Cf. Non-Christian Religions, 3.
19. Cf. *Ibid.*, 2.
20. Cf. *Ibid.*, 5; Modern World, 21.

Chapter V

1. This text is based on *Basic Teachings for Catholic Religious Education*, a document approved by the bishops of the United States in November 1972, and subsequently reviewed and approved by the Holy See. *Basic Teachings* was largely inspired by the *General Catechetical Directory*, articles 47-69. It has been modified to take into account some major documents published since 1972. Articles 14 through 19, on morality, have been revised, largely in the light of two documents: *To Live in Christ Jesus*, a collective pastoral approved by the bishops of the United States in November 1976; and *Declaration on Certain Questions Concerning Sexual Ethics*, issued by the Sacred Congregation for the Doctrine of the Faith in December 1975. The discussion of the sacraments has been placed in Parts A and B of Chapter VI, "Catechesis for a Worshiping Community," and articles 11-13 have been replaced with materials from the revised instructions and rituals.

  Also, of the topics discussed in the Introduction to BT, the importance of prayer is treated in Part C of Chapter VI, participation in the liturgy is dealt with throughout that chapter; familiarity with the Bible appears in several articles: 43, 52-53, 60a)i, 143, 179, 185, 190, 207, 223. Knowing and observing the Ten Commandments, the Beatitudes and the Precepts of the Church are mentioned in articles 100, 105, 154. The Ten Commandments and the precepts are in the Appendices.

2. Cf. Divine Revelation, 3; GCD, 51.
3. Cf. Encyclical Letter, *Humani Generis* (1950), Pope Pius XII, A.A.S., (Vol. 42, pp. 575-576); cf. Modern World, 12, 14.
4. Cf. Rom 20; Acts 15, 17; Ps 19,1; Wis 13,1-9.
5. Cf. Dogmatic Constitution *Dei Filius* of the First Vatican Council.
6. Cf. Modern World, 21.
7. Cf. *Ibid.*, 22.
8. Cf. Jn 7,39; Acts 2,33; Rom 4,25; 8,11;1 Cor 15,45; Heb 5,6.
9. Cf. Words of institution, eucharistic prayers.
10. Cf. Lv 19,18; Mt 5,44-48; 22,37-40; Lk 10,25-28.
11. Missionary Activity, 4.
12. Cf. Church, 12.
13. Cf. Missionary Activity, 1-2.
14. Cf. Church, 10.
15. *Ibid*.
16. Church, 29.
17. Bishops, 16.
18. Cf. Church, 25. "Magisterium" is the teaching of the bishops, successors of the apostles, in union with and never apart from the teaching of the successor of St. Peter, the pope, as well as the official teaching of the pope alone.
19. *Ibid*.
20. *Ibid*.
21. *Ibid.*, 12.
22. Cf. *Ibid.*, 32.
23. Cf. Ecumenism, 4-5.
24. Cf. Church 8, 14-16; cf. Religious Freedom, 1; cf. entire Ecumenism; cf. GCD, 27.
25. Cf. Church, 9; Missionary Activity in its entirety.
26. Modern World, 93.
27. *Ibid.*, 3.
28. Decree on the Sacraments of the Council of Trent, Denzinger-Schönmetzer, 1601, 1606.
29. Cf. Church, 1.
30. Cf. Sacred Liturgy, 59.
31. Cf. Modern World, 13.
32. *Credo of the People of God*, Pope Paul VI, June 30, 1968. United States Catholic Conference, p. 6.
33. The Holy See has rejected the opinion that mortal sin exists only "in the formal refusal directly opposed to God's will, or in that selfishness which completely and deliberately closes itself to the love of neighbor." It is not only in such cases that there comes into play the "fundamental option," i.e., the decision which is necessary for mortal

sin to exist. On the contrary, mortal sin is found "in every deliberate transgression in serious matter, of each of the moral laws," and not only in formal and direct resistance to the commandment of charity. Cf. *Sexual Ethics* (Doctrine of the Faith, 1975), 10.

34. *Paenitemini*, Apostolic Constitution of Pope Paul VI, February 17, 1966.
35. Cf. Roman Missal, Memorial Acclamation.
36. John Henry Newman, *Parochial and Plain Sermons*, V,7.
37. Roman Missal, Preface for the Feast of Christ the King.
38. Religious Freedom, 3; cf. St. Thomas Aquinas, *Summa Theologiae*, 1-2. 91,1 and 2; 94, 1.
39. Cf. Modern World, 16.
40. *Ibid*.
41. Religious Freedom, 14.
42. Church, 18.
43. Cf. Modern World, 51; *On the Regulation of Birth (Humanae Vitae)*, Encyclical Letter of Pope Paul VI, July 25, 1968; *Human Life in Our Day*, a collective pastoral of the American hierarchy issued November 15, 1968. United States Catholic Conference, 1968. ©Copyright 1968 by the United States Catholic Conference. All rights reserved.
44. For a discussion of premarital sex, homosexuality, and masturbation, cf. *Sexual Ethics* (Doctrine of the Faith, 1975).
45. Roman Ritual, First Eucharistic Prayer of the Mass.
46. Cf. Church, 52-59.
47. *Ibid*., 53.
48. The bishops' pastoral letter, *Behold Your Mother, Woman of Faith*, published in 1973, can be very helpful in catechizing on this subject. Cf. also *Devotion to the Blessed Virgin Mary (Marialis Cultus)*, an Apostolic Exhortation of His Holiness, Pope Paul VI, February 2, 1974. United States Catholic Conference, 1974.

In 1859, at the request of the bishops of the United States, Pope Pius IX placed the nation under the protection of Mary's Immaculate Conception.
49. Cf. Church, 49-51.
50. Cf. *Ibid*., 48.
51. *Ibid*., 49.

Chapter VI
1. GCD, 55.
2. Cf. *Ibid*., 57.
3. Cf. Church, 14.
4. The Roman Ritual, *Rite of Christian Initiation of Adults*. Sacred Congregation for Divine Worship, 1972.
5. The Roman Ritual, *Rite of Baptism for Children*. Sacred Congregation for Divine Worship, 1969.
6. *Ibid*., 8.
7. The Roman Pontifical, *Rite of Confirmation*, Apostolic Constitution on the Sacrament of Confirmation, Pope Paul VI, 1971.
8. *Ibid*., 11.
9. The Congregation of Rites published a very important *Instruction on Eucharistic Worship* on May 25, 1967. In that *Instruction* there is a seven-part article (3) that deals specifically with "The Principal Points of Doctrine."
10. Liturgy, 52.
11. Roman Ritual, Eucharistic Prayer III.
12. In the *Instruction on Eucharistic Worship, op. cit.*, there are eleven articles (5-15) under the title "Some General Principles of Particular Importance in the Catechesis of the People on the Mystery of the Eucharist." These principles should be a guideline for all catechists, writers, and publishers.
13. GCD, 58.
14. *The General Instruction of the Roman Missal* gives full information concerning the prayers and actions at Mass proper to the laity.
15. "[It will not] be easy to grasp the force of that love by which Christ was impelled to give us himself as our spiritual food except by fostering a special devotion to the Eucharistic Heart of Jesus." *Haurietis Aquas*. (1956), Pius XII, 185.
16. The Roman Ritual, *Rite of Penance*. Sacred Congregation for Divine Worship, 1973, 6a).
17. Cf. *Ibid*., 32.
18. *Quam Singulari*, decree of the Congregation for the Discipline of the Sacraments, 1910; letter (Prot. N. 2/76) of the Sacred Congregation for the Sacraments and Divine Worship and the Sacred Congregation for the Clergy, March 31, 1977, to Archbishop Joseph L. Bernardin, president of NCCB/USCC, signed by James Cardinal Knox and John Cardinal Wright. Cf. also GCD, Addendum.

19. Liturgy, 73.
20. The Roman Ritual, *Rite of Anointing and Pastoral Care of the Sick*. Sacred Congregation for Divine Worship, 1972, 5.
21. Cf. *Ibid.*, 8, 10-12.
22. Modern World, 50.
23. Cf. *On the Regulation of Birth (Humanae Vitae)*, Encyclical Letter of Pope Paul VI, July 25, 1968.
24. Cf. *The Ministerial Priesthood*, Second General Assembly of the Synod of Bishops, 1971. United States Catholic Conference, 1972, I, 4.
25. Cf. also, the Roman Pontifical, *The Ordination of Bishops*. Sacred Congregation for Divine Worship, 1972.
26. Cf. *Ibid.*, *The Ordination of Priests*.
27. *Ibid.*, *The Ordination of Deacons*.
28. It should be recalled, as the Second Vatican Council stated, and as the pope has many times confirmed, that regulation of the sacred liturgy depends on ecclesiastical authority. "Therefore no other person, not even a priest, may add, remove or change anything in the liturgy on his own authority." Liturgy, 22.
29. Cf. *Directory for Masses with Children*. Sacred Congregation for Divine Worship, November 1, 1974, 2.
30. *Ibid.*, 9.
31. Pius XII, in his encyclical *Haurietis Aquas* (1956), states: "If the evidence on which devotion to the Wounded Heart of Jesus rests is rightly weighed, it is clear to all that we are dealing here, not with an ordinary form of piety which anyone may at his discretion slight in favor of other devotions, or esteem lightly, but with a duty of religion most conducive to Christian perfection," 150. (National Catholic Welfare Conference, 1956). Cf. also *Annum Sacrum*, Leo XIII (1899); *Miserentissimus Redemptor*, Pius XI (1928).
32. General Decree and Instruction, *Maxima Redemptionis Nostrae Mysteriis*, Sacred Congregation of Rites, November 16, 1955, A.A.S. 47.
33. Moto Proprio, *Approval of the General Norms for the Liturgical Year and the New General Roman Calendar*, Pope Paul VI, February 14, 1969.
34. *General Norms for the Liturgical Year and the Calendar*, Sacred Congregation for Divine Worship, February 14, 1969, 1.
35. *Ibid.*, 3.
36. *Ibid.*, 4.
37. *Ibid.*, 8.
38. *Ibid.*, 18.
39. *Ibid.*, 22.
40. *Ibid.*, 27.
41. *Ibid.*, 32.
42. *Ibid.*, 39.
43. *Ibid.*, 43.
44. *Ibid.*, 1.
45. *Roman Calendar, Text and Commentary*, United States Catholic Conference, 1976.
46. Liturgy, 122.
47. *Ibid.*, 123; cf. Modern World, 62; Paul VI, discourse to the artists of Rome, A.A.S. 56 (1964), pp. 439-442.
48. Cf. Liturgy, 60-63.

Chapter VII

1. Modern World, 45.
2. Cf. JW, Introduction.
3. Cf. *On the Development of Peoples* (Paul VI, 1967), 27.
4. Cf. *Peace on Earth* (John XXIII, 1963), 8-33.
5. *The Eightieth Anniversary of Rerum Novarum (Octogesima Adveniens*, Paul VI, 1971), 4.
6. Cf. Modern World, 42.
7. Cf. JW, II. The Gospel Message and the Mission of the Church, The Mission of the Church, Hierarchy and Christians; III. The Practice of Justice, Cooperation Between Local Churches; Ecumenical Collaboration.
8. Modern World, 39.
9. Synodal documents do not have the same teaching authority as the documents of ecumenical councils, but they are certainly of great weight and stature in the Church.
10. JW, Introduction.
11. *On Evangelization* (Paul VI, 1975), 35.
12. Message to the United States bishops' "Call to Action" convocation, October 1976.
13. Cf. JW, III, The Practice of Justice, The Church's Witness.
14. Cf. Modern World, 69; cf. footnote 223 in the Abbott-Gallagher translation of this pastoral constitution.
15. *Sermo 10 in Quadragesima*, 3-5: Pl 54, 299-301.
16. Cf. Modern World, 69.
17. Cf. *Christianity and Social Progress (Mater et*

Magistra), Encyclical of Pope John XXIII, May 15, 1961, 6.

18. The specific papal, conciliar and synodal documents which embody much of the teaching include: Leo XIII's *On the Condition of Labor (Rerum Novarum,* 1891); Pius XI's *Reconstruction of the Social Order (Quadragesimo Anno,* 1931); Pius XII's Christmas Messages (1939-1957), his Radio Messages (1939-1957), and his Radio Message of Pentecost (1941); John XXIII's *Christianity and Social Progress (Mater et Magistra,* 1961) and *Peace on Earth (Pacem in Terris,* 1963); the Second Vatican Council's *Pastoral Constitution on the Church in the Modern World (Gaudium et Spes,* 1965) and *Declaration on Religious Freedom (Dignitatis Humanae,* 1965); Paul VI's *On the Development of Peoples (Populorum Progressio,* 1967), and the Apostolic Letter, *The Eightieth Anniversary of Rerum Novarum (Octogesima Adveniens,* 1971); the Second General Assembly of the Synod of Bishops, *Justice in the World* (1971).

19. Modern World, 30.

20. Cf. *Peace on Earth* (John XXIII, 1963), 35-38.

21. Sin is personal though it has social consequences.

22. JW, Introduction.

23. Cf. *Peace on Earth* (John XXIII, 1963), 30.

24. JW, II, The Gospel Message and the Mission of the Church, The Saving Justice of God Through Christ.

25. Major documents of the Holy See and the bishops are available from the Publications Office, United States Catholic Conference (1312 Massachusetts Avenue, N.W., Washington, D.C. 20005), soon after they appear. Papal and other Roman documents are printed in *The Pope Speaks* published by Our Sunday Visitor, Inc. (P.O. Box 920, Huntington, Ind. 46750).

26. Among the numerous documents on abortion and related topics, cf. *Declaration on Procured Abortion,* Sacred Congregation for the Doctrine of the Faith, 1974. Documentation and information on abortion and the right to life may be obtained from the Publications Office, United States Catholic Conference (1312 Massachusetts Avenue, N.W., Washington, D.C. 20005).

27. Cf. Religious Freedom, 5; Christian Education, 6.

28. Cf. Modern World, 10.

29. Cf. JW, III, The Practice of Justice, Educating for Justice.

30. Cf. *Ibid.*

31. Cf. *Ibid.*

Chapter VIII

1. Cf. GCD, 30, 38.

2. For the use of the social and psychological sciences in pastoral care, cf. Modern World 52, 62.

3. GCD, 131; cf. Christian Education, 1.

4. Cf. GCD, 121.

5. Cf. *Ibid.,* 72.

6. Cf. *Ibid.,* 74.

7. Cf. *Ibid.,* 73.

8. Cf. *Ibid.,* 78.

9. Cf. *Ibid.*

10. Cf. *Ibid.,* 79.

11. Cf. *Ibid.,* 83.

12. *Ibid.,* 88.

13. One method of discernment has been described as operating on three levels; the sociological (empirical reality — what is going on in society); anthropological (within the mind and heart — what is happening to men and women); theological (the acting out of God's designs — how do I act in the light of the gospel?).

14. Cf. *Catholic Schools in a Declining Church* (1976), p. 148.

15. Cf. GCD, 83, which invites study of the stage of young adulthood.

16. Cf. *Ibid.,* 94.

17. Cf. *Ibid.,* 97, for a treatment of the special functions of catechesis for adults.

18. Cf. Church, 14.

19. GCD, 63.

20. *Ibid.,* 95.

21. Cf. *Ibid.*

22. Cf. Laity 2, 7.

23. The catechist should always keep in mind that "the conscience of the faithful, even when informed by the virtue of prudence, must be subject to the magisterium of the Church, whose duty it is to explain the whole moral law authoritatively, in order that it may rightly and correctly express the objective moral order." GCD, 63.

24. Cf. TLCJ, 1, The Church.

25. *The Church in Our Day,* National Conference of Catholic Bishops. United States Catholic Conference, November 1967, p.

64. ©Copyright 1968 by the United States Catholic Conference. All rights reserved. Cf. also Gal 3, 23; 5,1.13ff.
26. *The Catholic School*, Sacred Congregation for Catholic Education. United States Catholic Conference, 1977, 84.
27. Cf. *Human Life in Our Day*, A Collective Pastoral of the American Hierarchy. United States Catholic Conference, 1968, p. 18.
28. For more on this subject, cf. *Sexual Ethics* (Doctrine of the Faith, 1975).
29. Christian Education, 1.
30. In one study, it was found that only 12 percent of young people are taught about sex by their parents. Most learn from their peers. *Adolescent Appraisals and Selected Institutions (Home, Church, School, Youth Organizations)*, Calderwood, Deryck. Oregon State University, 1970.
31. Cf. Christian Education, 1.
32. Cf. TJD, 57.
33. Cf. *Where Are the 6.6 Million? A Statistical Survey of Catholic Elementary and Secondary Formal Religious Education 1965-1974*, Paradis, Wilfrid H., Thompson, Andrew D. United States Catholic Conference, 1976; cf. also update for 1975 by the same authors.
34. Cf. *Religion and American Youth* (1976), pp. 8-9.
35. Cf. *Ibid.*, pp. 18-21.
36. Cf. *Ibid.*, pp. 11-21.
37. Cf. *Ibid.*, pp. 22-43.
38. Cf. *Ibid.*, pp. 43-49.
39. Cf. *Ibid.*, p. 24.

Chapter IX

1. GCD, 111.
2. TJD, 23.
3. *Ibid.*, 24.
4. *Ibid.*, 29.
5. Cf. Christian Education, 3; Laity, 11.
6. Cf. Laity, 24.
7. GCD, 71.
8. *Teach Them*, A Statement of the Catholic Bishops. United States Catholic Conference, May 6, 1976. United States Catholic Conference, 1976, p. 7.
9. *Directory on the Pastoral Ministry of Bishops*, Sacred Congregation for Bishops, February 22, 1973. Publications Service, Canadian Catholic Conference, 65.
10. GCD, 126.

Chapter X

1. Cf. GCD, 129; TJD, 142.
2. Cf. Revelation, 22.
3. Cf. *Directory on the Pastoral Ministry of Bishops*, Sacred Congregation for Bishops, February 22, 1973. Publications Service, Canadian Catholic Conference, 174.
4. Cf. Missionary Activity, 35-38; Church, chapters I and II.
5. *On Evangelization* (Paul VI, 1975), 71.
6. GCD, 78.
7. TJD, 118; cf. also, *The Catholic School*, Sacred Congregation for Catholic Education. United States Catholic Conference, 1977.
8. Cf. TJD, 92.
9. *Ibid.*, 103.
10. Christian Education, 8.
11. TJD, 108.
12. Christian Education, 9.
13. Letter of Pope Paul VI to French social action groups meeting in France, July 1, 1970.
14. *Engel v. Vitale*, 370. U.S. 421 (1961); *School District of Abington Township v. Schempp, Murray v. Curlett*, 374 U.S. 203 (1963).
15. Cf. *Illinois ex. rel. McCallum, Board of Education*, 333 U.S. 203, 227 (1948); and *Zorach v. Clauson*, 343 U.S. 306 (1952).
16. Cf. Bishops, 27; for the desirability of such councils, cf. *Directory on the Pastoral Ministry of Bishops, op. cit.*, 204.
17. GCD, 126.
18. Cf. *Ibid.*, 128.
19. *Program of Priestly Formation*, National Conference of Catholic Bishops. United States Catholic Conference, 1976, 151.

Chapter XI

1. Cf. *Pastoral Instruction on the Means of Social Communications*. Pontifical Commission for Social Communications, January 29, 1971, 14; *On Evangelization* (Paul VI, 1975), 45.
2. *Ibid.*, 15.
3. *Ibid.*, 65.
4. GCD, 121.
5. Cf. *Ibid.*, 122.

Appendix A

1. Cf. Ex 20, 2-17; Dt 5,6-21.

Appendix B

1. Cf. BT, p. 28.

Index

commissioning ceremony, parish catechists, 213
commitment:
    catechist's commitment to Church, 208
    making life decisions, 183
    pre-adolescence and puberty, 179
    religious commitment of youth, 201c
    sacraments/mysteries of commitment, 129-133
Committee for Pro-Life Activities (NCCB), 250
common doctrine of the Church, 16
communal celebrations:
    Anointing of the Sick, 127
    Sacrament of Reconciliation, 124
communications, 20, 22:
    dialogue and God's self-communication, 47
    hopeful signs in catechetics, 9
    organizational principles, 221e
    press and catechesis, 259-260
    skills required of catechists, 211
communications media:
    resources for catechesis, 251-258
    training media users, 262
    training media producers, 261
communion. see Holy Communion.
Communion of Saints, 107
community:
    call of Christians to community, 70
    campus ministry, 243
    catechesis in Catholic schools, 232
    catechesis in later adulthood, 186, 187
    catechesis of children, 229
    catechesis of the young, 181, 200e, 228b
    catechist's commitment to community, 208, 209, 213
    Catholic press, 259
    Catholic schools, 215
    childhood (ages 6-10), 178
    Church as a community, 94
    community prayer, 140
    development of social teaching, 163
    ecclesial signs, 45
    family and community in U.S., 25
    needs of minority groups, 194
    parish organizations, 224
    secular press, 260
    sense of community, 21
    social consequences of sin, 165b
compassion, biblical basis, 153
computers and data banks, 22
comunidad de base, 9
Condition of Labor, On the (Rerum Novarum), 164
conduct of life:
    catechesis in morality, 38, 102-105, 170
    characteristics of youth, 200
    elements of catechesis, 105
    human values, 102
confession. see Reconciliation, Sacrament of.
Confirmation/Chrismation, Sacrament of, 114, 118-119
Confraternity of Christian Doctrine, 8, 222b
conscience:
    conscience formation, 190
    element of catechesis, 103
    faith as a free response, 58
    moral basis for social teaching, 158
consultation:
    catechesis for persons with special needs, 196
    NCD, 4
contemplation, 143
continuing education, 189, 217
contraception:
    catechesis for Matrimony, 131
    duties to others, 105b

contrition, definition, 124
conversion of life:
    catechesis and evangelization, 35
    catechetical guidelines, 170
    element of catechesis, 99
    Sacrament of Reconciliation, 124, 125, 126
cooperation, provincial and regional cooperation, 239
coordinators of religious education, 214
core curriculum, 232
corporal works of mercy, 66, 160
correspondence courses, 265a
counseling:
    divorce, 131
    campus ministry, 243
country life. see city and country life.
courtesy, respect for others, 105b
covenants, Matrimony, 130
creation:
    biblical signs, 43
    dignity of human person, 156
    element of catechesis, 85-86, 88, 90
    God's self-manifestation, 51
    natural signs, 46
    viewed as a symbol, 114
creeds:
    ecclesial signs, 45
    moral principles and teachings, 59
crisis of faith, 179
criteria, catechetical, 7, 47
critical scholarship, Bible, 60a
"crowning" (ceremony), 130
cultural groups:
    catechesis, 194, 242
    college students, 201a
    ethnic parishes, 236
    Masses for cultural groups, 137, 139
    youth subculture, 197
culture:
    context for catechesis, 7
    media as part of, 261, 262
curricula, 218b:
    Catholic schools, 232
    catechesis of children, 229

D

daily life:
    God's manifestation, 55
    resources of catechesis, 60a
deacons:
    Church as hierarchical society, 69
    element of catechesis, 93
    Holy Orders, 132
    permanent deacons as catechists, 216
deaf and hearing disabled, 138, 195
death, 90, 108, 186
decalogue. see commandments of God.
decisions:
    formation of conscience, 190
    making life decisions, 183
    middle adulthood, 184
    planning groups, 221d
deduction, 176, 181
demography:
    changes in U.S. family life, 26-28
    characteristics of later adulthood, 202
    characteristics of youth, 200a
Department of Education (diocese), 238c
Department of Education (USCC), 223, 240, 242a
deposit of faith, 53

NOTES

NOTES